East from Huddersfield by Bus 1913-

Peter Cardno and Stephen Harling

ROBIN HOOD
PUBLISHING

CONTENTS

Front Cover
The replacements for County's Wulfrunians eventually arrived in February 1964 in the more conventional shape of a pair of Roe bodied Leyland Titan PD3A/1s. 105 (AVH 635B) is on the "Wakefield Direct" service in Lord Street. Around this time most of the fleet seemed to carry advertising for Typhoo tea.
[Photobus]

Title Page
In May 1953 Yorkshire Traction Kirkburton school buses are parked near the junction of Low Town (in the foreground) with Riley Lane, going off into the distance towards the left. Although the buses appear to be typical early postwar BET group front-engined saloons with forward entrance bodies, the bus on the left at least is actually a rebodied prewar Leyland Tiger. Originally a petrol engined coach, 1937 Leyland Tiger TS7 579 (HE 7775) had been given a new body by Roberts of Horbury in 1948. [Kirklees Image Archive ke09864]

Back cover left
Yorkshire Traction 390 (WVH 231), a Leyland Leopard/Willowbrook new to County in 1962, is parked out of service on the east side of Lord Street on 8 September 1973. It is unlikely to have run as a one-man bus on conductor operated route 63 from Wakefield via Flockton, unless on an early morning short working. The open doors remind us of the climb facing passengers when boarding so many British single deck buses of the fifties and sixties. [H J Black]

Back cover right
Yorkshire Woollen's first (1965) Daimler Fleetlines reintroduced cream relief to the drab all red double deck livery of the day. Alexander bodied 128 (BHD 218C) is in Lord Street on 13 May 1970 awaiting departure for Dewsbury via Savile Arms (route 26). [H J Black]

ISBN 978 0 948854 17 0
© July 2008 Peter Cardno & Stephen Harling
Designed and published by

ROBIN HOOD PUBLISHING

Attenborough, Notts.
NG9 6AP
mail@robinhood publishing.co.uk
www.robinhood publishing.co.uk

INTRODUCTION

This book is an account of company motorbus operations to the north east, east and south east of Huddersfield before the formation of West Yorkshire PTE (Metro) in 1974. The main activities covered are Waterloo based County Motors and the local routes of the three companies which jointly owned County for most of its existence, Dewsbury based Yorkshire Woollen, West Riding of Wakefield and Yorkshire Traction at Barnsley. Vehicles of these operators ran into and out of Huddersfield along Leeds Road or Wakefield Road for many years and the latter two were also regular visitors to Holmfirth. Smaller firms such as Harburn, Ideal and Mitchell are also included.

We have not set out to write a comprehensive account of coaching operations, especially by Yorkshire Traction and Yorkshire Woollen. Outlines are, however, included to illustrate the interests of various businesses outside local bus operation, especially for the late 1920s and early 1930s.

ACKNOWLEDGEMENTS

The authors are grateful to the following individuals for assistance: John Black, Amanda Booth, David Dodd, Ted Gadsby, John Gill, Geoff Lumb, Roy Marshall, Rev. John P. Senior, Norman Walker, Paul Watson and not least to Geoff Hodgson, who has made a major contribution, particularly in relation to County Motors.

Sources consulted include the Huddersfield Daily Examiner, Huddersfield Weekly Examiner, Huddersfield Borough Advertiser, Holmfirth Express, Brighouse and Elland Echo, Dewsbury and District News, Cleckheaton Advertiser and Spen Valley News and Barnsley Chronicle newspapers; minutes of the county borough, municipal borough or urban district councils of Huddersfield, Brighouse, Denby Dale, Kirkburton, Lepton, Penistone and Thurstonland; Notices and Proceedings of the Yorkshire Traffic Area and fleet records of the PSV Circle.

The following libraries, archives and museums provided access to material of interest and we thank their staff for the help given: The Geoff Lumb Transport Archive, Huddersfield, Halifax and Leeds local studies libraries, Kirklees Community History Service, Omnibus Society Library, Kirklees Photographic Archive www.kirkleesimages.org.uk, West Yorkshire Archives Service and the former West Yorkshire Transport Museum, Bradford.

We apologise to any individuals or organisations inadvertently omitted. Any errors or misinterpretations in the text are of course the authors' responsibility.

A Yorkshire Traction 1939 Leyland Tiger TS8/Burlingham coach on the Blackpool service heads a line of vehicles on the west side of Venn Street, Huddersfield on 3 June 1949. The former Progress garage can be seen on the right. From Progress the premises passed to Yorkshire Woollen who changed the paintwork to maroon; after the outbreak of war the building was taken over for civil defence use. The coach on the left is loading for London or Liverpool.
[Kirklees Image Archive ke01683]

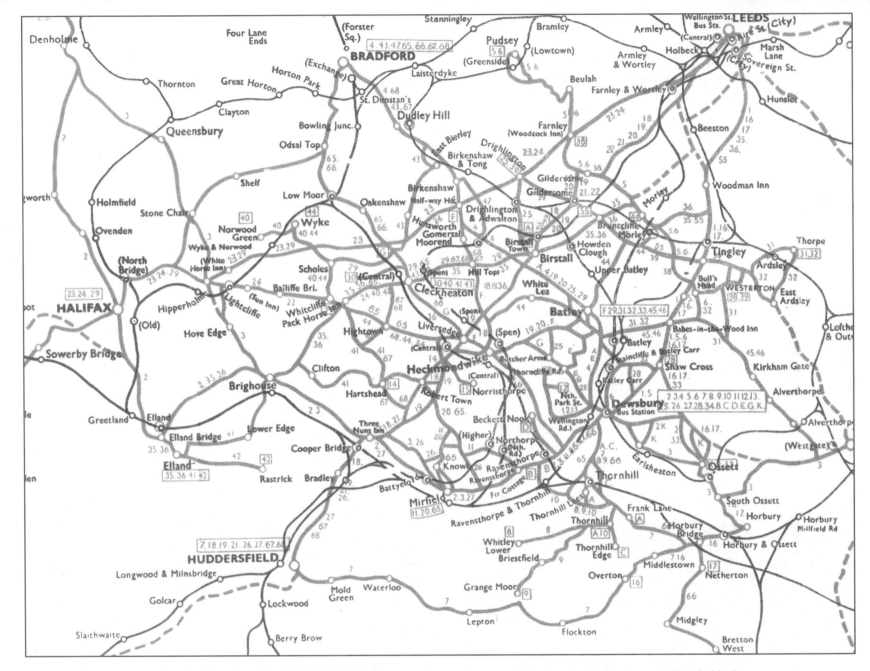

Section of a Yorkshire Woollen District 1949 route map showing bus services in grey and railways operations in black.
The map has been updated to include the 1940s route alterations, but forgetting to change the 19 shown between Heckmondwike and Birstall via Batley into a 21, yet at at the same time they have left the 7 running into Huddersfield, although it was withdrawn between Grange Moor and Huddersfield in September 1939.

Yorkshire Woollen District (Electric Tramways) Ltd, a company which ran a tramway network linking Dewsbury and other districts of the Heavy Woollen District, was the earliest significant bus operator in the Huddersfield area. Incompatibility of the Huddersfield Corporation and Yorkshire Woollen tramway gauges meant that, even if the gap between their termini at Bradley and Ravensthorpe were to be bridged, through running would not be possible. Instead Yorkshire Woollen purchased four 30 seater Daimler CC single deck front entrance motorbuses which were garaged at Savile Town, Dewsbury, where the head office was later located. These buses were used to inaugurate services between Cleckheaton and Scholes and, more to the point, between Bradley (Leeds Road/Colne Bridge Road junction) and Ravensthorpe (Fir Cottage) via Three Nuns and Mirfield from 18 November 1913. Passengers could now travel by tram and bus between Huddersfield and Dewsbury; the buses terminated at the tram termini at Bradley and Ravensthorpe. In 1914 Yorkshire Woollen offered to provide a service linking Milnsbridge [probably Manchester Road] and Golcar in return for a payment of £5 per day but this was declined by Golcar UDC. In the same year a pair of rear entrance Daimler B type single deckers were obtained and the services continued during the war; in 1917 some of the buses were converted to run on coal gas carried in a bag on the roof. On 27 February 1921, however, motorbus operation was temporarily suspended and the services were withdrawn. Huddersfield Corporation then started running between Bradley and Ravensthorpe but the Yorkshire Woollen service was reinstated in 1922 using

One of Yorkshire Woollen's 1913 Daimlers (C 7577) is captured at Shepley Bridge, Ravensthorpe. This Ravensthorpe (Fir Cottage) to Bradley route, which supplied the missing link between the Yorkshire Woollen (Dewsbury) and Huddersfield trams, ran from 1913 to 1921.
[Kirklees Image Archive K000330]

new Leyland single deckers.

Yorkshire Woollen buses had also reached Waterloo by 2 December 1922 on a very indirect route from Dewsbury. Buses left Dewsbury at 2.00pm, 5.00pm and 8.00pm, running via Thornhill, Middlestown, Flockton, Grange Moor Cross Roads and Lepton. By 31 March 1923 the service had been slightly accelerated and extended to Huddersfield, which was reached in 75 minutes. A morning service now left Dewsbury at 9.30am and on Saturdays a 90 minute freqency was operated throughout the day. Some journeys ran via Emley on Saturday only between Flockton and Lepton. It is interesting that during the last month when the service terminated at Waterloo it was used by 13,693 passengers; during the first month of through running into Town it was used by 15,426. Many of the extra passengers might previously have walked to the tram stop. By 1927 the terminus was in Lord Street and an hourly service was operated at weekends (possibly reduced on winter Sundays); during the week this route always remained relatively infrequent.

In September 1924 Yorkshire Woollen were granted a three month licence to run between Bradley and Leeds via Roberttown, Heckmondwike, Batley and Birstall. The service was hourly and, being at first unlicensed by Leeds Watch Committee, used a terminus on private land at Leeds Bridge. The Leeds authorities granted a licence on 17 November 1924. From 27 February 1925 they were allowed to project the Leeds-Bradley service from the borough boundary to a new terminus in Silk Street in Huddersfield; an hourly service took 90 minutes for a through fare of 1/6d. Ideal Bus Services (Kilburn) of Heckmondwike, who had run between Bradley and Heckmondwike since 1922, competed on this corridor

and started a through Huddersfield to Heckmondwike route in May 1925. Yorkshire Woollen never established an operational depot in Huddersfield and their buses ran into the town over the years from depots in Dewsbury, Liversedge or Heckmondwike.

The company was given a licence to extend the Bradley to Ravensthorpe route at both ends to run between Huddersfield and Dewsbury direct via the main road on 29 June 1925. An agreement was eventually reached with Huddersfield Corporation for running a joint service, which commenced on 15 March 1926. The basic hourly frequency doubled to 30 minutes on Wednesday, Friday, Saturday and Sunday afternoons; part of this extra traffic was generated by the popular Dewsbury open market. Terminal points were Kirkgate in Huddersfield and stand no. 9, Long Causeway in Dewsbury.

In the summer following the General Strike of 1926 the company, conscious that money would be in short supply, advertised a series of "holiday haunts" which could easily be reached by bus or tram from Batley or Dewsbury. In the Huddersfield area the virtues of Honley Pleasure Gardens, Holmfirth, Meltham and Nont Sarah's were extolled. Pleasure seekers were advised to change onto the Corporation tram to Outlane, from where it was apparently only a short walk to Nont Sarah's.

With increasing patronage, from 1 November 1926 on Tuesdays, Saturdays and Sundays the afternoon frequency to Leeds via Batley was doubled to half hourly. Early morning workmen journeys were soon to follow and it is interesting to compare the return fares applicable at the time from Huddersfield.

To:	Workman Return	Ordinary Return
Roberttown	8d	10d
Heckmondwike	10d	1/-
Batley	1/-	1/3d
Birstall	1/4d	1/6d
Leeds	-	2/6d

By December 1927 Kilburn had extended the Ideal Huddersfield-Heckmondwike route to Leeds and, unlike Yorkshire Woollen, he did not deviate via Batley before reaching Birstall. It is surprising that the larger company did not manage to respond more promptly but it was 27 June 1928 before, following the granting of the necessary licences, their new direct service between Huddersfield and Leeds ("Leeds direct") commenced. As the route was like the existing service but direct between Heckmondwike and Birstall, the through journey could be completed in 70 minutes (frequency

NEW DIRECT SERVICE COMMENCING
WEDNESDAY, JUNE 27th, 1928.

LEEDS - HUDDERSFIELD (Direct Route)

Via Gildersome, Birstall, Heckmondwike, Roberttown and Bradley.

	Week-Days.						Sundays.					
Leeds ... ... a				7- 5	7-35		10-35	11- 5	12- 5	.	10-35	11- 5
Gildersome (King's Arms) ...					7-28		10-58	11-28			12-28	10-58 11-28
Birstall (Smithies)		6- 8	6-40	7- 5	7-35	and	11- 5	11-35	11-35 12- 5 12-35		11- 5	11-35
Heckmondwike (Green) ...	5-55	6-15	6-50	7-15	7-45	every	11-15	11-45	11-45 12-15 12-45	and	11-15	11-45
Roberttown (Central)	6- 0	6-22	6-57	7-22	7-52	30	11-22		11-52 12-22 12-52		11-22	
Bradley (Tram Ter.)	6- 5	6-30	7- 5	7-30	8- 0	mins	11-30		12- 0 12-30 1- 0	every	11-30	
Huddersfield (Kirkgate)	6-20	6-45	7-20	7-45	8-15	until 10-50 p.m.	11-45		12-15 12-45 1-15	30	11-45	
Huddersfield (Kirkgate)			6-20				10-50	11-15		12-20	10-50	11-15
Bradley (Tram Ter.)			6-35	mins			11- 5	11-30		12-35	11- 5	11-30
Roberttown (Central)			6-43				11-13	11-38		12-43	11-13	11-38
Heckmondwike (Green)		6-20	6-50	until			11-20	11-45	11-20 11-50 12-20	12-50 until	11-20	11-45
Birstall (Smithies)		6-30	7- 0				11-30	11-53	11-30 12- 0 12-30		11-30	11-53
Gildersome (King's Arms) ...		6-38	7-10				11-38		11-38 12- 8 12-38	1- 8	11-38	
Leeds		7- 0	7-30				12- 0		12- 0 12-30 1- 0	1-30	12- 0	

m The Picking-Up point in Leeds is Aire St., City Square.

NOTE.—On Saturdays only the 11-50 a.m. from Batley to Leeds goes via Main Road from Gildersome.

YORKSHIRE MOTOR BUS SERVICE.

ALTERATION TO TIMES.

LEEDS, BATLEY, HUDDERSFIELD ROUTE.

As from WEDNESDAY, JUNE 27th, 1928, 'Buses will leave Batley for Leeds and Huddersfield, and Leeds and Huddersfield for Batley as follows:—

To Leeds—

Monday Wednesday, Thursday and Friday.

at 6-0 a.m., 6-25, 7-5, 7-25, 7-50, 8-5, 8-20, 8-50, 9-20, 9-50, 10-20, 10-50, 11-20, 11-50, 12-20 p.m., 12-50, 1-20, 1-50, 2-20, 2-50, 3-20, 3-50, 4-20, 4-50, 5-20, 5-50, 6-20, 6-50, 7-20, 7-50, 8-50, 9-20, 9-50, 10-50 p.m.

Tuesdays and Saturdays.

at 6-0 a.m., 6-25, 7-5, 7-25, 7-50, 8-5, 8-20, 8-50, 9-5, 9-20, 9-50, 10-5, 10-20, 10-35, 10-50, 11-5, 11-20, 11-35, 11-50, 12-5, 12-20, 12-35, 12-50, 1-5, 1-20, 1-35, 1-50, 2-5, 2-20, 2-35, 2-50, 3-5, 3-20, 3-35, 3-50, 4-5, 4-20, 4-35, 4-50, 5-5, 5-20, 5-35, 5-50, 6-5, 6-20, 6-35, 6-50, 7-5, 7-20, 7-35, 7-50, 8-5, 8-20, 8-35, 8-50, 9-5, 9-20, 9-35, 9-50, 10-5, 10-20, 10-50.

Sundays.

at 11-50 a.m., 12-20 p.m., 12-50, 1-5, 1-20, 1-35, 1-50, 2-5, 2-20, 2-35, 2-50, 3-5, 3-20, 3-35, 3-50, 4-5, 4-20, 4-35, 4-50, 5-5, 5-20, 5-35, 5-50, 6-5, 6-20, 6-35, 6-50, 7-5, 7-20, 7-35, 7-50, 8-5, 8-20, 8-35, 8-50, 9-5, 9-20, 9-35, 9-50, 10-5, 10-20, 10-50.

From LEEDS. Times as now.

To Huddersfield—

Mondays Wednesdays, Thursdays and Fridays.

at 6-20 a.m., 7-25, 7-54, 8-54, 9-54, 10-54, 11-54, 12-54, 1-54, 2-54, 3-54, 4-54, 5-54, 6-54, 7-54, 8-54, 9-54.

Tuesdays and Saturdays.

at 6-20 a.m., 7-25, 7-54, 8-54, 9-54, 10-54, 11-54, 12-24, 12-54, 1-24, 1-54, 2-24, 2-54, 3-24, 3-54, 4-24, 4-54, 5-24, 5-54, 6-24, 6-54, 7-24, 7-54, 8-24, 8-54, 9-24, 9-54, 10-24, 10-54.

Sundays.

at 11-55 a.m., 12-25 p.m., 12-55, 1-24, 1-54, 2-24, 2-54, 3-24, 3-54, 4-24, 4-54, 5-24, 5-54, 6-24, 6-54, 7-24, 7-54, 8-24, 8-54, 9-54, 10-24, 10-54.

From Huddersfield—

Monday, Wednesday, Thursday, Friday.

at 7-10 a.m., 8-10, 9-10, 10-10, 11-10, 12-10 p.m., 1-10, 2-10, 3-10, 4-10, 5-10, 6-10, 7-10, 8-10, 9-10, 10-10, 11-15.

Tuesday and Saturday.

at 7-10 a.m., 8-10, 9-10, 10-10, 11-10, 11-40, 12-10 p.m., 12-40, 1-10, 1-40, 2-10, 2-40, 3-10, 3-40, 4-10, 4-40, 5-10, 5-40, 6-10, 6-40, 7-10, 7-40, 8-10, 8-40, 9-10, 9-40, 10-10, 10-40, 11-15.

Sundays.

at 12-10 p.m., 12-40, 1-10, 2-10, 2-40, 3-10, 3-40, 4-10, 4-40, 5-10, 5-40, 6-10, 6-40, 7-10, 7-40, 8-10, 8-40, 9-10, 9-40, 10-10, 10-40, 11-15.

Yorkshire (W.D.) Electric Tramways Ltd.,
Frost Hill, Liversedge.

was every 30 minutes). Both the Leeds services started from Kirkgate in Huddersfield. By this time Kilburn was fully licensed and in the following month he matched Yorkshire Woollen by increasing his service to half hourly. On 14 August 1928 one of the Yorkshire Woollen "direct" single deck buses came to grief in Whitehall Road, Leeds. The fully laden bus skidded on the greasy road and crashed into a tram standard which became embedded in the rear of the saloon, injuring a Lockwood man, Mr Joe Hoyle. While many of the passengers chose to walk the short distance into the centre of Leeds, Mr and Mrs Hoyle continued their journey by ambulance to the Leeds Infirmary.

After standardising on Leylands, between 1925 and 1928 a large number of Dennis single deckers were placed in service, especially Dennis E types. These buses were used to extend the company's route network and interurban routes from the Heavy Woollen District to Halifax and Bradford besides those to Leeds and Huddersfield were established.

During 1927 several licence applications for a route from Huddersfield to Bradford via Cleckheaton had been declined but eventually there was a change of heart and on 5 December 1927 a licence was granted. On 30 January 1928 buses started running from Lord Street to Bradford via Bradley, Roberttown (Central), Liversedge, Cleckheaton, Gomersal and Birkenshaw with a journey time of 58 minutes. An hourly frequency was operated on weekdays, increased to half hourly on Saturday

and Sunday afternoons. In June 1929 application was made to combine this service at Bradford with a route to Ilkley; the through service was to be jointly operated with the Harrogate based West Yorkshire Road Car bus company. Huddersfield Watch Committee had no objections provided that no extra buses ran within the borough on this route. The joint through service started on 15 July 1929, taking one hour and 50 minutes to reach Ilkley. The route beyond Bradford was via Shipley, Guiseley and Burley and through fares were 2/4d single and 3/6d return.

Meanwhile fully licensed competitor Kilburn had continued to compete in many parts of the company's territory, including the Huddersfield to Leeds corridor. In order to eliminate this competition and maximise their revenue, Yorkshire Woollen bought out Kilburn's business in May 1929. Twenty fairly new Leyland vehicles were part of the deal, including a pair of the recently introduced Leyland Titan TD1 double deckers with Leyland lowbridge bodies. Yorkshire Woollen had bought four of these, their first double deckers, in the previous year and the company was again standardising on Leylands for single deck purchases. By July 1929 the Leeds direct service was operating every 30 minutes until 7.50am, then every 15 minutes for the rest of the day. An hourly Sunday morning service was provided and Leeds was reached in 55 minutes. From 5 October 1929 the Emley variant of the Dewsbury via Flockton route was withdrawn.

Around April 1930 route numbers were introduced and those used on Huddersfield routes were:

6 Dewsbury-Flockton-Huddersfield
7 Dewsbury-Mirfield-Huddersfield (joint with Huddersfield Joint Omnibus Committee)
18 Leeds-Birstall-Heckmondwike-Huddersfield ("Leeds direct")
19 Leeds-Birstall-Batley-Heckmondwike-Huddersfield
39 Ilkley-Bradford-Cleckheaton-Roberttown-Huddersfield (joint with West Yorkshire)

Joint operator Huddersfield JOC did not yet use route numbers. Three years later they initially allocated 47 to the joint service (7 would have been in the Huddersfield tram routes sequence). The other joint operator, West Yorkshire, also did not use route numbers in 1930. Their numbers were first shown in their 18 July 1932 timetable where 105 was allocated to Huddersfield-Ilkley.

The management were left with egg on their faces after an interesting court case in October 1932. A commercial traveller had purchased a return ticket for a Leeds to

YORKSHIRE
(W.D.) Electric Tramways Ltd.

Amended Service commencing 23rd January, 1933.

DEWSBURY - HUDDERSFIELD

via MIDDLESTOWN, FLOCKTON, LEPTON and WATERLOO (Route No. 6).

MONDAYS TO FRIDAYS. | SATURDAYS. | SUNDAYS

Dewsbury → Huddersfield — Mondays to Fridays:

Stop	a.m.	a.m.	p.m.	p.m.	p.m.	p.m.	p.m.	p.m.	p.m.	p.m.
DEWSBURY (Omnibus Station)	5.35	6.55	1.30	3.30	4.30†	5.30	7.30	8.30†	9.30	10.50
Thornhill Station	5.39	6.59	1.34	3.34	4.34†	5.34	7.34	8.34†	9.34	10.54
Thornhill (Combs)	5.42	7.2	1.37	3.37	4.37†	5.37	7.37	8.37†	9.37	10.57
Sandy Lane Viaduct	5.50	7.10	1.45	3.45	4.45†	5.45	7.45	8.45†	9.45	11.5
Middlestown (Co-op.)	5.52	7.12	1.47	3.47	4.47†	5.47	7.47	8.47†	9.47	11.7†
Overton (Black Swan)	5.55	7.15	1.50	3.50		5.50	7.50		9.50	
FLOCKTON (Angel Inn)	6.3	7.23	1.58	3.58		5.58	7.58		9.58	
Grange Moor (Blacksmith's Arms)	6.8		2.3	4.3		6.3	8.3		10.3	
Lepton (Red Lion)			2.8	4.8		6.8	8.8		10.8	
Waterloo Tram Terminus			2.15	4.15		6.15	8.15		10.15	
Mold Green (Junction Inn)			2.20	4.20		6.20	8.20		10.20	
HUDDERSFIELD (Lord Street)			2.25	4.25		6.25	8.25		10.25	

Dewsbury → Huddersfield — Saturdays (and every hour until):

Stop	a.m.	a.m.	a.m.	noon	p.m.	p.m.	p.m.	p.m.
DEWSBURY (Omnibus Station)	5.35	6.55	11.30	12.0	12.30	9.30	10.50	
Thornhill Station	5.39	6.59	11.34	12.4	12.34	9.34	10.54	
Thornhill (Combs)	5.42	7.2	11.37	12.7	12.37	9.37	10.57	
Sandy Lane Viaduct	5.50	7.10	11.45	12.15	12.45	9.45	11.5	
Middlestown (Co-op.)	5.52	7.12	11.47	12.17	12.47	9.47	11.7	
Overton (Black Swan)	5.55	7.15	11.50		12.50	9.50		
FLOCKTON (Angel Inn)	6.3	7.23	11.58		12.58	9.58		
Grange Moor (Blacksmith's Arms)	6.8		12.3		1.3	10.3		
Lepton (Red Lion)			12.8		1.8	10.8		
Waterloo Tram Terminus			12.15		1.15	10.15		
Mold Green (Junction Inn)			12.20		1.20	10.20		
HUDDERSFIELD (Lord Street)			12.25		1.25	10.25		

Dewsbury → Huddersfield — Sundays:

Stop	p.m.	p.m.	p.m.	p.m.	p.m.	p.m.	p.m.
DEWSBURY (Omnibus Station)	1.30	3.30	5.30	7.30	8.30	9.30	10.50
Thornhill Station	1.34	3.34	5.34	7.34	8.34	9.34	10.54
Thornhill (Combs)	1.37	3.37	5.37	7.37	8.37	9.37	10.57
Sandy Lane Viaduct	1.45	3.45	5.45	7.45	8.45	9.45	11.5
Middlestown (Co-op.)	1.47	3.47	5.47	7.47	8.47	9.47	11.7
Overton (Black Swan)	1.50	3.50	5.50	7.50	8.50	9.50	
FLOCKTON (Angel Inn)	1.58	3.58	5.58	7.58	8.58	9.58	
Grange Moor (Blacksmith's Arms)	2.3	4.3	6.3	8.3	9.3	10.3	
Lepton (Red Lion)	2.8	4.8	6.8	8.8	9.8	10.8	
Waterloo Tram Terminus	2.15	4.15	6.15	8.15	9.15	10.15	
Mold Green (Junction Inn)	2.20	4.20	6.20	8.20	9.20	10.20	
HUDDERSFIELD (Lord Street)	2.25	4.25	6.25	8.25	9.25	10.25	

Huddersfield → Dewsbury — Mondays to Fridays:

Stop	a.m.	a.m.	p.m.	p.m.	p.m.	p.m.	p.m.	p.m.	p.m.
HUDDERSFIELD (Lord Street)				2.30	4.30	6.30	8.30	10.30	
Mold Green (Junction Inn)				2.35	4.35	6.35	8.35	10.35	
Waterloo Tram Terminus				2.40	4.40	6.40	8.40	10.40	
Lepton (Red Lion)				2.47	4.47	6.47	8.47	10.47	
Grange Moor (Blacksmith's Arms)	6.15			2.52	4.52	6.52	8.52	10.52	
FLOCKTON (Angel Inn)	6.20	7.25		2.57	4.57	6.57	8.57	10.57	
Overton (Black Swan)	6.28	7.33		3.5	5.5	7.5	9.5	11.5	
Middlestown (Co-op.)	6.31	7.36	2.8†	3.8	5.8	6.8†	7.8	9.8	11.8
Sandy Lane Viaduct	6.33	7.38	2.10†	3.10	5.10	6.10†	7.10	9.10	11.10
Thornhill (Combs)	6.41	7.41	2.18†	3.18	5.18	6.18†	7.18	9.18	11.18
Thornhill Station	6.44	7.49	2.21†	3.21	5.21	6.21†	7.21	9.21	11.21
DEWSBURY (Omnibus Station)	6.48	7.53	2.25†	3.25	5.25	6.25†	7.25	9.25	11.25

Huddersfield → Dewsbury — Saturdays:

Stop	a.m.	a.m.	p.m.	p.m.	p.m.	p.m.	p.m.	p.m.	p.m.
HUDDERSFIELD (Lord Street)			12.30	1.30	10.30	2.30	4.30	...	10.30
Mold Green (Junction Inn)			12.35	1.35	10.35	2.35	4.35	...	10.35
Waterloo Tram Terminus			12.40	1.40	10.40	2.40	4.40	...	10.40
Lepton (Red Lion)			12.47	1.47	10.47	2.47	4.47	...	10.47
Grange Moor (Blacksmith's Arms)	6.15		12.52	1.52	10.52	2.52	4.52	...	10.52
FLOCKTON (Angel Inn)	6.20	7.25	12.57	1.57	—	2.57	4.57	...	10.57
Overton (Black Swan)	6.28	7.33	1.5	2.5	11.5	3.5	5.5	...	11.5
Middlestown (Co-op.)	6.31	7.36	12.38	1.8	2.8	11.8	3.8	5.8	11.8
Sandy Lane Viaduct	6.33	7.38	12.40	1.10	2.10	11.10	3.10	5.10	11.10
Thornhill (Combs)	6.41	7.41	12.48	1.18	2.18	11.18	3.18	5.18	11.18
Thornhill Station	6.44	7.49	12.51	1.21	2.21	11.21	3.21	5.21	11.21
DEWSBURY (Omnibus Station)	6.48	7.53	12.55	1.25	2.25	11.25	3.25	5.25	11.25

Huddersfield → Dewsbury — Sundays:

Stop	p.m.	p.m.	p.m.	p.m.	p.m.	p.m.	p.m.
HUDDERSFIELD (Lord Street)	2.30	4.30	6.30	8.30	9.30	10.30	
Mold Green (Junction Inn)	2.35	4.35	6.35	8.35	9.35	10.35	
Waterloo Tram Terminus	2.40	4.40	6.40	8.40	9.40	10.40	
Lepton (Red Lion)	2.47	4.47	6.47	8.47	9.47	10.47	
Grange Moor (Blacksmith's Arms)	2.52	4.52	6.52	8.52	9.52	10.52	
FLOCKTON (Angel Inn)	2.57	4.57	6.57	8.57	9.57	10.57	
Overton (Black Swan)	3.5	5.5	7.5	9.5	10.5	11.5	
Middlestown (Co-op.)	3.8	5.8	7.8	9.8	10.8	11.8	
Sandy Lane Viaduct	3.10	5.10	7.10	9.10	10.10	11.10	
Thornhill (Combs)	3.18	5.18	7.18	9.18	10.18	11.18	
Thornhill Station	3.21	5.21	7.21	9.21	10.21	11.21	
DEWSBURY (Omnibus Station)	3.25	5.25	7.25	9.25	10.25	11.25	

†WEDNESDAYS ONLY.

FOR THE DIRECT SERVICE BETWEEN DEWSBURY AND HUDDERSFIELD SEE TIME TABLE FOR "DEWSBURY—HUDDERSFIELD via MIRFIELD," ROUTE No. 7.

Heckmondwike journey and when he later tried to use the return half for another journey in the same direction the conductor refused to accept the ticket. The traveller claimed he was entitled to a second journey and would not pay a fare so he was taken to court. However, as the company were unable to produce a bye-law relating to the validity of return tickets, the case was dismissed. Similar cases in north east England usually involved miners who often walked to their colliery to save money but after a hard shift underground preferred to ride home, using a cheaper return ticket twice in the same direction.

By January 1933 alterations had been made to the direct Leeds route with the Monday to Friday frequency reduced to 20 minutes. There were now three versions of the route but all buses still showed 18. From Huddersfield the variations were as follows [the letters are ours]:

(variant A) at 5 minutes past the hour via Roberttown (Central), Liversedge (Globe), Heckmondwike, Liversedge (Swan), Gildersome Station and Gildersome Green, taking 57 minutes

(variant B) at 25 minutes past via Roberttown (Fountain and Yew Tree), Union Road, Heckmondwike, New North Road and Gildersome Station, taking 53 minutes

(variant C) at 45 minutes past via Roberttown (Central and Yew Tree), Liversedge (Globe), Heckmondwike, New North Road, Gildersome Station and Gildersome Green taking 56 minutes

Most passengers referred to the 25 minutes past bus, which bypassed the centres of Roberttown and Gildersome, as the "direct bus". [At the same time the whole of the 18 was still referred to as "Leeds direct" to distinguish it from 19 via Batley.] On Saturday afternoons the 15 minute frequency was retained with departures at 05, 20, 35 and 50 minutes past and route variations in the sequence A B C C. Slower route 19 via Batley followed our variant C (seemingly the original route) on common sections and ran hourly (half-hourly on Saturday afternoons). This pattern of operation continued, apart from the inevitable wartime temporary cutbacks, until 1948.

On the 18 conductors' booking up points were at White Gate Inn, Heckmondwike, Birstall Smithies and Gildersome Green as well as at the termini. Fares were 7d to Heckmondwike, 9d to Birstall Smithies, 11d to Gildersome and 1/4d to Leeds. There was also an ordinary return at 2/- to Leeds.

By 1 January 1935 some Wednesday and Saturday journeys on route 6 (Huddersfield-Flockton-Dewsbury) were diverted to run direct via Smithy Brook (instead of Sandy Lane) between Middlestown and Thornhill. Meanwhile in June 1934 the 7 (Huddersfield-Mirfield-Dewsbury) route had been renumbered 27 by joint operator Huddersfield JOC. It was not until 1935 (by 1 June) that Yorkshire Woollen started using 27 instead of 7 - an arithmetical compromise as Huddersfield JOC had previously used 47. At the same time 6 (Huddersfield-Flockton-Dewsbury) was renumbered 7. It was in 1935 that the company name was changed to Yorkshire Woollen District Transport Co. Ltd, reflecting the abandonment of the tramway system. From January 1937 the joint operators on the Huddersfield-Cleckheaton-Bradford-Ilkley route also reached a compromise when that service was renumbered 68. Yorkshire Woollen had previously used 39 while West Yorkshire had only recently (by 28 May 1936) switched from their initial choice of 105 to 62.

Although Yorkshire Woollen and their joint operator had introduced double deckers on the Dewsbury via Mirfield route in the early 1930s, the Leeds and Ilkley via Bradford routes continued to be single deck operated during this decade. This entailed a good deal of duplication on the Leeds routes. Originally "duplicate car" would be shown as the destination but later a flap labelled "duplicate" could be hung down and "Leeds" was displayed. Throughout the 1930s Yorkshire Woollen continued to standardise on Leyland buses. Among the single deckers, Leyland Tigers with front entrance 32 seat Roe bodywork were particularly common; there were also some Leyland Lions. Leyland Titan double deckers used on interurban routes were mostly of the lowbridge variety; highbridge buses with centre entrances were bought for tramway replacement.

Like all operators Yorkshire Woollen had to introduce emergency timetables on the outbreak of war. From 23 September 1939 services to Huddersfield were reduced on average by about 50% but this first round of cuts proved too severe and in December 1939 another timetable, showing only a 25% cut compared with prewar service levels, came into operation. At this point the stand for the Leeds routes (18/9) was transferred from Kirkgate to Rosemary Lane; the Bradford (68) buses joined them there later in the war. As the fuel situation deteriorated towards the end of 1942, Sunday services were further curtailed and last evening buses ran at about 9.00pm.

The direct Dewsbury service (27) initially fared very

Yorkshire Woollen Roe bodied Leyland Tigers such as TS7 401 (HD 6317), new in 1937, were a common sight on the Huddersfield to Leeds and Ilkley services in the late 1930s. This bus is seen on the parking ground at the "bottom end of Town" and was sold to Hebble in 1950. [P.J. Cardno collection]

badly on Monday to Friday and from Huddersfield there was a four hour gap each morning between 8.03am and 12.03pm. A two hour frequency followed until the evening peak but the timetable advised passengers to use alternative services between Three Nuns and Dewsbury: 2 (Ossett-Keighley) and 3 (Dewsbury-Brighouse). Through passengers could use the train. The revisions of December 1939 gave an 80 minute morning off peak frequency. By November 1942 the last ordinary departure of the day was at 8.55pm; a final bus at 9.35pm was only available to shift workers who were contributing to the war effort at the mills and factories along Leeds Road.

The direct Leeds service (18) was initially cut to hourly off peak on Monday to Friday and all day on Sundays. This was totally inadequate and the revision of December 1939 gave an irregular off peak service with buses leaving Huddersfield at 5 and 45 minutes past the hour; all off peak journeys followed the same route, omitting the sections serving the Fountain Inn at Roberttown and the Swan Hotel at Liversedge. By November 1942 the last bus for Leeds left Town at 8.05pm on Monday to Saturday with the 8.45pm running only as far as Gildersome Green.

The Leeds via Batley service (19) initially became irregular on Monday to Friday with only ten departures; there were considerable gaps in the off peak timetable. The hourly frequency was restored in the revision of December 1939 but further cuts in November 1942 saw the last bus scheduled to depart for Leeds as early as 7.25pm. As on the Dewsbury route, a 9.35pm short working to Heckmondwike was reserved for shift

workers.

From 23 September 1939 the Huddersfield-Bradford-Ilkley joint service (68) was split at Bradford. West Yorkshire Road Car buses were not seen in Huddersfield, except on long distance coach services, for another 30 years. Yorkshire Woollen continued the Huddersfield to Bradford section under the same number but it was severely pruned; the Sunday service was withdrawn completely and there were only 11 through return journeys on Monday to Friday and 13 on Saturdays. Also from 23 September 1939 route 7 (Dewsbury-Flockton-Huddersfield) was cut back to run no further than Grange

Moor Cross Roads and never reached Huddersfield again.

By the end of 1939 Yorkshire Woollen had reduced overall mileage by more than 40% and many single deck buses and coaches were no longer required. It was not surprising that by July 1940 the Ministry of War Transport had requisitioned 19 coaches and 27 single deck buses, many of which were never returned. Double deck buses were more widely used and appeared on the Huddersfield-Leeds routes.

With no excursions or holiday tours to sell, management embarked on an advertising campaign aimed at explaining the difficulties under which they were trying to operate. Headed "Yorkshire Bus Bulletin", most of these adverts were illustrated with an appropriate cartoon in an effort to get the message home.

Intending passengers were implored not to blind the driver in the blackout by shining a torch in his face but to signal with a folded newspaper or white handkerchief. On board the bus, passengers were reminded that conductresses found punching tickets and giving the correct change difficult in the blackout.

The importance of buses in serving the country by carrying essential war workers to and from work was stressed and shoppers and non essential travellers were urged to avoid the rush hour. Being short of platform staff (many men were away on active service), the company wanted to reduce the number of conductors absent with 'flu or heavy colds. Under the heading

YWD's first utility Guy Arab, Duple bodied Mark I 481 (HD 7307) new in 1942, is in Dewsbury Bus Station after the war bound for Huddersfield on the indirect route 26 via Savile Arms introduced in 1947. [R.D. Mills – R. Marshall collection]

"Keep It To Yourself", passengers were reminded of the effects of coughing and sneezing, even though buses were disinfected every night.

As passengers had to be reassured that everything was mechanically sound, under the title "Perfectly Tuned" it was stressed that engines were still overhauled at regular intervals. After all "It's the engine that drives the bus that carries the people who go to work to win the war."

From 1943 a new series of advertisements appeared under the heading "British Buses" which stressed the importance of buses to the war effort in general and were patriotic in tone. In one, passengers were urged to make the local "Wings for Victory Week" their own battle for Britain by putting as much money as possible into war savings. In another they were reminded that long distance coach services, suspended by government order, would only be restored when the job of winning the war was finished.

Between 1943 and 1945 the company received substantial numbers of Guy Arab double deckers, wartime utility buses with wooden seats. Their bodywork was constructed from inferior materials which soon deteriorated but most were later rebodied. After the war double deckers could be seen on all Yorkshire Woollen services into Huddersfield, although single deckers also still appeared on the Bradford route and as duplicates elsewhere.

Prewar frequencies were restored first on the Dewsbury route, with the Bradford and Leeds routes following on 3 August 1946. As with other companies, difficulties were being experienced in maintaining elderly vehicles and new buses were in short supply. Nevertheless by the end of 1948 121 new vehicles had entered the fleet since the end of the war: 6 Leyland Tiger coaches, 75 Leyland Tiger single deck buses and 40 highbridge double deckers (25 Guy Arabs and 15 Leyland Titans).

Higher protective fares were always charged for local journeys between Town and Bradley (and between Town and Waterloo on the prewar indirect Dewsbury route), in order to encourage short distance passengers to use the more frequent Corporation services. Because of the unreliability of the Bradley trolleybus service in early 1947 many Huddersfield bound passengers were regularly boarding inward bound Yorkshire Woollen buses. Some crews, however, were not keen to pick up extra passengers and several drivers ignored the signals of the would be passengers. Complaints to the company elicited a promise to investigate.

Route development had become possible again and

on 25 October 1947 a second service between Dewsbury and Huddersfield jointly operated with Huddersfield JOC (26) was started. This deviated from the existing main road route (27) between Fir Cottage and Three Nuns by running via Church Lane, Savile Arms, Nab Lane and Stocks Bank Road.

From 8 November 1948 the Leeds direct services, which up to that point were all still numbered 18, were reorganised. Departures at 05 and 45 minutes past the hour from Huddersfield (our variants A and C –see page 7) both now followed the C, running via the New Inn and Yew Tree Inn at Roberttown and direct via New North Road beyond Heckmondwike; they retained number 18. The 25 minutes past departure (our variant B) via the Fountain and Yew Tree on the outskirts of Roberttown and via Union Road was renumbered 19 and diverted between Heckmondwike and Six Lane Ends via Liversedge (Swan) [instead of direct via New North Road] and also via Gildersome Green. Consequently existing 19 (Leeds via Batley) was renumbered 21.

Existing hourly 68 (Bradford via Cleckheaton) was supplemented from 6 August 1949 by new hourly service 67 which differed from the 68 only by running between Three Nuns and Hightown via Hartshead instead of Roberttown. Although double deckers were used on these routes, single deckers from the huge batch of 75 Leyland Tiger PS1s with Brush B34F bodies purchased in 1948 (558-632) were frequently seen in Huddersfield on the 67/8 and also as Saturday duplicates on the Dewsbury and Leeds routes. On one occasion, for the benefit of Fartown rugby league supporters, a Leyland Tiger duplicate on the 27 which had just reached Dewsbury Bus Station

immediately became a special to the ground at Crown Flatt. Rebooking was possible without alighting and the conductor had to rush round again with his Bellgraphic machine as the bus was driven non-stop to the ground.

The railway bridge with a headroom of 14 feet 6 inches on the A62 at Cooper Bridge could be negotiated by highbridge buses but was often a problem for drivers, particularly in bad weather. Three passengers were injured on 20 December 1949 when 480, a Leyland Titan TD7 of 1942 with Roe H30/26R body, being driven from Dewsbury by John Hemingway on the 27 route, failed to pull out far enough towards the centre of the road to gain the maximum headroom. As a result the top of the bus was badly buckled and several upstairs windows were smashed. The conductor, who had just come downstairs,

This image of YWD's solitary 1942 Leyland TD7/Roe 480 shows the damage caused by collision with the bridge near Cooper Bridge Station on 20 December 1949. Three passengers on the Dewsbury to Huddersfield bus were injured.[Kirklees Image Archive ke02348]

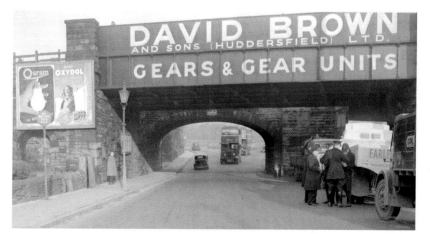

A December 1949 general view of the railway bridge near Cooper Bridge Station over the busy A62, then the main Leeds to Manchester road, shows how bus drivers had to pull out towards the centre of the road to negotiate the bridge safely until the road surface was lowered in 1952. [Kirklees Image Archive ke02349]

YWD Guy Arab III/Northern Coach Builders 535 (HD 7818), new in 1947 and still in original maroon and cream livery, picks up in Aire Street off City Square, Leeds, en route to Huddersfield. 535 was withdrawn and scrapped in 1958. [W.J. Haynes]

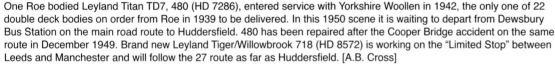

One Roe bodied Leyland Titan TD7, 480 (HD 7286), entered service with Yorkshire Woollen in 1942, the only one of 22 double deck bodies on order from Roe in 1939 to be delivered. In this 1950 scene it is waiting to depart from Dewsbury Bus Station on the main road route to Huddersfield. 480 has been repaired after the Cooper Bridge accident on the same route in December 1949. Brand new Leyland Tiger/Willowbrook 718 (HD 8572) is working on the "Limited Stop" between Leeds and Manchester and will follow the 27 route as far as Huddersfield. [A.B. Cross]

YWD 1950 Leyland Tiger/Willowbrook service buses 700/5 (HD 8554/9) are posed outside the Three Nuns. Many single deckers were painted mainly cream because they would be needed as duplicates on coach services on summer weekends. The Three Nuns Inn, Leeds Road, Cooper Bridge, two minutes ride beyond Bradley trolleybus terminus on a YWD bus from Huddersfield and a request stop on the "Tyne Tees Mersey", was supposedly established in 1539 by three nuns turned out of nearby Kirklees Priory, the site of Robin Hood's grave. [R. Marshall collection (courtesy Yorkshire Woollen District Transport Co. Ltd)]

was thrown from the platform into the lower saloon. Eventually in April 1952 workmen began the six weeks task of lowering the road surface under the bridge, a task made more difficult by the presence of a large water main underneath it. Only after this had been completed was it possible for double deckers to pass each other safely under the bridge.

A new service was introduced from 27 January 1950 between Dewsbury and Skelmanthorpe via Thornhill, Middlestown, Flockton and Emley. Route 48 ran on Wednesday (a Dewsbury market day) afternoons and evenings only and short workings between Flockton and Skelmanthorpe were a particularly unusual feature. Kirkburton UDC felt that this entirely new route should not have been introduced until all withdrawn prewar services had been reinstated; they were still asking for the restoration of the Dewsbury-Flockton-Huddersfield facility but it never reappeared.

In 1950 35 Leyland Titan PD2/3s with Roe H31/25R bodies were purchased (647-81). Many of these remained in the fleet until 1964 and they were regular performers on the Huddersfield-Leeds routes. In their

Yorkshire Woollen's terminus in Leeds for the Huddersfield via Heckmondwike routes was in Queen Street on the western fringes of the city centre, although most passengers boarded at a slightly less inconveniently located stop in Aire Street not far from City Station. 1950 Roe bodied Leyland PD2/3s 670/1 (HD 8524/5), examples of a large batch (647-81) associated with these routes in the fifties and early sixties, display their original elegant livery of maroon with cream bands in a deserted Queen Street. The first bus is on the hourly shortworking of route 21. [R. Marshall collection]

1951 integrally constructed Yorkshire Woollen Leyland Olympic/Weymann 737 (HD 9128) is on the 67/8 (Bradford via Cleckheaton) stand in Rosemary Lane, Huddersfield. Dewsbury's very slow issuing of its original sequence of HD registrations made YWD's buses seem older than they were. Following on from HD, AHD was still being issued in 1955 – Huddersfield had used up its ACX and AVH in the mid 1930s. [R.F. Mack]

latter years the varnished woodwork in the saloons was covered with light grey gloss paint which did nothing for their appearance. They were the last rear entrance double deckers bought new and indeed no further new double deckers were placed in service until 1958.

The distinguished maroon and cream livery was replaced from 1953 onwards by unrelieved lighter red which was economical to apply but very drab. Some single deck buses which were sometimes used on coach duties were mainly cream with red relief. Further modernisation of the double deck fleet was achieved by the rebodying of the wartime Guy Arabs with new Roe bodies. As the Guys went to Roe at Crossgates, Leeds for their new bodies, other vehicles had to be hired as replacements so that, for example, Ribble lowbridge Guy Arab utilities worked for a short period on the 26/7 (Dewsbury) routes. Most of the rebodied Guys lasted until 1967 and could regularly be seen on the 26/7 routes until very late in their lives. More double deckers were

Top left-
For many years YWD had to use bus stands in various dingy streets on the edge of Huddersfield town centre. From 1939 to 1959 buses to Leeds picked up in the none too fragrant Rosemary Lane in the middle of an undeveloped prewar slum clearance site east of the present Kirkgate/Southgate junction. Roe bodied Leyland Titan PD2/3 662 (HD 8516) is seen almost new in 1950 in Rosemary Lane. A Leyland Tiger on the Bradford via Cleckheaton services is partly visible. [A.B. Cross]

Above
Yorkshire Woollen's 1950 Roe bodied Leyland Titan PD2/3 668 (HD 8522) has been repainted in the unrelieved red scheme introduced in 1953, making an instructive comparison with the photograph of HD 8516. The new livery at least matches the drab surroundings in Rosemary Lane, Huddersfield, where 668 is awaiting departure for Leeds. [R. Marshall collection]

Left
In 1945 eight nearly new Guy Arab utilities were acquired by Yorkshire Woollen from the Maidstone and District bus company, which then received eight Daimler CWA6s allocated to but unwanted by YWD. 513 (GKP 445) was rebodied by Roe in 1954 and is seen later at the Queen Street, Leeds terminus of the Huddersfield routes. [P. J. Cardno collection]

obtained by rebodying 24 of the 1948 intake of Leyland Tiger single deckers with new lightweight highbridge bodies of the ugly MCCW Orion design in 1954; these buses looked exceptionally unattractive in the allover red livery and most also survived until 1967.

As a result of the Suez Crisis from 15 December 1956 some modest temporary service reductions were made to Huddersfield area services (until April 1957). The combined Monday-Saturday evening and Sunday frequency on 18/9 (Leeds direct) was cut from 20 to 30 minutes. On the Dewsbury (26/7) services the Saturday only 9.55pm departure from Dewsbury and return were deleted.

A more permanent economy measure was the withdrawal of the Sunday to Friday evening service on 67 (Bradford via Hartshead) from 21 December 1957; sister service 68 remained hourly in those periods. At the same time the combined daily evening service on 18/9 (Leeds direct) was reduced to half-hourly.

From 8 March 1958, to replace infrequent route

The conductor of YWD 1962 Leyland Leopard/ Marshall 912 (HHD 876) has already reset the blind for the return journey from Huddersfield and is giving signals to his driver in the days when traffic already on a roundabout did not automatically have priority. The bus is negotiating the roundabout from Leeds Road into Northgate to reach its Brook Street terminus. The company's very attractive mainly cream single deck livery of the early sixties was applied with an eye to weekend express work. [W.J. Haynes]

YWD 895 (GHD 767), a 1962 Metro-Cammell bodied Leyland Titan PD3A/1, has stopped outside the Bradley branch of the Co-op, complete with loading hoist, at the Colne Bridge Road and Leeds Road junction, a place better known as Bradley trolleybus terminus. 895's all red "livery" contrasts with that of the overtaking Leopard – for most of the sixties all YWD saloons were predominantly cream with red relief. 895 is on route 21 from Leeds via Batley while the Leopard is on even more indirect service 68 from Bradford via Cleckheaton. [S.T. Harling collection]

15 (Heckmondwike-Norristhorpe), alternate daytime journeys on the 18 (and all evening journeys) were rerouted between Yew Tree Inn and Heckmondwike via Norristhorpe as new route 18A. Further changes occurred on 4 January 1959 when the Sunday daytime and Monday to Friday daytime off peak "Leeds direct" services were reduced to a combined half hourly frequency by the withdrawal of the route 18 journeys. The 18 now ran only during Monday to Friday peaks and on Saturdays until early evening. These cuts possibly reflected a decrease in the number of through passengers travelling between Huddersfield and Leeds, a number which probably fell further when British Railways introduced a competing half hourly diesel train service. In July 1959 the terminus for the services to Bradford and Leeds was moved from Rosemary Lane to Kirkgate (the section now known as Oldgate) where it remained for four years before moving again to Brook Street; the Dewsbury routes were transferred to Brook Street at the same time.

In 1956 the maximum length permitted for double deckers had been increased to 30 feet. Between 1958 and 1961 Yorkshire Woollen bought several batches of AEC Regent Vs with 70 seat front entrance bodywork and driver controlled doors (not used on Huddersfield routes when new) and these were followed by Leyland Titan PD3As. From 1959 new single deckers were AEC Reliances featuring the brighter livery of mainly cream with red relief which would be applied to all single deckers delivered for the next few years. Buses in this livery were regularly used on express service duplication. From 12 February 1961 route 21 (Leeds) was diverted via the newly opened Batley bus station.

Yorkshire Woollen were also quick to take advantage of new regulations which permitted 36 feet long single deckers and from 1962 Leyland Leopards of this length appeared. The attractive brighter livery used on the Reliances was adapted to good effect to suit the stylish BET specification Marshall and Weymann bodywork supplied on several batches of Leopards between 1962 and 1966. These vehicles became a familiar sight in Huddersfield. They worked alongside double deckers on the Leeds routes while the Bradford routes became mainly single deck operated.

As late as 1963 a further six Leyland Tiger single deckers were rebuilt as double deckers, this time receiving new front entrance Roe bodies. These appeared on the Leeds routes and could be seen from time to time in Huddersfield until conductors were dispensed with.

A vehicle shortage in February 1964 resulted in two elderly County Motors Leyland Titan PD2s (87/8) running on loan on the Dewsbury (26/7) routes into Huddersfield. Entry into service of a batch of Albion Lowlanders had been delayed by a strike at the bodybuilders, Weymanns, whose product was incidentally better proportioned than that of their rivals. The first six of these lowheight double deckers, which are said to have been purchased because of clearance problems as a result of road resurfacing, appeared on the Leeds (18/18A/19/21) routes from 12 February, where they ran alongside Leyland Leopard single deckers for a number of years.

Yorkshire Woollen had placed their first rear engined double deckers, Daimler Fleetlines, in service in 1965 but it was only from 1967 onwards, when further Fleetlines and also some Leyland Atlanteans with the same very modern looking Alexander bodies entered service, that these buses were regularly seen in Huddersfield on the Dewsbury routes. Older buses such as Leyland Tiger rebuilds still appeared on the peak hour journeys between Trafalgar Mills and Dewsbury. By this stage all double deckers were gaining a single cream band, which certainly improved their appearance.

The company was 100% state owned from March 1968, when the BET group voluntarily sold their UK bus and coach interests, and from 1 January 1969 became part of the newly established National Bus Company

alongside neighbours Yorkshire Traction and West Riding. West Riding and Yorkshire Woollen would soon be placed under common management and became known as the "West Riding Group".

From 1 October 1969 there was a change of partner on 26/7 (Dewsbury) as a result of Huddersfield Corporation's purchase of the National Bus Company's share of the Huddersfield Joint Omnibus Committee. As part of the deal the JOC's workings on 26/7 passed to Yorkshire Traction, who would later share the operation of other Yorkshire Woollen routes into Huddersfield.

A steady decline in passenger numbers resulted in the familiar economies of abolishing return tickets (4 January 1970), substantial fare increases, service cuts and the expansion of one man operation. Worked mainly by single deckers since the early/mid 1960s, routes 67/8 (Huddersfield-Cleckheaton-Bradford) were Yorkshire Woollen's first Huddersfield routes to lose their conductors, on 4 July 1970. Route 48 (Dewsbury-Skelmanthorpe) was converted to one man operation

from the same date. From 27 February 1971 the Huddersfield-Dewsbury (26/7) routes were reduced and speeded up on Sundays to use just two buses (one from each operator) on a combined half-hourly frequency.

From 28 June 1971 Yorkshire Woollen foresook the dismal and inconveniently situated stands at the east end of Brook Street and moved to Byram Street for the Bradford routes and to Lord Street for the Leeds routes; the Dewsbury routes had moved to a stand in Lord Street which had become surplus to Huddersfield JOC's requirements in April 1967. [All the routes would be reunited in Byram Street soon afterwards.] Although passengers still had no seats or shelters, the new stands, which were surplus to the Corporation's requirements following their 1970 reorganisation, were at least more central and less lonely and unpleasant at night.

A major reorganisation of almost the entire route network took place on 14 August 1971. The combined "Leeds direct" group (18/18A/19) became half hourly at all times with the deletion of the existing 18 journeys;

Many of Yorkshire Woollen's rebodied wartime utility Guys gave lengthy service. 485 (HD 7373), a Guy Arab II with newer Roe body, lasted until 1967 and in June 1965 is turning from Northgate into Brook Street, with the Huddersfield terminus of these joint (with Huddersfield JOC) routes to Dewsbury in the foreground. [R. Marshall collection]

YWD's Albion Lowlanders had Weymann bodywork which looked less ill proportioned than other manufacturers' products on this lowheight chassis. 116 (KHD 408) of 1964 had gained a welcome cream band when pictured on the Leeds stand in Brook Street, Huddersfield on 21 November 1969. As usual no "via" blind was displayed. [H.J. Black]

this number was, however, reused because 18A via Norristhorpe was renumbered 18. 19 was rerouted between Three Nuns and Yew Tree Inn to follow the 18/18A route via the centre of Roberttown and Lumb Lane. Some of its old route direct along the A62 was left without buses but Fountain Inn was now served by 21, rerouted via Mirfield.

21 (Leeds via Batley) was combined with former route 20 (Leeds-Mirfield) as new service 21, now jointly operated with Yorkshire Traction with an increased running time of 75 minutes from Huddersfield. This service was converted to one man operation with double deckers and during Monday to Saturday daytimes it was interworked in Huddersfield with new routes 1 to 3. New 21 was hourly via Three Nuns, Mirfield, Roberttown (Fountain), Heckmondwike, the Healey by-pass and Batley. On Monday to Saturday evenings and all day on Sundays this new 21 was at first operated only between Mirfield and Leeds.

67 (Bradford via Hartshead) was completely withdrawn, the Sunday service on this route having met the same fate four years earlier. 68 (Bradford via Roberttown and Cleckheaton) survived but was renumbered 60; this too was now jointly operated with Yorkshire Traction.

Finally the most obvious change to affect Huddersfield was the combination of routes 26/7 to Dewsbury (jointly operated with Yorkshire Traction) with former route 1 from Dewsbury to Leeds (Sovereign Street) via Shaw Cross, Woodkirk and Tingley Cross Roads. Three different routes were followed between Three Nuns and Fir Cottage and new hourly joint services were numbered 1, 2 and 3, giving an overall 20 minute frequency:

1 via Church Lane, Savile Arms and Stocks Bank Road [former 26 route]
2 via Huddersfield Road [former 27 route]
3 via Huddersfield Road, Nettleton Road and Stocks Bank Road

These routes were run with one man double deckers, the first examples of such working by Yorkshire Woollen into Huddersfield. The three routes were interworked and during Monday to Saturday daytime they were further interworked with the 21.

All the company's services into Huddersfield now terminated in Byram Street and all except 18/9 were operated jointly with Yorkshire Traction. The 60 (Bradford) continued to be worked by single deckers but the other routes were mainly double deck operated; new Daimler Fleetlines with Alexander bodies could be seen. From July 1972 new ECW bodied Fleetlines also appeared, at first especially on routes 1 to 3.

From 27 November 1971 route 21 was extended on Monday to Saturday evenings and all day on Sundays to run through to Huddersfield again rather than being curtailed at Mirfield at those times. The journey time was increased from 75 to 85 minutes because it had proved insufficient for the one man operated buses.

A minor change took place on 2 February 1972 on the Monday to Saturday evenings and Sunday service on the 1-3 (Huddersfield-Dewsbury-Leeds) group. The previous pattern of two journeys per hour, one on route 1 and one on route 2, was changed in favour of routes 1 and 3. This gave a service via Nettleton Road and doubled the frequency to Stocks Bank Road at those times, at the expense of the main Mirfield to Three Nuns road. This corridor had, however, enjoyed an alternative hourly service since November on route 21.

By the end of 1972 vehicles were starting to appear in the National Bus Company poppy red and white livery, less attractive than the deeper shade of red and cream which preceded it. The NBC's new standard integral single decker, the Leyland National, also started to appear on the 60 (Bradford).

Various elderly double deckers, including secondhand tin-fronted Leyland Titans from Sheffield, could still be seen on the 18/9 (Leeds via Heckmondwike) but this did not last for long. In September 1973 routes 18/9, the remaining conductor operated Yorkshire Woollen buses in Huddersfield and their only routes into the town not operated jointly with Yorkshire Traction, were converted to one man operation with journey times increased from 56 to 63 minutes. Five buses were now required for the Monday to Saturday service instead of the previous four. On Sundays just an hourly service was provided by the 18 as the 19 had been withdrawn, presumably part of the price to be paid for one man conversion.

Heckmondwike UDC and Morley Borough Council objected unsuccessfully to these changes. There were also complaints about the refusal of one man drivers to open doors to allow passengers to board during layover periods in Queen Street, Leeds, even during bad weather. The traffic commissioners suggested that Leeds City Council should be asked to provide shelters and issued an instruction that drivers had to allow passengers to board during the layover period. Whether this had any effect is not known but keeping passengers standing outside in cold and rain was a common practice, particularly of National Bus Company drivers, during this period which must have lost the bus industry countless "customers".

Yorkshire Woollen Leyland Tiger 49 (HD 8552), rebuilt and rebodied by Roe in 1963, advertises the South-West Clipper coach services to Devon in a quiet Brook Street on the Leeds stand on 16 September 1970. The single fare to Leeds had recently been increased to three shillings, return fares having been abolished earlier in the year.
[H.J. Black]

TICKETING

For many years Yorkshire Woollen favoured the use of composite Bell Punch tickets on interurban bus routes. These measured 3.5" by 1.25" and had a perforated tab to a design very similar to those used by Huddersfield JOC. The title was initially Yorkshire (WD) Electric Trams Ltd, changing in May 1935 to YWD Transport Co Ltd. On the Leeds-Huddersfield routes the maximum single fare was 1/4d for many years and tickets up to the value of 2/- were required for returns. Known values and colours include the following: 1d white; 1½d green; 2d pink; 2½d white with red stripe; 3d orange; 3½d white with blue stripe; 4d sepia; 5d sage; 6d blue; 7d pale brick; 8d beige; 9d mauve; 10d yellow; 11d pink with green o/p; 1/- green; 1/1d grey; 1/2d white; 1/3d green with o/p; 1/4d sage; 1/5d purple; 1/6d white; 1/9d dark plum; 1/11d green; 2/- mauve.

Punch tickets were initially replaced on the longer routes by Bellgraphic machines and later the Setright speed system was favoured. A few of the Bellgraphic machines were used as late as the early 1960s when specific traffic statistics were required.

One fault of the Bellgraphic ticket system as used by Yorkshire Woollen was the ease with which dishonest conductors could defraud the company. One conductor who could not resist the temptation was given a four month prison sentence in March 1950. On the Leeds-Huddersfield routes on two separate occasions he had issued a 2/- return ticket with the carbon copies registering 2½d and 3d singles respectively, thus obtaining 3/6½d for himself. The fraud was proved by the presence of a thumb print on the counterfoil, which in normal use could not be touched by the conductor. A piece of metal such as a razor blade had been inserted between the carbon and the counterfoil.

THE LIMITED STOP (TYNE TEES MERSEY)

Apart from operating bus services centred on the Heavy Woollen area of the West Riding, Yorkshire Woollen were one of the pioneers of the famous limited stop service which from 15 May 1929 linked Liverpool and Manchester via the A62 over Standedge with Huddersfield, Dewsbury, Leeds, Harrogate, Ripon, Darlington, Durham and Newcastle. There was also a branch from Thirsk which served Middlesbrough. The "Limited Stop", as it was affectionately known, had developed by May 1933 into a joint operation between Lancashire United Transport, North Western Road Car, Northern General, United Automobile, West Yorkshire Road Car and Yorkshire Woollen. For some years there was a basic hourly service after 8.00am from Kirkgate (later Venn Street), Huddersfield to Manchester and Liverpool (journey times 1 hour 25 minutes and 3 hours 25 minutes respectively). In the other direction Leeds, served hourly, was reached in 45 minutes but unfortunately for Huddersfield passengers this was usually followed by a 35 minute refreshment stop at the cramped Wellington Street coach station. From Leeds, the route ran via Harrogate and Ripon, after which alternate departures served Newcastle via Darlington and Durham and Middlesbrough via Thirsk and Northallerton.

The service was very popular with holidaymakers who would use it to connect with other bus services and on summer Saturdays many duplicates were to be seen in Venn Street, swallowing up lengthy queues of excited passengers and their bulky luggage. The advantage of the Limited Stop from the passenger's point of view was that advanced booking was not required so fares could be paid on the bus. With so many operators, it was relatively easy to provide duplicates but a nightmare for anyone trying to reclaim lost belongings. As most of the vehicles used were service buses rather than coaches, accommodation for holiday luggage was limited and often suitcases had to occupy seats, limiting seating capacity even further. Two ladies found their own solution to this problem. As far as clothing was concerned, they simply wore two of each kind of garment; anything else fitted into a shopping bag along with refreshments for the journey.

The service always avoided the main streets of the town. For many years coaches ran between Longroyd Bridge and Venn Street via St Thomas's Road, Colne Road and Queen Street South; from the early 1960s they would be rerouted via Manchester Road and the new inner ring road, Queensgate. Prewar period return fares from Huddersfield were: Leeds 3/6d, Harrogate 5/-, Middlesbrough 12/6d, Newcastle 16/-, Manchester 4/- and Liverpool 8/-.

With the declaration of war in September 1939 there was an immediate reduction in frequency, followed by a complete suspension after Sunday 9 June 1940. Services were resumed on 6 October 1946 but with through passengers being required to change vehicles at Leeds unless they were on board one of the duplicate vehicles.

As a result of the Suez crisis the number of journeys was drastically reduced from 30 December 1956; on the Leeds-Huddersfield-Manchester section the number of weekday return journeys was halved to seven. By the end of March 1957 the emergency was over but the operating companies decided that the time had come for economies to be made. The Suez timetable was to become the permanent winter timetable as well as the Tuesday to Thursday summer timetable and the authorised summer timetable would only operate from Friday to Monday.

On 6 August 1948 Yorkshire Woollen 1938 Leyland Tiger TS8/Duple coach 414 (HD 6613) arrives at the stand on the east side of Venn Street, Huddersfield. 414 is bound for Liverpool on the "Limited Stop". Part of the queue could have been waiting for a London coach.[Kirklees Image Archive Ke00266]

Single deck coaches (or buses) were almost invariably used. There were, however, several occasions during the 1950s when Leyland Titan double deckers of both Yorkshire Woollen and North Western could be seen on the Leeds-Huddersfield-Manchester section, for example during the 1955 train strike and also in May 1958.

Route numbers were introduced for Summer 1960: X97/8 Liverpool-Newcastle and X99 Liverpool-Middlesbrough. In September 1970, following the formation of the National Bus Company in the previous year, Yorkshire Woollen's licences were transferred to Hebble Motor Services, which was being restructured as the coaching arm of the West Riding and Yorkshire Woollen companies.

The Limited Stop continued, albeit in a much reduced form, and lasted long enough to pass into the control of National Travel North East in April 1974. The services, renumbered 397-9, became part of the National Express network.

OTHER YWD EXPRESS SERVICE OPERATIONS

For many years Yorkshire Woollen had also run summer coach services to Scarborough, Filey and Bridlington from Dewsbury and the Heavy Woollen District. In the early 1930s there was a daily through service from Huddersfield but by 1937 this had been replaced by a special connecting service on Sundays only; on other days passengers caught the Leeds service bus and changed onto a coach at Heckmondwike. After the war coaches typically ran daily from Dewsbury between May and September. On Saturdays during July, August and September there would be a through coach from Huddersfield but at other times passengers used the service bus as far as Heckmondwike. Through booking from Huddersfield was always available.

Further Yorkshire Woollen express services run jointly with other "area agreement" bus companies are described in the Yorkshire Traction section of this book.

Yorkshire Woollen 743 (HD 9151) was a Leyland Royal Tiger with a centre entrance Windover coach body, one of six. When new in 1951 it would have looked ultra-modern alongside traditional half-cab coaches and front seat passengers could have enjoyed the excellent views. It is about to return to Huddersfield on an express service. [P.J. Cardno collection]

2: IDEAL (KILBURN) AND OTHER EARLY OPERATORS ON THE LEEDS ROAD

At least three other bus operators in addition to the Corporation and Yorkshire Woollen tried their hand at running bus services in Leeds Road or beyond Bradley in the 1920s. Foremost among these was GH Kilburn and Sons Ltd of Parkside Garage, Heckmondwike, who traded as Ideal Bus Services. From 19 August 1922 Kilburn advertised an hourly service between Bradley (Corporation tram terminus), Robertown and Heckmondwike. His first bus left Heckmondwike at 1.30pm daily with one hour allowed for the round trip.

The Ideal was not without competitors. Robert Barr of Leeds may well have been the first to run a service over the "direct" route (via Liversedge and Birstall; not via Batley) between Huddersfield and Leeds in 1923 but if so he was unlicensed; his first licence was granted by the Leeds authorities on 17 November 1924. He later withdrew an application for a route via Batley and soon left this scene. Barr's real claim to fame came in 1926 when, after purchasing the Wallace Cunningham and Arnold Crowe business, he formed the Wallace Arnold company.

An advertisement in November 1924 revealed that Scotia Motor Services of Seed Hill, Huddersfield had started a direct service from Bradley to Leeds via "Mirfield Moor", Liversedge, Birstall and Gildersome. The bus ran every two hours starting at 6.30am from Bradley; the Leeds terminus was on private land at the Marlborough garage near Lyon Arcade in Briggate as the service was unlicensed. Nothing more is known of this operation.

Meanwhile in September 1924 a more powerful competitor, Yorkshire (Woollen District) Electric Tramways Ltd, had appeared on this corridor for the first time after they had been granted a three month licence to run an hourly bus service between Bradley and Leeds via Heckmondwike, Batley and Birstall. In February 1925 Yorkshire Woollen were allowed to project their hourly Leeds-Bradley route from the borough boundary to a new terminus in Silk Street in Huddersfield town centre; in the following year on Tuesday, Saturday and Sunday afternoons the frequency was doubled.

In April 1925 Kilburn too was granted a licence to extend his Bradley-Heckmondwike service into Huddersfield via Leeds Road. No objections were raised by the Corporation because a fare of 5d was to be charged between Town and Bradley to prevent abstraction of passengers from the trams and also Kilburn was willing to allow Huddersfield inspectors to board and check his buses within the borough. The new timetable from 1 May 1925 provided an hourly service out of Huddersfield from 1.30pm and the journeys were clearly shown extending beyond Heckmondwike to Dewsbury. By April 1926 the Huddersfield terminus was on the west side of New Silk Street between Beast Market and Rosemary Lane (today this translates roughly into Southgate near the bottom of Kirkgate).

On one occasion in January 1926 an Ideal bus brought the tram service on Leeds Road to a halt for over two hours when a head-on collision took place near Woodlands Road between a Huddersfield bound bus and a heavy wagon travelling to Mirfield. Both vehicles were so extensively damaged that they were eventually towed away from the scene. By November 1926 Kilburn was actually authorised to extend the service to Dewsbury and officially he ran through hourly from 1.30pm to 10.30pm, taking 58 minutes. He did not, however, always do so and complaints were made to the Watch Committee. The timetable for September 1927 shows that the section to Dewsbury was no longer served by the Huddersfield buses, which ran as far as Heckmondwike only with a faster journey time of 30 minutes and a through fare of 8d. An extra bus was provided on Tuesday, Saturday, and Sunday afternoons. The basic timetable was:

	am		pm
Huddersfield	7.30	every	10.30
Bradley	7.40	60mins	10.40
Three Nuns	7.42	until	10.42
Roberttown	7.50		10.50
Bar House	7.53		10.53
Heckmondwike	8.00		11.00
Heckmondwike	7.00	every	10.00
Bar House	7.05	60mins	10.05
Roberttown	7.10	until	10.10
Three Nuns	7.15		10.15
Bradley	7.20		10.20
Huddersfield	7.30		10.30

The faster running times led to driver Alfred Mayman being summoned for exceeding the 12 mph speed limit in Leeds Road when two police constables armed with stop watches found that his bus covered the measured mile in less than five minutes. Mayman admitted the offence, claiming that he had fallen behind schedule because cattle had been on the road. He was fined £2 but the chairman of the Bench commented that insufficient time was now allowed for the journey and that Kilburn ought to pay the fine himself.

On 12 September 1927 Kilburn started a new direct service from Heckmondwike to Leeds running via Birstall and Gildersome; unlike the Yorkshire Woollen service, this did not deviate via Batley before reaching Birstall. At first unlicensed in Leeds, Kilburn ran hourly during the morning, increasing to half hourly from mid afternoon. Very soon there were complaints to Huddersfield Watch Committee that he was linking the Huddersfield to Heckmondwike and Heckmondwike to Leeds journeys without permission; by 14 December 1927 the two services had been combined to operate as a through service and were advertised as such. Basic frequency was hourly but doubled from 1.00pm on Tuesdays, Saturdays and Sundays. One bus on this service did not have a guard rail between the wheels for more than two weeks, for which Kilburn was fined and criticised for his carelessness by the Huddersfield Bench. The Ideal Huddersfield-Leeds service was fully licensed from 30 March 1928 following a successful appeal to the Minister of Transport.

Yorkshire Woollen belatedly responded to Kilburn's direct through route to Leeds by introducing their own half hourly service over the same roads from 27 June 1928. This was advertised daily for two weeks in the Huddersfield Examiner newspaper. For his part from 27 July 1928 Kilburn increased the Ideal frequency to half hourly on a daily basis, with buses allowed 75 minutes outwards from Huddersfield with 68 minutes for the return.

From the Parkside and Beck Lane garages in Heckmondwike Kilburn also operated other services in the Dewsbury area. One major service ran between Dewsbury and Bradford via Heckmondwike and Cleckheaton but Yorkshire Woollen also operated over it. A route between Dewsbury and Brighouse was shared with County Motors on a combined 45 minutes frequency with one bus contributed by each company. A service also ran between Mirfield (Black Bull) and Dewsbury. Kilburn's presence could no longer be tolerated by Yorkshire Woollen and in May 1929 he sold his business to the larger firm, with twenty fairly new vehicles changing hands. By then all were of Leyland manufacture, mostly a mixture of A13 and Lion PLSC1 and PLSC3 single deckers. Earlier in the year he had introduced double deckers and these newest buses were two Leyland Titan TD1s with Leyland lowbridge (L27/24R) bodies. The Ideal livery was red and white.

IDEAL BUS SERVICE.

LEEDS and HUDDERSFIELD HALF-HOUR SERVICE
Commencing To-morrow (Saturday).

	a.m.	a.m.	a.m.		p.m.	S. p.m.	p.m.	p.m.	p.m.
Huddersfield				7.30		10-0	10-30	11-0	11-30
Bradley		and	7.50		and	10-20	10-50	11-20	11-50
Roberttown		every	7.55		every	10-25	10-55	11-25	11-55
Heckmondwike	5-45	half	7-45	8-5	half	10-35	11-5	11-35	12-5
Birstall	5-50	hour	7-50	8-15	hour	10-45	11-15		
Gildersome	5-55	until	7-55	8-25	until	10-55	11-25		
Leeds	6-15		8-15	8-45		11-15	11-45		

S. This 10-30 Bus is from Huddersfield to Heckmondwike only, except Saturdays.

	a.m.		a.m.	p.m.	p.m.	p.m.
Leeds	6-20		10-20	10-50	11-20	11-50
Gildersome	6.40	and	10-40	11-10	11-40	11-10
Birstall	6-45	every	10-45	11-15	11-45	11-15
Heckmondwike	6-55	half	10-55	11-25	11-55	11-25
Roberttown	7-5	hour	11-5			
Bradley	7-10	until	11-10			
Huddersfield	7-28		11-28			

* The 11.50 p.m. Bus from Leeds Saturdays only.

First Bus on Sundays from Heckmondwike to Huddersfield 11-25 a.m.
„ „ „ „ „ Leeds 11-35 „
„ „ „ „ Huddersfield to Leeds 12-0 noon
„ „ „ „ Leeds to Huddersfield 12-20 p.m.

G. H. KILBURN & SONS, Proprietors, Heckmondwike.   Telephone 215.

Ideal Bus Service timetable for the Leeds - Huddersfield service, commencing on Saturday 27th July 1928.

Another 1927 Leyland Lion PLSC1 in the fleet of Ideal was 36 (WW 3397), seen here after the May 1929 sale of the company as Yorkshire Woollen 139. On the extreme right can be seen a YWD single decker on route 7 for Huddersfield.
[P.J. Cardno collection]

Ideal (Kilburn) 38 (WW 3853), a 1927 Leyland Lion PLSC1 with Leyland bodywork, is parked on the east side of Queen Street, Leeds, before departing for Huddersfield. On the other side of the road was the stand used for many years by YWD buses for Huddersfield. After the May 1929 takeover this bus became YWD 141.
[P.J. Cardno collection]

More details of the fleet can be found in PSV Circle publication PB 10 (Yorkshire Woollen District).

3.1: PEARSON AND MITCHELL: KIRKBURTON BUS PROPRIETORS

Arthur Pearson of Dean Bottom Garage, Kirkburton first advertised his Kirkburton and Waterloo motorbus service in the Huddersfield Examiner in early April 1919. At Waterloo passengers could complete their journey by changing onto one of the frequent Corporation trams running to and from Town. This pioneering bus service to Kirkburton probably started on 5 April; a small charabanc left Waterloo hourly on Monday to Saturday between 10.00am and 9.00pm, returning 30 minutes later from Kirkburton. On Sundays a similar service started at 2.10pm. Pearson's route was mentioned in the journal Tramway and Railway World (15 May 1919) as the "motor omnibus service recently instituted between Waterloo and Kirkburton". It was reported to be appreciated by visitors to Storthes Hall Hospital, as there were no trains to Kirkburton on Sundays. By 14 June a large charabanc was in use and the Monday to Saturday service now started at 9.30am from Kirkburton. It is not known when Pearson ceased but his operation was shortlived. Another firm active in this area (in 1919-20) was Kirkburton Motors Ltd but bankruptcy had removed it from the scene by June 1920.

Tom Mitchell of Kirkburton was first mentioned in the minutes of Lepton UDC in July 1919 as the proprietor of a large charabanc and a 10 seater bus. Between July and November 1919 he began operating a service from Kirkburton to Waterloo tram terminus and was paying Kirkburton UDC 2d per mile for the privilege of running on their roads. The Commercial Motor magazine of September 1919 included a photograph of his 29 seater AEC bus WY 1171. Route details were displayed on a board below the saloon windows: Kirkburton-Storthes Hall Lane-Dogley-Fenay Bridge-Waterloo. From 30 December 1920 Mitchell was also licensed by Huddersfield Corporation to run between Waterloo and Kirkburton.

When Harburn (Blue and White) applied to run between Huddersfield and Barnsley via Kirkburton, in May 1921 Mitchell objected to Harburn being allowed to ply for hire between Waterloo and Kirkburton and sought the support of Kirkburton UDC in his attempt to safeguard his own route. He was unsuccessful and from September 1921 Harburn ran from the town centre to Barnsley. It was not until 1923 that Mitchell himself

was licensed to use a stand in Lord Street, Huddersfield. Whether before this he had continued to operate only as far as Waterloo or ran into Town unlicensed on the return ticket system is not clear. By 9 August 1921 Mitchell was based at Dean Bottom Garage (no relationship with earlier occupant Pearson is known).

On 20 March 1922 Mitchell had submitted an application to Brighouse council for a licence to run from the Smithy tram stop in Bradford Road, Huddersfield to Brighouse via Rastrick. The Brighouse tram service was not to start until March 1923. It is not known for how long, if at all, Mitchell ran on this route – Baddeleys had been running on it earlier but had probably already relinquished it.

On 1 May 1923 Mitchell started a service from Huddersfield to Barnsley via Denby Dale and Cawthorne with departures at 8.45am and 1.30pm from Huddersfield, returning from Barnsley at 10.45am and 4.45pm. He also offered an extra journey on Wednesdays, Saturdays and Sundays. This Barnsley service competed with parts of Harburn's existing routes and from the following day Harburn retaliated by starting a service over exactly the same roads. In May 1925 Mitchell planned to run a feeder service from Thorncliffe (Highburton) to Dogley Bar to connect with his main Kirkburton service but owing to the poor condition of the roads the UDC would not grant permission. Towards the end of his tenure he does seem to have run on Saturdays to Storthes Hall via Dean Bottom and Storthes Hall Lane for the benefit of hospital visitors.

In the early evening of 27 October 1925 a Mitchell's bus returning from Kirkburton was involved in a nasty accident on Wakefield Road. It had been raining very heavily and the driver's vision was obscured so that he did not see a stationary wagon until the last moment. He swerved in an attempt to avoid the wagon but the nearside of the bus struck the wagon with such force that most of the side was ripped out. George Taylor, a youth who was travelling to the technical college, was thrown out of the bus and sustained a badly broken leg.

Latterly Mitchell used a plot of land by Penistone Road at Waterloo as his garage. From 1 December 1925 he sold his business to Barnsley and District Traction, who were expanding their operations in the area and had already bought Harburn's routes, for £1,300. The vehicles involved in the sale were not operated by Barnsley and District and his garage site eventually passed to County Motors.

Mitchell's fleet is known to have included at least

the following eight vehicles, painted in a red and white livery:

WY 1171	AEC	B29-
WY 3632	Thornycroft J	B32-
WR 8357	Ford	Ch14
CX 4610	AEC	
CX 5596	GMC K16	
CX 4371	Chevrolet*	
CX 5602	GMC K16*	
CX 6864	Chevrolet*	

*Taken over but not operated by Barnsley & District

3.2: HARBURN AND THE BLUE AND WHITES

Another early operator on Penistone Road was Frank Kilner Harburn of 3 Sufton Street, Birkby. He started in business in May 1919 with a Mr Hudson of 49 Lea Street, Lindley, trading as Vindictive Luxury Coaches (named after the warship) from Prince Royd Garage at Birchencliffe. Both partners contributed £200 and a Karrier was obtained on hire purchase. On 27 March 1920 Huddersfield Town played Bristol City in the cup semi-final at the Chelsea ground in London. For this occasion the Vindictive charabanc left Huddersfield at 5.00pm on the previous day, stopping for the night at a hotel en route and reaching London at 11.00am on the Saturday in good time for the match. The night was spent in another hotel and the supporters arrived home on Sunday evening; the entire package, including travel and bed and breakfast, cost £4 10s.

By mid 1920 the partnership had been dissolved and Harburn was in business on his own from Rugby Garage, Percy Street, Fartown. He took over the coach, on which £1,800 was still owing, and during the Huddersfield August holiday week ran a daily excursion from the clock tower at Lindley.

He then advertised Karrier charabanc CX 4743 equipped with a folding hood, using the slogan "For joyous outings try the Vindictive Superbe coach". Within a year the outstanding debt was settled. Three other charabancs were owned including a Lancia and a Thornycroft and Harburn's private company had an authorised capital of £8,000.

Harburn, trading as Blue and White in honour of Huddersfield Town football club, applied to operate a bus service from St George's Square, Huddersfield to Barnsley. The service started on 27 September 1921 and ran daily except on Sundays, using a new Karrier

For Joyous Outings Try "The "Vindictive Superbe" Coach.

Frank Harburn is seen with his 30 seater Karrier charabanc CX 4743, new in 1921. Harburn had actually worked for Karriers. This was among the vehicles which passed to Barnsley & District Traction in April 1925. [P.J. Cardno collection]

the roadside en route and within a radius of 200 yards of the Peel Street terminus in Barnsley.

From 8 October the Huddersfield terminus was moved to Byram Street, on the east side at the Kirkgate end just above the Parish Church. At the same time the morning departure was retimed to 9.00am and the Saturday short journey to Birdsedge was extended to Penistone. The Thursday service was withdrawn from 3 November owing to poor patronage but Sunday journeys were run for the first time. A new faster "saloon bus" placed in service on 15 November allowed the running time to Barnsley to be reduced to 1½ hours, while tea, coffee and Bovril could now be served during the journey and travelling rugs were supplied. The route was even operated on Christmas Day 1921.

A further improvement during 1922 was an early morning return workmen's bus to Shelley (Bank Bottom). An extra late service to Barnsley ran on Saturday and Sunday evenings leaving at 7.00pm and "pleasure seekers" were invited to "give it a trial to enjoy the panoramic views and the moorland air".

A new route from Huddersfield to Clayton West via Shepley and Denby Dale started on 25 November 1922. The initial timetable was as follows:

Huddersfield dep.	Clayton West dep.
9.30am	10.00am
1.00pm	2.00pm
2.30pm (Sunday)	3.00pm (Sunday)
4.30pm	5.30pm
7.45pm (Sunday)	8.30pm (Sunday)
8.40pm (Saturday)	10.10pm (Saturday)

Also by this date it is believed that a Huddersfield-Skelmanthorpe-Scissett-Denby Dale service was being operated.

As a result of competition provided by Mitchell's Barnsley service, from 2 May 1923 two of the Denby Dale via Shepley departures (Tuesday and Sunday excepted 1.15 and 6.00pm; also Sunday 2.30pm) were extended to Barnsley via Cawthorne and Silkstone with a journey time of 75 minutes. About a week later a potentially more dangerous competitor, major company Barnsley & District Traction, started running into Huddersfield for the first time from Barnsley via Cawthorne, Denby Dale and Skelmanthorpe. Harburn advertised the invigorating virtues of his service with claims such as "A dose of Kruschen salts and a ride on my bus and you could be pushing tramcars over". He reminded his patrons that he had provided the first bus service to Barnsley and had not stolen what someone

of the latest type. This was the first bus service of any operator to start from the town centre on a regular basis rather than connecting in the suburbs with a tram route. Initially just two return trips were offered over the full route, leaving Huddersfield at 8.45am and 2.30pm via Kirkburton (Spring Grove), Shepley, Ingbirchworth,

Penistone, Oxspring and Silkstone and reaching Barnsley 1 hour 45 minutes later. An additional journey was operated as far as Birdsedge on Tuesday and Saturday at 12.45pm. Return fares were 11d to Shepley, 1/11d to Penistone and 2/11d to Barnsley and parcels up to 56 pounds in weight were carried and delivered anywhere at

Harburn's timetable dated the 2 May 1923, incorrectly headed as the White & Blue Motor Service

TIME TABLE, commencing Saturday, September 29th, 1923.

BLUE & WHITE MOTOR SERVICES.

↙ The First Service to start between Huddersfield and Barnsley, in Sept., 1921. ↘
We lead, others follow.   "The others followed as usual."

BARNSLEY, Silkstone, Cawthorne, Penistone Thurlstone, Denby Dale, Ingbirchworth, High Flatts, Birdsedge, Sovereign Inn, Shepley, Shelley, Kirkburton (For Storthes Hall), HUDDERSFIELD.

——— The Blind Carried Free of Charge. ———

Byram Street, Top Side of Parish Church.	Daily not Sun.	Every Day.	Daily not Sun.	Daily not Sun.	Daily not Sun.	Sun. only.	Sun. only.	Sat. only.	Every Day.	Sat. Sun. only.	Sat. Sun. only.
	a.m.	a.m.	a.m.	p.m.	p.m.	p.m.	p.m.	p.m	p.m.	p.m	p.m
HUDDERSFIELD Depart	7-30	9-0	11-0						2-30	7-0	9-30
KIRKBURTON, Spring Grove	7-50	9-20	11-20						2-50	7-20	9-50
SHELLEY, Bank Bottom	7-55	9-25	11-25						2-55	7-25	9-55
SHEPLEY, Black Bull	8-0	9-30	11-30						3-0	7-30	10-0
SOVEREIGN INN	8-5	9-35	11-35						3-5	7-35	10-5
BIRDSEDGE, Post Office	8-10	9-40	11-40						3-10	7-40	10-10
HIGH FLATTS, Post Office	8-13	9-43	11-43						3-13	7-43	10-13
INGBIRCHWORTH, Club	8-20	9-50	11-50						3-20	7-50	10-20
PENISTONE, Bridge End	8-28	9-58	11-58						3-28	7-58	10-28
THURLSTONE, Post Office			12-0								
MILLHOUSE, Blacksmiths' Arms Arr. Dep.			12-5 12-10	2-0	5-30		6-20				
PENISTONE Church			12-15	2-5	5-35		6-25				
	8-30	10-0	12-20	2-10	5-40		6-30		3-30	8-0	10-30
OXSPRING, Toll Bar	8-37	10-7	12-27	2-17	5-47		6-37		3-37	8-7	10-37
SILKSTONE COMMON, Station Hotel	8-45	10-15	12-35	2-25	5-55		6-45		3-45	8-15	10-45
SILKSTONE, Ring o' Bells			12-40	2-30	6-0		6-50				
DODWORTH, Cross Roads	8-50	10-20	12-45	2-35	6-5		6-55		3-50	8-20	10-50
BARNSLEY, Peel Street Arrive.	9-0	10-30	12-55	2-45	6-15		7-5		4-0	8-30	11-0
Depart.	9-15	11-0	1-0	4-30	7-30	5-30		2-45	5-5	9-0	11-0
Cross Roads	9-25	11-10	1-10	4-40	7-40	5-40		2-55	5-15	9-10	11-10
SILKSTONE, Ring o' Bells			1-15	4-45	7-45	5-45					
SILKSTONE COMMON, Station Hotel	9-30	11-15	1-20	4-50	7-50	5-50		3-0	5-20	9-15	11-15
OXSPRING, Toll Bar	9-37	11-23	1-28	4-58	7-58	5-58		3-8	5-28	9-23	11-23
PENISTONE Church	9-45	11-30	1-35	5-5	8-5	6-5		3-15	5-35	9-30	11-30
THURLSTONE, Post Office			1-40	5-10	8-10	6-10					
MILLHOUSE, Blacksmiths' Arms Arr. Dep.			1-45	5-15	8-15	6-15					
THURLSTONE, Post Office					8-20						
PENISTONE, Bridge End					8-25						
INGBIRCHWORTH, Club	9-47	11-32			8-30			3-17	5-37	9-32	11-32
HIGH FLATTS, Post Office	9-55	11-40			8-40			3-25	5-45	9-40	11-40
BIRDSEDGE, Post Office	10-2	11-47			8-47			3-32	5-50	9-47	11-47
SOVEREIGN INN	10-5	11-50			8-50			3-35	5-55	9-50	11-50
SHEPLEY, Black Bull	10-10	11-55			8-55			3-40	6-0	9-55	11-55
SHELLEY, Bank Bottom	10-15	12-00			9-0			3-45	6-5	10-0	12-0
KIRKBURTON, Spring Grove	10-20	12-5			9-5			3-50	6-10	10-5	12-5
HUDDERSFIELD Arrive.	10-45	12-10			9-30			4-15	6-35	10-30	12-30

Byram Street, Top Side of Parish Church.	not Thur. Sun.	not Thur. Sun.	Sat. Sun. only.	Sat. Sun. only.
	p.m.	p.m.	p.m.	p.m.
HUDDERSFIELD Depart.	1-15	6-0	2-30	2-30
KIRKBURTON, Spring Grove	1-35	6-20	2-50	2-50
SHELLEY, Bank Bottom	1-40	6-25	2-55	2-55
SHEPLEY, Black Bull	1-45	6-30	3-0	3-0
SOVEREIGN INN	1-50	6-35	3-5	3-5
CUMBERWORTH, Star Inn	1-53	6-38	3-8	3-8
DENBY DALE, Viaducts	2-2	6-43	3-13	3-13
DUNKIRK, Junction Inn	2-5	6-46	3-16	3-16
CAWTHORNE Church	2-10	6-53	3-24	3-24
SILKSTONE Church	2-15	6-58	3-29	3-29
DODWORTH, Cross Roads	2-20	7-5	3-34	3-34
BARNSLEY, Peel Street Arrive.	2-30	7-15	3-45	3-45
Depart.	7-0 n't Th. S't S'n	8-0 not Thur.		8-0
DODWORTH, Cross Roads	3-10	8-10		8-10
SILKSTONE Church	3-15	8-15		8-15
CAWTHORNE Church	3-20	8-20		8-20
DUNKIRK, Station Inn	3-28	8-28		8-28
DENBY DALE, Viaducts	3-33	8-33		8-33
CUMBERWORTH, Star Inn	3-38	8-38		8-38
SOVEREIGN INN	3-45	8-45		8-45
SHEPLEY, Black Bull	3-50	8-50		8-50
SHELLEY, Bank Bottom	3-55	8-55		8-55
KIRKBURTON, Spring Grove	4-0	9-0		9-0
HUDDERSFIELD Arrive.	4-20	9-20		9-20

PARCELS may be left at HUDDERSFIELD, Mr. Fox, Picture Framer, Byram Street; PENISTONE, Mr. Bradley, Florist, etc., Market Place; THURLSTONE, Mr. Oliver Lockwood, Fruiterer, Townend; BARNSLEY, Mr. Harry Dale, Hairdresser, etc., Peel Street.

EXCURSION TICKETS are issued on the 11-0 a.m. and 1-15 p.m. 'Buses out of Huddersfield to Barnsley.   Return Fare 2/11.

WORKMEN'S TICKETS are issued on the 7-30 a.m. Bus out of Huddersfield to all places en route.

Telephone : 861, Huddersfield.

F. K. HARBURN, Rugby Garage, Percy Street, Fartown, Huddersfield.

else had spent his time and money in working up. Moreover, his buses had safely travelled over 80,000 miles without accident. In an advertisement in the Barnsley Chronicle he reminded patrons that his bus always departed from Peel Street, opposite the clock on Mr Hatton's shop. From 2 November 1923 cheap excursion fares to Barnsley were now offered from Huddersfield on Monday to Wednesday only on the 11.00am and 1.15pm departures with returns at 7.30pm or 8.00pm. The blind were carried free of charge.

On summer Sundays Harburn operated a special circular bus service leaving Barnsley at 5.15pm, out via Cawthorne and Denby Dale to the Sovereign Inn, returning via Ingbirchworth, Penistone and Oxspring.

By September 1923 he also ran a service from Millhouse via Thurlstone and Penistone to Barnsley: two return journeys on Monday to Saturday afternoons and one on Sundays. Total journey time was 45 minutes and from Penistone to Barnsley the route was the same as that for the service from Huddersfield. The Millhouse route was worked by the bus that had formed the 11.00am departure from Huddersfield on Monday to Saturday.

Early in 1924 rumours, possibly initiated by his competitors, were circulating to the effect that Harburn was about to cease trading. He denied this and offered a £10 reward for information about the source of the rumours.

During a railway strike (24 to 29 January 1924) Harburn doubled his normal services to Barnsley and one innovation was a 9.00am express bus stopping only at Penistone and Barnsley. At the annual inspection in May 1924 Huddersfield Watch Committee commended Harburn for the cleanliness of his vehicles. In June 1924 he invited the travelling public to try a circular ticket. They could take a bus to the Sovereign Inn on the Penistone route, walk down to the Prospect Hotel at Denby Dale and return (presumably) on the other route via Skelmanthorpe. By then it is believed that buses ran from Huddersfield to Denby Dale via Skelmanthorpe every two hours from 7.00am to 9.00pm. During the Huddersfield holiday weeks he provided extra buses every two hours to Barnsley via Penistone from 7.00am. The annual Penistone agricultural show also generated much needed extra passengers and they were catered for by an additional hourly service running as far as Penistone.

As the Blue and White routes fell entirely within the territory regarded by the expanding Barnsley & District undertaking as its own, it was not surprising that Harburn sold the "stage carriage" (local bus) side of his business along with the following seven buses to that company in the first week of April 1925 for £5500.

CX 5271	Karrier K3	B30-	new 1921
CX 5654	Karrier JS4	B20-	new 1923
CX 4743	Karrier CY	B30-	new 1921
CX 6096	Leyland RAF	B30-	new 1924
CX 6853	Leyland RAF	B30-	new 1924
CX 6670	Gotfredson WTU	B20-	new 1924
CX 6643	Berliet VMB	B16-	new 1924

The above became B & D 131-7 respectively. As these buses were still fairly new, after being overhauled at a further cost of £750 they gave up to five years service with their new owners. At least two other buses, a Leyland and a twenty seater Berliet, are known to have been operated.

After Harburn and Mitchell had sold out to Barnsley & District, two other local proprietors were still operating out of Huddersfield via Penistone Road. Ernest Sellers ran to Farnley Tyas via Dean Bottom and Storthes Hall.

An account of this service, which eventually passed via Barnsley & District to Huddersfield Corporation, is included in the authors' book Huddersfield: the Corporation motorbus story. Richard Henderson was first refused a licence to operate from Huddersfield to Lepton in June 1925 and shortly afterwards his request for a Kirkburton licence was also turned down but he seems to have operated both services on the return ticket system. Barnsley & District took exception to Henderson's Kirkburton service and early in 1926 they started running a bus just in front of Henderson's to poach his passengers. On behalf of the local man, Kirkburton UDC wrote a letter of objection to the company. The practice continued and in March the UDC wrote again, saying that while they neither supported nor opposed the Barnsley company's bus they took exception to it not running to a fixed timetable. In March 1926 Huddersfield Watch Committee granted Henderson a licence to operate from Lord Street via Almondbury to Farnley Tyas and his Kirkburton service probably ceased at this time. Henderson's Farnley Tyas route was later extended to Thurstonland and, like the Sellers business, was acquired by Huddersfield Corporation via Barnsley & District. Details of its development are included in Huddersfield: the Corporation motorbus story.

3.3: HARBURN'S COACHING INTERESTS

When Harburn had sold the local service bus side of his business and discharged his liabilities, he concentrated on private hire and coach tours, publishing a professionally produced illustrated souvenir and guide of over one hundred pages for the 1926 season. This included photographs of two new coaches:

| CX 7378 (1925) | Lancia | 20 seats |
| CX 8064 (1926) | Bean | 12 seats |

Seating arrangements were shown for the vehicles and in both the driver shared a double seat with a passenger. The Bean had seats for two on the offside and single seats on the nearside while the larger coach had the more usual pairs of seats on both sides of the gangway. Both coaches had powerful twin headlamps to ensure safety at night and each carried two spare wheels mounted on either side of the bonnet. The larger coach was used by Huddersfield Town football club for travelling to away matches in this period.

According to Harburn, the Blue and White coaches offered a mode of travel far superior to the railways. There was no scrambling for seats, no draughty carriages and no waiting or changing. The drivers were said to be fully experienced and passengers fully insured against all risks while rigid all weather side curtains and rugs assured comfort irrespective of the weather.

Party organisers had to supply a deposit of £2 on booking a coach. There had to be a minimum of 18 passengers for the 20 seater coach and 10 for the smaller coach and all excursions had to be completed by 11.00pm the same day, otherwise an extra charge of £1 per hour was levied. This rule was meant to ensure that drivers had a reasonable night's rest so another party would not be riding behind a tired man the next day. Passengers had to pay all tolls and ferry charges separately.

The 1927 Blackpool Illuminations attracted enormous crowds with as many as 300,000 people thronging the promenades on Saturday nights; the roads were so congested that coaches were taking five hours for the eighteen miles between Blackpool and Preston. To avoid this unpleasant late night travel, Harburn offered a special package for 19/6d which included bed and breakfast in Blackpool; patrons could leave St George's Square at 8.30am daily (Fridays excepted) and return from Blackpool at 6.00pm the following day.

An innovation for summer 1929 was a daily trip to Blackpool which for 9/- on weekdays and 10/- on Saturdays included a "first class" tea and supper. Harburn was prepared to offer a refund to any passenger who was not satisfied with the meals. For the August Holiday Week in 1929 Harburn advertised four trips daily and one special excursion was to Lilleshall in Shropshire to the former home of the Duke of Sutherland. The pictures of the house and 600 acres of gardens and woodlands displayed in his Kirkgate booking office persuaded about 100 passengers to book for the 190 mile round trip.

Harburn had diverse business interests. He claimed to own the most up to date battery charging station in the district and also had a small number of private hire cars. In partnership with Mr JT Thornton he invested £300 in the Venus Radiophone Company which manufactured single- and multi-valve wireless sets but this was not a success and the partnership ceased after June 1930.

The coach business went into decline in 1930 and losses of £1000 were incurred in selling the small coaches. To some extent Harburn joined forces with Joe Kaye of Thornton Lodge as excursions were ad-

BLUE AND WHITE
Motor Coach Tours

Illustrated Souvenir
and Descriptive Guide

BLUE AND WHITE COACHES
Rugby Garage,
Percy Street, Fartown,
TEL. 861. HUDDERSFIELD. TEL. 861.

THE PROPRIETOR OF
Blue & White Coaches

WISHES THAT HIS PATRONS HAVE A MOST ENJOYABLE OUTING AND THE GOOD HEALTH TO ENJOY MANY MORE.
Yours Sincerely,
F. K. HARBURN.

vertised as jointly operated by the Blue & White and Conqueror coaches. Very cheap midweek trips were offered. Free gifts were even promised to all passengers who booked in advance for the August holiday week, when up to six tours daily were advertised (but not necessarily operated); all the coaches were described as detachable head sunshine saloons. The poor summer weather of 1931 coupled with extra expenses en-

tailed in meeting the requirements of the new Road Traffic Act added to his problems.

Harburn's first application for licences to the new traffic commissioners was reasonably successful. Five half day tour licences were granted (Knaresborough, Bolton Abbey, Studley Royal, York and Burnsall) and three full day licences (Blackpool, Bridlington and Scarborough) for the period April to October but his maximum vehicle allowance on any one day was only two. Unfortunately when he applied to renew these licences in February 1932, two of the half day tour licences were not granted.

A more serious setback was a fire in September 1932 which caused considerable damage to his premises and coaches, now at Woodbine Road, Fartown. Much of the £590 insurance compensation was used to settle debts. In March 1933 Harburn filed for bankruptcy and probably stopped running coaches, owing to increasing competition, after the summer of 1933. His final application for renewal of licences in August 1933 was refused.

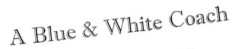

A Blue & White Coach

SHOWING SEATING ARRANGEMENT

NOTE Powerful Headlights—this ensures **YOUR SAFETY** when travelling at night.

Blue & White Coaches

OUR FREE
Battery Collection and Delivery Van
is at your service.

WHY KEEP CARRYING YOUR HEAVY BATTERY AND SPILLING ACID DOWN YOUR CLOTHES?

Drop us a post-card and your battery will be called for, charged and delivered to your door in TWO DAYS.

Light Haulage up to 7 cwt.

RING UP 851 HUDDERSFIELD

Blue & White Coaches

ARE ALL ELECTRICALLY EQUIPPED.

A small Blue and White Coach shewing seating arrangement.

Compare our Coaches with others

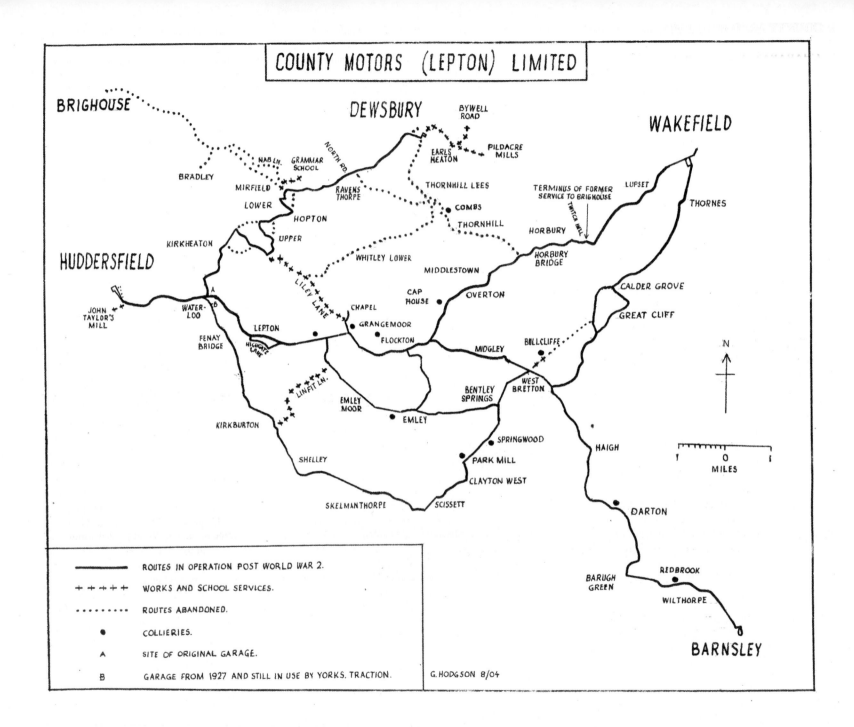

COUNTY MOTORS (LEPTON) LIMITED

BRIGHOUSE

DEWSBURY

BYWELL ROAD

WAKEFIELD

BRADLEY

NAB LN.   GRAMMAR SCHOOL

NORTH RD.

EARLS HEATON

PILDACRE MILLS

MIRFIELD

THORNHILL LEES

LUPSET

TERMINUS OF FORMER SERVICE TO BRIGHOUSE

LOWER

RAVENS THORPE

THORNES

HOPTON

COMBS

THORNHILL

HORBURY

KIRKHEATON

UPPER

HORBURY BRIDGE

HUDDERSFIELD

WHITLEY LOWER

MIDDLESTOWN

LILEY LANE

CALDER GROVE

WATER-LOO

CHAPEL

CAP HOUSE

OVERTON

GREAT CLIFF

JOHN TAYLOR'S MILL

A
B

GRANGEMOOR

FLOCKTON

BILLCLIFFE

N

FENAY BRIDGE

LEPTON

HIGHGATE LANE

MIDGLEY

LINFIT LN.

EMLEY MOOR

BENTLEY SPRINGS

WEST BRETTON

KIRKBURTON

EMLEY

SPRINGWOOD

HAIGH

SHELLEY

PARK MILL

0

MILES

CLAYTON WEST

SKELMANTHORPE

SCISSETT

DARTON

BARUGH GREEN

REDBROOK

WILTHORPE

BARNSLEY

——————   ROUTES IN OPERATION POST WORLD WAR 2.

+ + + + +   WORKS AND SCHOOL SERVICES.

• • • • •   ROUTES ABANDONED.

●   COLLIERIES.

A   SITE OF ORIGINAL GARAGE.

B   GARAGE FROM 1927 AND STILL IN USE BY YORKS. TRACTION.

G. HODGSON 8/04

28

4: COUNTY MOTORS (LEPTON) LIMITED

4.1 CHARABANCS AND PURPLE SALOONS

Arthur and Brinton Farrar started trading as the County Bus Service on 11 October 1919. They were the directors of the Farrars cotton doubling mill on Wakefield Road just beyond the Huddersfield borough boundary at Waterloo; Brinton Farrar was also a Lepton and later Kirkburton councillor. They were soon joined by Mr T Greenhalge and a timber yard owned by Fred Greensmith between Tandem and Cowmes (in "Lower Lepton") served as the first garage. The first manager seems to have been Mr E Midgeley of Lepton. It is believed that one of the driving forces behind the venture was Alfred Gale, who had previously worked in local collieries until obliged to leave following a serious accident. He saw the possibility of a viable business venture based on providing transport for miners to the many pits then open in the area. Lacking the finance himself, he persuaded the relatively well off Farrars to back the venture.

The first two vehicles were charabancs, one based on the chassis of an ex-Army vehicle, the other a Karrier. At first Alf Gale did most of the driving.

The proprietors set their sights on the villages of Flockton and Emley, whose residents in those days had to make do with very limited public transport by waggonettes. Joe Eastwood ran market day services from Emley Cross at 10.00am on Tuesdays and Saturdays to the Pack Horse Hotel in Huddersfield and at the same time on Tuesdays to the York Hotel at Wakefield, return fares to both towns being 1/6d. The journey offered little comfort for the 16 passengers seated facing each other in two rows of eight; in summer they were open to the elements and in winter the sailcloth cover was very draughty. Lepton Edge often proved too much for the horsepower and the men were obliged to alight and walk up the hill, so decreasing the load. Otherwise Emley villagers would either walk the two miles to Clayton West station to catch infrequent trains to Huddersfield or four miles to Haigh station for trains to Barnsley and Wakefield. [The waggonette operator later reappeared as a motorbus proprietor; in June 1933 Joe Eastwood & Son was granted a licence to run a workmen's service between Emley Cross and Park Mill Colliery, near Clayton West.]

The first County Bus Service route seems to have operated daily from October 1919 between Lepton and Waterloo, where passengers had to change onto trams for Town as it was not licensed within the Huddersfield borough. That there were teething troubles is suggested by an advertisement in the Huddersfield Daily Examiner on 21 October announcing that the Lepton bus would be running normally (hourly) from 2.00pm the same day. On Tuesdays from 1.00pm onwards and on Saturdays from 10.00am journeys were extended from Lepton to Emley via Grange Moor Cross Roads and Flockton and at least one lorry-bus (CX 3439) was 'route branded' for the service. Within a month the residents were complaining to Whitley Upper UDC about poor timekeeping; they also pointed out that they would be "more appreciative of the service" if the bus ran to the Chapel in Grange Moor but for another decade they would have to walk to the cross roads (unless such a service was operated for a short period from 1919).

The first County charabanc excursions may well have been those to the races at Doncaster on 23 and 24 October 1919. Passengers were able to book their seats and pay the 10 shillings fare at the Waterloo Hotel. The business was registered as a limited company on 22 December 1919 with a nominal capital of £3,000 in £1 shares, the directors being Arthur and Brinton Farrar. Henry Cooper was a further early director. Many other local people gave financial backing.

From 4 April 1920 a "summer" Sunday service was added on the Emley bus route. Regular country drives were also offered on summer Sundays from 1920 onwards, leaving the Waterloo Hotel at 3.00pm and the Woolpack in Almondbury at 6.00pm. Longer tours were advertised for the holiday weeks in 1920 and by the following year two charabancs and two lorries on which bus seats could be fitted as required were owned. During the week the lorries transported goods to Manchester, Liverpool and Birkenhead docks for shipment overseas. All types of motor vehicles could be repaired and overhauled at the garage, which also stocked tyres and accessories. During the summer of 1921 private hire trips were advertised at new lower rates and a weekly Saturday service was offered to Blackpool. For the September holiday week, which coincided with Leger week at Doncaster, four trips were made to the races there and three to Blackpool.

Alf Gale himself is believed to have been responsible for developing new routes. The licensed "direct" bus service from Huddersfield to Wakefield started on Saturday 3 March 1923, running via Waterloo, Lepton, Grange Moor Cross Roads, Flockton, Overton, Middlestown and Horbury. [There has never been a regular bus service using the truly direct road between Grange Moor and Middlestown, but this route was direct compared with the service via Kirkburton and Scissett introduced in 1926.] County's first route to reach Huddersfield town centre, the new service boasted three Monday to Friday departures at 9.00am, 1.00pm and 5.30pm from a stand in Lord Street, a thoroughfare which was to remain closely associated with County - and other bus operators - for nearly half a century. On Saturdays a later bus left at 8.45pm and the single fare was 1/6d. On 7 April a much improved every two hours frequency was announced for Saturdays and Sundays, starting at 9.00am on Saturdays and 1.00pm on Sundays. The 9.00am, 1.00pm and 7.00pm departures ran between Lepton and Flockton via Emley instead of via Grange Moor. It is not clear whether the existing Lepton and Emley journeys were also extended through to Lord Street. An earlier Wakefield departure on weekdays was introduced in July 1924 with a special return fare of 2/- for workmen. By 1923 Mr J Clegg was the manager and soon afterwards Alf Gale was designated traffic manager. The two men worked together in these positions until at least January 1927.

On 2 June 1923 County started running an unlicensed service from private land at Waterloo to Dewsbury on Wednesdays and Saturdays, Dewsbury market days. The original route was via Waterloo Road, Kirkheaton Station, Kirkheaton, Cockley Hill Lane, Bellstring Lane, Liley Lane, Tanhouse Lane, Whitley Road. and Thornhill Lees to the centre of Dewsbury. By August 1923 an application had been made for a licence for a revised route which County also wished to extend from Waterloo to Huddersfield. The new route proposed between Kirkheaton and Dewsbury was via Mirfield and Ravensthorpe instead of Whitley and Thornhill Lees. This was rejected by Huddersfield Watch Committee, probably because they feared abstraction of passengers from their own Corporation bus service between Bradley, Mirfield and Ravensthorpe. Passengers wishing to travel from Huddersfield to Dewsbury by Huddersfield Corporation were still obliged to change from tram to bus at Bradley and from bus to [Yorkshire Woollen] tram again at Ravensthorpe so some of them might well have preferred to switch to County's proposed through route. The Watch Committee, however, used the excuse that because in their view there was no community of interest between Kirkheaton and Mirfield, there was no need for a bus service between the two places. Whether that was true or not, this argument also ignored the needs of Hopton people in the middle.

The company appealed against the decision but, instead of waiting for the judgement, then committed what the Corporation later described as a "breach of faith". Towards the end of 1923 the Corporation granted County a licence for an extra bus to be used on their existing and fully licensed Huddersfield-Flockton-Wakefield route. From December 1923 or early January 1924 County extended the Dewsbury-Waterloo route to Huddersfield, using buses licensed for the Wakefield route and presumably terminating at the Wakefield stand on Lord Street. These buses were licensed to run on the road between Town and Waterloo but on another service; the unlicensed service on which they were running was the subject of an appeal against refusal of licence.

When Huddersfield Corporation discovered what was happening, Mr Spivey, County's company secretary, had to write a very apologetic letter. He claimed that this was merely a mistake on the part of the managers, who were "rough and uneducated working men" who ran the buses but did not understand the complexities of licensing. Huddersfield quickly extended their own Kirkheaton bus route, a feeder to the trams at Moldgreen, into the town centre. County were fortunate to be granted their licence and a stand in Lord Street, officially from 5 May 1924.

Very soon after the introduction of the through Huddersfield to Dewsbury service, the route had been altered to run via Mirfield and Ravensthorpe, as proposed. It is possible that the original route between Kirkheaton and Mirfield ran via Heaton Moor Road, Hollin Hall Lane, Jackroyd Lane, Hopton Hall Lane, Hopton Lane and Station Road. If this version was introduced, it lasted for a very short time before buses started running via the original route as far as Freemasons Arms then via Hopton Hall Lane and the lower section of the shortlived variant just described; the main road through Ravensthorpe was then followed into Dewsbury. Also, by January 1927 the buses ran between Hopton and Mirfield via Calder Road and Newgate, to serve Lower Hopton.

During 1925 a shortlived service was also run from Bradley (the tram terminus) to Dewsbury via Mirfield and Ravensthorpe in competition with the Corporation and Yorkshire Woollen. In April 1925 the County representative, George Browne was refused permission to project this unlicensed service into Town (he had proposed an hourly service with a through fare of 10d). The Ministry of Transport inquiry which followed found

in favour of a joint Corporation/Yorkshire Woollen service between Huddersfield and Dewsbury.

County nevertheless managed to maintain a presence in this area by introducing a service entirely outside the borough. On Saturday 15 August 1925 they started running between Brighouse, Mirfield and Dewsbury; with a 90 minutes frequency and a running time of 35 minutes each way only one bus was required. The route between Three Nuns and the Black Bull at Mirfield was initially via Stocks Bank Road and Nab Lane although by 1927 this had been changed to the main road; over the rest of the route, the bus had always kept to the main roads. Ideal (Kilburn) of Heckmondwike also ran over this route and his timetable was coordinated with County's to offer a combined 45 minutes frequency

Barnsley was first served by County from Monday 27 July 1925 by a two hourly feeder service from the Angel Inn at Flockton, where it connected with Wakefield journeys leaving Huddersfield from 8.00am to 8.00pm; the Wakefield route was increased from the same date

to operate hourly. A passenger bound for Barnsley could leave Huddersfield on the even hour, change at Flockton and, travelling via Emley and Bretton, arrive in Barnsley only 80 minutes after leaving Huddersfield, all for 1/6d, both the cheapest and quickest way at the time of travelling to Barnsley. As far as County were concerned, this arrangement had the advantage of not requiring a licence from Huddersfield Watch Committee and only one bus was needed to provide the connection. On 5 October 1925, however, the watch committee granted permission for stand B in Lord Street to be used for a service to Barnsley via Lepton, Emley, Flockton, Midgley, Bretton and Darton and this through service actually started on 7 November 1925. Departures were at 30 minutes past the hour from 7.30am to 5.30pm with the exception of 8.30am, 10.30am, 12.30pm and 3.30pm. The round trip took three hours so this timetable was maintained using just two buses.

The Reo Motor Car Company of Michigan, USA run by Ransome E Olds was by 1925 exporting large

COUNTY BUS SERVICE
BETWEEN
BRIGHOUSE & DEWSBURY,
Via THREE NUNS, NAB LANE, BLACK BULL, FIR COTTAGE & RAVENSTHORPE.
Commencing SATURDAY, AUGUST 15th, 1925, Daily.

		Not on Sundays.									
		a.m.	a.m.	a.m.	p.m.	p.m.	p.m.	p.m.	p.m.	p.m.	p.m.
BRIGHOUSE...	dep.	8-45	10-15	11-45	1-15	2-45	4-15	5-45	7-15	8-45	10-15
Bar House	...	8-50	10-20	11-50	1-20	2-50	4-20	5-50	7-20	8-50	10-20
Three Nuns	...	8-55	10-25	11-55	1-25	2-55	4-25	5-55	7-25	8-55	10-25
Nab Lane	...	8-58	10-28	11-58	1-28	2-58	4-28	5-58	7-28	8-58	10-28
Black Bull	...	9-3	10-31	12-3	1-31	3-3	4-31	6-3	7-31	9-3	10-31
Fir Cottage	...	9-8	10-36	12-8	1-36	3-8	4-36	6-8	7-36	9-8	10-36
DEWSBURY ...	arr.	9-20	10-50	12-20	1-50	3-20	4-50	6-20	7-50	9-20	10-50
DEWSBURY ...	dep.	9-30	11-0	12-30	2-0	3-30	5-0	6-30	8-0	9-30	11-0
Fir Cottage	...	9-40	11-10	12-40	2-10	3-40	5-10	6-40	8-10	9-40	11-10
Black Bull	...	9-45	11-15	12-45	2-15	3-45	5-15	6-45	8-15	9-45	11-15
Nab Lane	...	9-50	11-20	12-50	2-20	3-50	5-20	6-50	8-20	9-50	11-20
Three Nuns	...	9-53	11-23	12-53	2-23	3-53	5-23	6-53	8-23	9-53	11-23
Bar House	...	10-0	11-30	1-0	2-30	4-0	5-30	7-0	8-30	10-0	11-30
BRIGHOUSE...	arr.	10-5	11-35	1-5	2-35	4-5	5-35	7-5	8-35	10-5	11-35

FARES :

Brighouse to Coal Pit Lane...	1d.	Brighouse to Nab Lane...	5d.	Brighouse to Calder Road...	8d.
„ Bar House ...	2d.	„ Black Bull...	6d.	„ Temple Rd. ...	9d.
„ Malt Kilns ...	3d.	„ Fir Cottage...	7d.	„ Dewsbury ...	10d.
„ Three Nuns ...	4d.				

Minimum Fare into or out of Dewsbury ... **4d.**

County Motors (Lepton), Ltd.,
Waterloo Garage, Huddersfield.
Tel. 1998.

J. CLEGG, Manager.
A. E. GALE, Traffic Manager.

M. Woffenden's Sons, Printers, Birkby, Huddersfield

"COUNTY" BUS SERVICE.

Revised Services to commence on SATURDAY, FEBRUARY, 13th, 1926.
BETWEEN
Huddersfield (Lord Street, Stand D). Waterloo, Lepton, Grange Moor, Emley, Flockton, Overton, Middlestown, Horbury Bridge and Wakefield (Top of Westgate).

TIME TABLE.

Route No 1 · Route No 2

		WEEK DAYS						Sat. only.	Extra Service via EMLEY Saturdays only.					SUNDAYS.		
		a.m.	a.m.	a.m.		p.m.	p.m.	a.m.	a.m.	p.m.	p.m.	p.m.	noon.		p.m.	p.m.
Huddersfield	dep.	7-0	8-0	9-0		9-0	10-0	10-0	11-15	2-15	5-15	8-15	12-0		9-0	10-0
Waterloo	..	7-12	8-12	9-12		9-12	10-12	10-12	11-23	2-23	5-23	8-23	12-12		9-12	10-12
Lepton (Red Lion)	..	7-20	8-20	9-20		9-20	10-20	10-20	11-30	2-30	5-30	8-30	12-20		9-20	10-20
Grange Moor	..	7-25	8-25	9-25	And every	9-25	10-25	10-25					12-25		9-25	10-25
Beaumont's Arms	..				hour until	9-0 p.m.			11-40	2-40	5-40	8-40		And every		
Emley (Cross)	..								11-50	2-50	5-50	8-50		hour until		
Flockton (Church)	..	7-30	8-30	9-30	and	9-30	10-30	10-30	12-0	3-0	6-0	9-0	12-30	9-0 p.m.	9-30	10-30
Overton (Black Swan)	..	7-40	8-40	9-40	10-0 p.m.	9-40		10-40	12-5	3-5	6-5	9-5	12-40		9-40	
Middlestown	..	7-45	8-45	9-45	on	9-45		10-45	12-10	3-10	6-10	9-10	12-45		9-45	
Horbury Bridge	..	7-50	8-50	9-50	Saturdays.	9-50	Back	10-50	12-15	3-15	6-15	9-15	12-50		9-50	
Highfield Road	..	7-53	8-53	9-53		9-53	to Car-	10-53	12-20	3-20	6-20	9-20	12-53		9-53	
Wakefield	arr.	8-5	9-5	10-5			10-5	age	11-5	12-34	3-35	6-35	9-35	1-5		10-5

Wakefield	dep.	8-10	9-10	10-10		10-10		11-10	12-45	3-45	6-45	9-45	1-10		10-10	
Highfield Road	..	8-22	9-22	10-22		10-22		11-22	12-57	3-57	6-57	9-57	1-22		10-22	
Horbury Bridge	..	8-25	9-25	10-25	And every	10-25		11-25	1-0	4-0	7-0	10-0	1-25		10-25	
Middlestown	..	8-30	9-30	10-30	hour until	10-30		11-30	1-5	4-5	7-5	10-5	1-30		10-30	
Overton (Black Swan)	..	8-35	9-35	10-35	10-10 p.m.	10-35		11-35	1-10	4-10	7-10	10-10	1-35		10-35	
Flockton (Church)	..	8-45	9-45	10-45	and	10-45		11-45	1-20	4-20	7-20	10-20	1-45	And every	10-45	
Emley (Cross)	..				11-10 p.m.				1-30	4-30	7-30	10-30		hour until		10-40
Beaumont's Arms	..				on				1-40	4-40	7-40	10-40		10-10 p.m.		10-45
Grange Moor	..	8-50	9-50	10-50	Saturdays	10-50		11-50					1-50		10-50	
Lepton (Red Lion)	..	8-55	9-55	10-55		10-55	Back	11-55	1-50	4-50	7-50	10-50	1-55		10-55	11-5
Waterloo	..	9-5	10-5	11-5		11-5	to Car-	12-5	1-55	4-55	7-55	10-55	2-5		11-5	11-15
Huddersfield	arr.	9-15	10-15	11-55		11-15	age.	12-15	2-5	5-5	8-5	11-5	2-15		11-15	11-15

Connections at Flockton for Emley and Barnsley every day.

COUNTY MOTORS (LEPTON) Ltd.,
Waterloo Garage, HUDDERSFIELD.

A. E. GALE, Traffic Manager.
J. CLEGG, Manager.

J. Broadbent & Co., Printers, Ltd., High Street, Huddersfield.— 7550bb

numbers of chassis to this country. The Pullman was the largest and, costing £595, it was faster than anything else available at the time. County obtained nine of these through an agency in Dewsbury and had them fitted with B20F bodies by Taylor of Barnsley. Some passengers, used to the sedate speed of the original buses, complained that the Reos were being driven at dangerous speeds and one driver, Harold Benjamin Auty

County 14 (WU 3335) was a Reo Pullman with 20 seater bodywork by Taylor of Barnsley, new in 1925 but withdrawn under the new management in 1929.
[G. Lumb collection]

of Honley, was summonsed by Dewsbury Police Court for dangerous driving through Dewsbury Market Place on 26 February 1926. For speeding at 25 miles per hour he was fined 27 shillings (the alternative was 28 days imprisonment).

These buses allowed the rapid expansion of this period to be made; another pair plus seven AECs also with Taylor B25F or B26F bodies supplemented them and by the end of 1926 the fleet strength was eighteen. On Easter Monday 1926 the seating capacity of these buses was quite inadequate, as conductor Lewis Hodge was to find to his cost when he was fined 20 shillings. At Lepton, Constable Redmile had seen 14 passengers alight from Hodge's bus and then observed a further 43 adults remaining on the bus. As ten children were also sitting on adults' knees this brought the original total to 67 people! Hodge claimed that he was working to instructions and could not stop people boarding his bus.

The General Strike started on Tuesday 4 May 1926 and a crowd of 700 people at Barnsley refused to let passengers board a County bus but they did not damage the vehicle. Similar disturbances took place at Dewsbury, Flockton, Horbury and Wakefield. By the afternoon of 6 May a restricted emergency bus service was operated and from the morning of 7 May until the end of the strike the following services were operated at half hourly intervals:

Kirkheaton to Huddersfield from 6.45am
Kirkburton to Huddersfield from 6.30am
Lepton to Huddersfield from 7.00am

After the strike was over the company employed several out of work miners; three of them, conductors Arthur Heywood and Arthur Walker and driver Bill Pickering (all later inspectors) each gave over 40 years of loyal service.

In June 1926 permission was granted to use stand D in Lord Street for a new route to Wakefield via Waterloo, Kirkburton, Shelley, Skelmanthorpe, Scissett, Clayton West, Bretton Cross Roads, Calder Grove and Durkar and this started on Saturday 26 June, running hourly. All was not plain sailing, however, as licences for routes to Sheffield via Penistone and to Barnsley via New Mill were refused and in January 1927 a licence request for a service to Bradford via Bradley and Brighouse met a similar fate. [It is possible that County ran between Huddersfield and Brighouse via Bradley around this time.]

In the early days all the County conductors had been men but this changed from October 1926 when six

County Bus Service.

A THROUGH SERVICE, commencing Saturday, June 26th, 1926,

WILL BE RUN BETWEEN

HUDDERSFIELD (Lord St. Stand D.) & WAKEFIELD (Top of Westgate)

Via KIRKBURTON, SHELLEY, SKELMANTHORPE, SCISSETT, CLAYTON WEST, CALDER GROVE, DURKAR and THORNES.

	a.m.	a.m.		p.m.	Saturday only. p.m.	Every Night except Sat. p.m.	
HUDDERSFIELD Dep.	6-20	7-20		8-20	9-20	9-20	Saturday 10-20 p.m. to Scissett only. Leave Scissett for Huddersfield 11-10.
Waterloo	6-30	7-30	And every hour	8-30	9-30	9-30	
Spring Grove	6-40	7-40	until	8-40	9-40	9-40	
Kirkburton (George)	6-45	7-45	8-20 p.m.	8-45	9-45	9-45	
Shelley	6-50	7-50	and	8-50	9-50	9-50	
Skelmanthorpe	6-55	7-55	9-20 p.m.	8-55	9-55	9-55	SUNDAYS.
Scissett	7-5	8-5	on	9-5	10-5	10-5	First Bus leaves Huddersfield 10-20 a.m. and every hour as on Week-days.
Park Mill	7-10	8-10	Saturdays.	9-10	10-10		
Bretton Cross Roads	7-20	8-20		9-20	10-20		
Calder Grove	7-30	8-30		9-30	10-30		
Durkar	7-33	8-33		9-33	10-33		
Thornes	7-38	8-38		9-38	10-38		
WAKEFIELD Arr.	7-45	8-45		9-45	10-45		

	a.m.	a.m.		p.m.	p.m.	Every night except Saturday	
WAKEFIELD Dep.	7-50	8-50		9-50	10 50		
Thornes	7-56	8-56	And every hour	9-56	10-56		SUNDAYS.
Durkar	8-2	9-2	until	10-2	11-2		Leave Wakefield 11-50 a.m. and every hour until 9-50 p.m.
Calder Grove	8-5	9-5	9-50 p.m.	10-5	11-5		
Bretton Cross Roads	8-15	9-15	and	10-15	11-15		
Clayton West	8-25	9-25	10-50 p.m.	10-25	11-25		
Scissett	8-30	9-30	on	10-30	11-30	10-10	
Skelmanthorpe	8-35	9-35	Saturdays.	10-35	11-35	10-15	
Shelley	8-40	9-40		10-40	11-40	10-20	
Kirkburton (George)	8-45	9-45		10-45	11-45	10-25	
Spring Grove	8-50	9-50		10-50	11-50	10-30	
Waterloo	9-0	10-0		11-0	12-0	10-40	
HUDDERSFIELD Arr.	9-10	10-10		11-10	12-10	10-50	

County Motors (Lepton), Ltd.,
Waterloo Garage, Huddersfield.

A. E. GALE, Traffic Manager.
J. CLEGG, Manager.

M. Woffenden's Sons, Birkby, Huddersfield.

young ladies were employed. They were taken by Alf Gale to Beevers the Tailors to be measured for their uniforms, the colours of which were similar to the buses' livery, being dark purple with black facings. The girls were then kitted out with cash bag, ticket rack, punch and whistle and given three days training. The first day was spent in observation, the second in learning fares and fare stages and the complexities of the waybill while on the third day the conductor/trainer sat back and watched while the new recruits tried their hand.

Sitting in St Peter's Gardens, Huddersfield some forty years later watching the smart blue and cream County buses in Lord Street and seeing the Esso advertisement "Put a tiger in your tank" brought back happy memories to one of the original conductresses. Ethel Milnes recalled that the small Reo buses could certainly have done with something extra in the tank when climbing Lepton Edge. On many occasions the passengers had to alight to allow the bus to struggle empty to the top of the hill. She recalled that from Lepton to the outskirts of Barnsley and Wakefield regular passengers were known by name, as were their destinations before they asked for a ticket. Mrs Gill, who travelled from Haigh Lane to Emley, always climbed down the steep steps backwards. Mr Haigh, a poultry farmer from Flockton who regularly travelled to Wakefield, was late one morning but his wife held up the bus, shouting that he was just putting on his collar. Two local policemen, Constables Mowbray of

Emley and Cooper of Flockton, rode on the buses and were very helpful whenever a bus broke down on the notorious Emley Clough switchback between Flockton and Emley.

If the regular passengers for the 8.00am Huddersfield to Wakefield bus were late the crew would wait for them. Bank clerks were picked up at Grange Lane and Middlestown; a lady who ran a drapers shop at Ossett also caught the bus at Middlestown but she never waited at the proper stop (similarly when she returned she was always dropped off outside her garden gate). For this favour she gave cigarettes to the men and something from the shop, such as a pair of garters, to the conductresses.

Alf Gale was fondly remembered as wearing an ordinary suit and a bowler hat; later, after the sale of the business, he sported a navy uniform with "Traffic Manager" on his cap band. He would arrive at the garage before 6.00am and did not leave until after the return of the last bus. As pressure mounted, particularly on Saturdays when every bus was in service, the bowler hat was tilted further and further back. He used to fling out his arm in an almost Nazi-like salute as he consulted his pocket watch, particularly if he thought someone was late. Alf Gale's daughter worked as a conductress at one time.

Another character of this period was the cashier, Ezra Jaggar, with snow white beard and rimless glasses who was also the local Methodist preacher. It was of course his job to point out any shortfalls in the conductresses' takings and he was the custodian of the much used ready reckoner (no pocket calculators in those days).

By mid 1927 the following timetabled services were in operation. Times shown are for Monday to Saturday unless otherwise indicated; on Sundays the buses started later but ran to the same frequencies. Huddersfield-Flockton-Overton-Wakefield (Wakefield Direct) Hourly from stand D on Lord Street from 7.00am to 9.00pm. Journey time was 65 minutes each way with a five minute layover at Wakefield; three buses were required. Fares from Town were: Lepton 5d; Grange Moor 6d; Flockton 8d; Overton 10d; Middlestown 11d; Horbury Bridge 1/1d and Wakefield 1/5d. [The Wakefield based West Riding company ran a similar service every two hours but with alternate buses via Midgley and Netherton, instead of Overton.]. Huddersfield-Emley-Flockton-Overton-Wakefield. Saturdays only from 11.15am, one extra bus running every 3 hours as above but via Emley instead of Grange

Moor.

Huddersfield-Kirkburton-Scissett-Wakefield.
Another hourly service leaving stand D, Lord Street, from 6.20am to 8.20pm. This longer route required 85 minutes running time each way and five minutes were allowed at each terminus; three buses were needed.

Huddersfield-Lepton-Bretton-Darton-Barugh Green-Barnsley By now this service had been improved to run hourly, departing from stand B from 6.15am to 9.15pm. In Lepton buses were routed via Highgate Lane and Rowley Lane, whereas the Wakefield service did not deviate from the main Wakefield Road. Nevertheless the 80 minute journey was considerably shorter than that on the Barnsley & District buses which ran via Penistone Road. With ten minute layovers at the termini, three buses were needed to maintain the service. By now there were alternative routes between Lepton Edge and Bretton Cross Roads. Most buses continued to run via Emley Moor, Emley, Flockton and Midgley but those leaving at three hour intervals from 8.15am were routed via Grange Moor Cross Roads, Flockton, Emley and Emley Woodhouse.

Huddersfield-Kirkheaton-Mirfield-Dewsbury
Contrary to advertisements proclaiming that all County Bus Services routes ran hourly, this service from stand F was only every two hours before midday but hourly afterwards. The journey took 50 minutes so the afternoon service was conveniently provided by two buses. Whilst the minimum protective fare in or out of Huddersfield was 3d (this applied to all operators running over the tram route between Town and Waterloo), it was 4d in and out of Dewsbury. Other fares from Huddersfield were: Kirkheaton 4d; Hopton 7d; Black Bull, Mirfield 10d; Fir Cottage 11d; Dewsbury 1/2d.

Brighouse-Dewsbury
This route was operated every 90 minutes by one bus. Kilburn's Ideal also ran one vehicle over the same route to give a combined 45 minutes frequency. After Three Nuns buses continued direct via the main road (Pear Tree) to the Black Bull at Mirfield; thereafter the route, also remaining on the main road, was identical to that of the Huddersfield to Dewsbury buses. A through fare of 10d was charged for the 35 minutes journey.

The published timetables for these services needed 13 vehicles, out of a fleet of 18 purple saloons, all running on pneumatic tyres. By 1926/7 the registered office was in Albany Road, Waterloo, where at least some of the vehicles were garaged, and George E Browne, Thomas W Murphy and A Collier had joined the list of directors.

The authorised capital was £6,000 and there were twenty shareholders. The buses ran about 6,000 miles per week, carrying 17,000 passengers at fares quoted as 1d per stage with a 2d minimum.

4.2: TRIUMVIRATE TAKES OVER

The company was first advertised for sale early in 1927 with an asking price of £36,000 but it was 17 August before it was sold - for just £27,500. A joint purchase was made by the three major bus companies with territory to the east of Huddersfield: Barnsley & District Traction (soon renamed Yorkshire Traction), Yorkshire Woollen District of Dewsbury and Wakefield based West Riding Automobile. This was an unusual partnership as it featured two tramway based BET group companies plus an independent or "non-combine" firm in the shape of West Riding. The authorised capital was increased, at first to £15,000 and in 1934 to £25,000.

In March 1927 Huddersfield Corporation too had started running buses from Lord Street as far as Lepton and Kirkburton. West Riding ran alongside County on the Wakefield direct route while most other sections of the County route network were also covered by one or more of the three parent companies with the exception of the Hopton area.

Herbert Burgin was appointed as manager and Herbert Jones, who had been on B&D's staff at Barnsley since 1923, was promoted to the post of chief clerk and cashier at Waterloo. [Jones stayed at Waterloo until 1935 when he joined another company part owned by Yorkshire Traction, the new Sheffield United Tours; he later lectured on transport studies at a Sheffield college.]

When Tom Mitchell had sold his business to Barnsley & District in 1925, his Penistone Road, Waterloo depot site was included in the sale. At first this was used as a non operational store but from August 1927 it was transferred to County Motors to become their new depot. Earlier the site had been a tip, to which at the close of the nineteenth century Corporation steam trams had hauled refuse wagons on behalf of the Corporation's Sanitary Department.

County's buses had been in poor condition. Nine buses had to be reconditioned by Yorkshire Woollen and the other nine by Barnsley & District, while West Riding loaned some 2-ton buses to County. The cost of refurbishing these buses was £3,346 2s 11d – much more than County's average monthly income in 1928.

The lightweight small capacity Reos were quickly sold off, although the last three survived until 1930, and the AECs too had all disappeared by 1934. For replacements County turned to Leyland and by the end of 1934 the fleet consisted of 18 petrol engined Leyland Lions, a mixture of PLSC3, LT1, LT2 and LT5 models seating between 32 and 35. Later prewar deliveries would be diesel engined Leyland Tigers. The three parent companies also either standardised on or were at least partial to Leylands. County adopted a new livery of dark blue (similar to that in use on prewar Leeds trams) below the saloon windows with ivory window frames and roofs; the fleetname County appeared in gold on the waist panels. The all single deck fleet carried a single line destination blind above the second nearside window to supplement the main front blind; both blinds were always turned and set correctly for each journey.

By 1928 the Brighouse-Dewsbury service was rerouted after Ravensthorpe to become Brighouse-Thornhill-Horbury, where passengers could change buses for Wakefield.

On 23 June 1928 a new Saturday only route was introduced from Huddersfield to Grange Moor Chapel, direct via Wakefield Road and Liley Lane. County's request for a licence for a daily service was later refused by Huddersfield Watch Committee and Grange Moor residents wishing to ride into Huddersfield on other days still had to walk to the cross roads at Shuttle Eye on Wakefield Road until 1951. On 18 October 1928 it was found necessary to reduce fares on the Dewsbury route between Huddersfield and Kirkheaton to the level charged by Huddersfield Corporation.

The new licensing system introduced in 1931 did not have a significant effect on County. It was intended to project the Brighouse-Horbury service through to Wakefield but the licence granted by the traffic commissioners in October 1931 was only for Brighouse-Horbury; opposition to through running to Wakefield had come from two of County's owners, West Riding and Yorkshire Woollen. It is surprising that this family disagreement had not been settled before reaching the traffic courts (a year later they were again refused the extension!) One bus entered service at Brighouse and ran from there every two hours, an inefficient operation with 20 minutes out of every hour spent standing idle at a terminus – hence the proposed Wakefield extension. From the following faretable it will be noted that between Three Nuns and Mirfield buses once again ran via Stocks Bank Road and Nab Lane.

Brighouse
```
     Coal Pit Lane
1    Kirklees Bar House
2  1    Dumb Steeple
3  2  1    Nab Lane
4  3  2  1    Ing Grove Park
5  4  3  2  1    Fir Cottage
6  5  4  3  2  1    North Road
7  6  5  4  3  2  2    Ingham's Road
8  7  6  5  4  3  2½  2    Thornhill
9  8  7  6  5  4  3½  3  2½    Frank Lane
9  8  7  6  5  4  3½  3  2½  2    Sandy Lane
10  9  8  7  6  5  4  3½  3  2½  2    Horbury Bridge
10  9  8  7  6  5  4  3½  3  2½  2  1    Horbury Station
11  10  9  8  7  6  5  4  3½  3  2½  1  1    Horbury Town Hall
11  10  9  8  7  6  5  4  3½  3  2½  1½  1½  1
```

Also in October 1931 it was found to be possible to accelerate the direct Wakefield service by ten minutes. With a new journey time of only 55 minutes, one bus was saved so just two were needed. The wasteful 45 minutes layover, previously spent parked up on the west side of Castlegate at the Seed Hill end, was eliminated.

In late April 1932 the Dewsbury route was rerouted to run much more directly between Kirkheaton and Lower Hopton via Heaton Moor Road, Hollin Hall Lane and Hopton Lane. Unfortunately this left much of Upper Hopton unserved so shortly afterwards it had to be rerouted again, this time via Heaton Moor Road, Highgate Lane, Bellstring Lane, Freemasons Arms, Hopton Hall Lane, Jackroyd Lane and Hopton Lane. This very circuitous route seemed to satisfy everyone and was to survive beyond the demise of County. Loadings soon justified an all day hourly frequency, increased to every 30 minutes on Saturday and Sunday afternoons and evenings, and the Dewsbury terminus was moved into the new bus station. For some years it

County 39 (VH 3683) was a Leyland Lion LT2 bodied by Leyland, seen here when new in June 1931. It was requisitioned on the outbreak of war in September 1939 but returned to County in 1941, passing to T. Burrows of Wombwell in 1943. [R. Marshall collection]

had been in Old Westgate, near the top of Daisy Hill.

From mid afternoon on Friday 24 February 1933 blizzard conditions prevailed in Huddersfield and surrounding districts and by Saturday morning over 12 inches of snow had fallen with severe drifting in places. Gradually all the County services ground to a halt and even on the direct Wakefield route eight feet drifts prevented the buses getting beyond Lepton. No buses ran on the Sunday and gangs of drivers worked day and night on snow clearance duties. It was 4.00pm on the Monday before a bus climbed to Lepton and the first bus to reach Wakefield did so via the main road (Denby Grange) on Tuesday morning as Flockton was still cut off.

During this period County employed one conductress who was never likely to encounter trouble from late night drinkers or indeed anyone else on her bus. Miss Fanny Storey who lived at Big Valley was a former gym instructress, weight lifter and wrestler. She challenged and beat the former English women's champion in a bout at a Barnsley theatre. She also had a passion for riding motor cycles.

From 1 September 1933 the Wakefield via Kirkburton service was diverted at Bretton Bar to serve Bretton West by a double run. This bus connected with the Barnsley service at 15 minutes past the hour at Bretton Cross Roads, making it was possible for passengers from, say, Skelmanthorpe on the Wakefield bound bus to change at Bretton for Darton and Barnsley. Similarly passengers from Emley on board the Barnsley bus could connect with the bus for Calder Grove and Wakefield. In the opposite direction buses connected at 20 minutes past each hour. These connections at Bretton Bar were still being made in 1969 after the absorption of County into Yorkshire Traction. A further rerouting of the Wakefield via Kirkburton service – direct via the main A636 road between Scissett and Park Mill – proved to be unpopular and from 8 January 1934 the route once again served Clayton West Church.

In the mid to late 1930s the maximum number of vehicles, without duplication, required for the main services was 15 on Saturday afternoon:
Wakefield (direct), hourly 2 buses
Wakefield via Emley (Sat only), every 3 hours 1 bus
Wakefield via Kirkburton, hourly 3 buses
Barnsley via Emley [2 routes], combined hourly 3 buses
Dewsbury, every 30 mins 4 buses
Brighouse to Horbury, every 2 hours 1 bus
Grange Moor Chapel (Sat only), hourly 1 bus

This Roe bodied Leyland Lion LT5A was new in June 1934 as County 46 (VH 6541). Withdrawn on the outbreak of war in 1939, it was taken by the War Department in 1940 but returned (to County's one-third owner West Riding) at the end of 1942. 46 was withdrawn again from the County fleet in 1943 and eventually passed to Heather Bell Motor Services of Tow Law, who used it until 1952.
[C.H. Roe, courtesy G. Lumb collection]

Roe bodied Leyland Tiger TS8 61 (BVH 142) is seen when new in 1939 in County's prewar livery outside Roe's premises. After withdrawal in 1950, 61 (and 60) passed to Sussex bus operator Southdown for their engines.
[C.H. Roe, courtesy G. Lumb collection]

Alongside these regular routes were some "workman's" schedules. Four buses left Waterloo depot between 5.50 and 6.05am on Monday to Saturday mornings and all returned at 7.58am:

5.50am Waterloo-Town-Flockton-Town-Emley Cross-Town –Waterloo (7.58am)

5.55am Waterloo-Flockton-Emley Cross-Town-Emley Cross-Town-Waterloo (7.58am)

6.00am Waterloo-Town-Grange Moor-Town-Lepton-Town-Waterloo (7.58am)

6.05am Waterloo-Flockton-Waterloo-Flockton-Town-Waterloo (7.58am)

Three other early morning duties were required to transport workers to the Broadhead and Graves Mill at Kirkheaton and John Taylor's Mill, Firth Street, Huddersfield.

5.55am Waterloo-Kirkheaton-Town followed by two more return trips to Kirkheaton

6.20am Waterloo-Kirkheaton-Town-Kirkheaton-Town

6.50am Waterloo-Kirkheaton-Town

These three buses then appear to have entered normal service from Huddersfield. At shift changeover times specials also took miners to Darton Main, Emley Moor, Park Mill, Royd House and Springwood collieries; ordinary passengers could be carried on the return journeys.

The annual Rockwood Hunt at Upper Midgley also required a special service, operated by two buses. Departures from Lord Street were at half hour intervals between 12.00noon and 2.00pm via Lepton and Flockton Green, with local passengers not carried between Town and Lepton. The two buses waited at Midgley before making return trips from 4.00pm onwards. Other specials were provided for this event by West Riding and Yorkshire Traction.

From January 1939 County's terminus in Barnsley was moved from St Mary's Gate to Yorkshire Traction's new bus station. This was a great improvement for County. The old terminus to the north of the Town Hall (referred to in early timetables as "War Memorial") was an uphill trek from the town centre. The County company had thus been at a disadvantage in attracting passengers compared with Yorkshire Traction, whose buses all started in the centre (Kendray Street and Peel Street in the case of their Huddersfield routes). On several occasions County had tried unsuccessfully to have their terminus moved into the centre before the opening of the bus station.

In February the company's final prewar batch of Roe bodied Leyland Tigers (60-3: BVH 141-4) entered service, bringing the number of these buses in stock to sixteen (48-63). The earlier Leyland Lions had been withdrawn by now but there were still nine of these petrol engined vehicles (39-47) in use; total fleet strength was 25 single deckers.

4.3: WARTIME AND DOUBLE DECKERS

As a result of the "wartime emergency", on Saturday 16 September 1939 what was described as one third of the workforce, 16 drivers, 16 conductresses and 10 garage hands, were dismissed with effectively no notice. It was anticipated that 1206 miles per week (30% of the company's mileage) would be saved by reducing frequencies and withdrawing routes. On 30 September 1939 swingeing cuts were made to the timetabled services and most last buses departed an hour earlier than normal. The Dewsbury service was standardised at hourly with the extra Saturday and Sunday journeys cancelled. The direct Wakefield service remained hourly but the Saturday only route via Emley was withdrawn and never reinstated after the war. On the Wakefield via Kirkburton route, the hourly frequency was maintained, probably because of the collieries served. The Barnsley service was severely curtailed with only five through trips (three on Sundays). On Saturdays from 12.15pm an extra bus maintained an hourly frequency as far as Emley; the variant route via Grange Moor was not served during the war as all buses ran via Emley Moor. Finally the Brighouse-Horbury service was withdrawn and never ran again.

From 11 December 1939 it was necessary to make further economies so the Wakefield via Kirkburton route was curtailed. Only the 8.20pm journey now ran through to Wakefield on most days as all other buses terminated at either Springwood Colliery or Bretton West. Connections were made every two hours at Bretton with the West Riding Holmfirth-Wakefield service (itself withdrawn between Holmfirth and Bretton). Only on Saturdays from 11.20am did all departures continue to run through to Wakefield. From the same date the service was rerouted between Bretton West and Calder Grove to run direct via Bretton Lane and Branch Road, instead of returning to Bretton Bar and continuing along the A636 through Bullcliffe Wood. Bullcliffe Colliery was, however, still served at shift change times by buses doing a double run over the short distance from Bretton Bar.

Even on a Saturday afternoon only ten buses were

HUDDERSFIELD—BARNSLEY (via Emley and Flockton)

	NS	NS	SO	NOS	SO	SO	D	SO	D	D	D	D	D
	am	am	pm	pm	pm	pm	pm	pm	pm	pm	pm	pm	pm
HUDDERSFIELD—Lord Street ..	6 15	9 25	12 15	12 25	1 15	2 15	3 25	4 15	5 15	7 15	8 15	10 5	
WATERLOO—Tram Terminus ...	6 23	9 33	12 23	12 33	1 23	2 23	3 33	4 23	5 23	6 23	7 23	8 23	10 13
LEPTON—Red Lion ...	6 32	9 40	12 32	12 40	1 32	2 32	3 40	4 32	5 32	6 32	7 32	8 32	
EMLEY—Cross ...	6 50	9 58	12 50	12 58	1 49	2 49	3 58	4 49	5 49	6 49	7 50	8 49	
FLOCKTON—School ...	7 0	10 5	1 0	1 5			4 5		6 0		8 0		
BRETTON BAR HOUSE ...	7 15	10 15	1 15	1 15			4 15		6 15		8 15		
DARTON—Rose and Crown ...	7 30	10 30	1 30	1 30			4 30		6 30		8 30		
BARNSLEY—Bus Station ...	7 45	10 45	1 45	1 45			4 45		6 45		8 45		

	NS	NS	SO	D	SO	SO	D	D	D	D
	am	am	pm	pm	pm	pm	pm	pm	pm	pm
BARNSLEY—Bus Station ...	7 50	10 50	1 50				4 50		6 50	8 50
DARTON—Rose and Crown ...	8 2	11 2	2 2				5 2		7 2	9 2
BRETTON BAR HOUSE ...	8 15	11 15	2 15				5 15		7 15	9 15
FLOCKTON—School ...	8 25	11 25	2 25				5 25		7 25	9 25
EMLEY—Cross ...	8 35	11 35	1 50	2 35	2 50	4 50	5 35	6 50	7 35	8 50	9 35
LEPTON—Red Lion ...	8 45	11 45	1 59	2 45	2 59	4 59	5 45	6 59	7 45	8 59	9 45
WATERLOO—Tram Terminus ..	5 55	8 55	11 55	2 6	2 55	3 6	5 6	5 55	7 6	7 55	9 6	9 55
HUDDERSFIELD—Lord Street ..	6 5	9 5	12 5	2 14	3 5	3 14	5 14	6 5	7 14	8 5	10 5

NS—Not on Sundays.   SO—Sats. Only.   D—Daily.   NOS—Not on Saturdays.

HUDDERSFIELD—WAKEFIELD (via Lepton and Flockton)

	Weekdays.					Sundays.			
	am	pm	pm	pm	pm	pm	pm	pm
HUDDERSFIELD—Lord Street ..	7 0	8 0	9 0	9 55	1 0	8 0	9 0	9 55
WATERLOO—Tram Terminus ..	7 8	and	8 8	9 8	10 3	1 8	and	8 8	9 8	10 3
LEPTON—Red Lion ...	7 15	every	8 15	9 15		1 15	every	8 15	9 15
FLOCKTON—Angel Inn ...	7 25	hour	8 25	9 25		1 25	hour	8 25	9 25
MIDDLESTOWN—White Swan ...	7 35	until	8 35			1 35	until	8 35
WAKEFIELD—Westgate ...	7 55		8 55			1 55		8 55
WAKEFIELD—Westgate ...	8 0		9 0			2 0		9 0
MIDDLESTOWN—White Swan ...	8 20	and	9 20			2 20	and	9 20
FLOCKTON—Angel Inn ...	8 30	every	9 30			2 30	every	9 30
LEPTON—Red Lion ...	8 40	hour	9 40			2 40	hour	9 40
WATERLOO—Tram Terminus ...	8 47	until	9 47			2 47	until	9 47
HUDDERSFIELD—Lord Street ..	8 55		9 55			2 55		9 55

HUDDERSFIELD—DEWSBURY (via Kirkheaton & Mirfield)

	Weekdays.				Sundays.			
	am	pm	pm	pm	pm	pm	pm	pm
HUDDERSFIELD—Lord Street ..	7 40	7 40	8 40	9 30	12 40	7 40	8 40	9 30
WATERLOO—Tram Terminus ..	7 48	and	7 48	8 48	9 38	12 48	and	7 48	8 48	9 38
KIRKHEATON—Moor Bottom ...	7 56	every	7 56	8 56		12 56	every	7 56	8 56
HOPTON—W.M. Club ...	8 5	hour	8 5			1 5	hour	8 5
MIRFIELD—Black Bull ...	8 15	until	8 15			1 15	until	8 15
DEWSBURY—Bus Station ...	8 26		8 26			1 26		8 26
DEWSBURY—Bus Station ...	8 45		8 45			1 45		8 45
MIRFIELD—Black Bull ...	8 56	and	8 56			1 56	and	8 56
HOPTON—W.M. Club ...	9 5	every	9 5			2 5	every	9 5
KIRKHEATON—Moor Bottom ...	9 14	hour	9 14	9 14		2 14	hour	9 14	9 14
WATERLOO—Tram Terminus ...	9 20	until	9 20	9 20		2 20	until	9 20	9 20
HUDDERSFIELD—Lord Street ..	9 30		9 30			2 30		9 30

HUDDERSFIELD—WAKEFIELD (via Kirkburton & Scissett)

	am	am	am	am	am		pm	pm	pm		pm	pm	pm
HUDDERSFIELD—Lord Street ..		6 20	7 20	8 20	9 20	and	1 20	2 20	3 20	and	8 20	9 20	10 10
WATERLOO—Tram Terminus ...	6 15	6 28	7 28	8 28	9 28	every	1 28	2 28	3 28	every	8 28	9 28	10 18
KIRKBURTON—George Hotel ...	6 28	6 40	7 40	8 40	9 40	hour	1 40	2 40	3 40	hour	8 40	9 40
SCISSETT—Church ...	6 46	7 0	8 0	9 0	10 0	until	2 0	3 0	4 0	until	9 0	10 0
PARK MILL—Junction Inn ...		7 5	8 5	9 5	10 5		2 5	3 5	4 5		9 5	10 5
SPRINGWOOD COLLIERY ...	6 55							3 8				10 8
BRETTON WEST—Post Office ...		7 16	8 16		10 16		2 16		4 16		9 16
BRETTON WEST—Post Office ...		7 23	8 23		10 23		2 23		4 23		9 23
SPRINGWOOD COLLIERY ...	7 0					and		3 26		and		10 10
PARK MILL—Junction Inn ...		7 29	8 29	9 29	10 29	every	2 29	3 29	4 29	every	9 29
SCISSETT—Church ...		7 6	7 33	8 33	9 33	10 33	hour	2 33	3 33	4 33	hour	9 33	10 16
KIRKBURTON—George Hotel ...		7 17	7 50	8 50	9 50	10 50	until	2 50	3 50	4 50	until	9 50	10 27
WATERLOO—Tram Terminus ...												10 37
HUDDERSFIELD—Lord Street ..		7 35	8 10	9 10	10 10		3 10	4 10	5 10		10 10

NOTE:—Connection will be made at Bretton West at 23 minutes past the even hour from 8.23 a.m. until 8.23 p.m. with the West Riding Automobile Co., Ltd., service to and from Wakefield.
SATS.:—As on weekdays until 10.20 a.m. Through service to Wakefield from 11.20 a.m. and every hour until 6.20 p.m. arriving in Wakefield at 12.45 p.m. and hourly until 7.45 p.m. As on weekdays from 7.20 p.m.
Departures from Bretton West as on weekdays from 12.23 p.m. Through service from Wakefield to Huddersfield from 12.50 p.m. and hourly until 7.50 p.m.
SUNDAY:—Hudd.—Bretton West. As on weekdays from 12.20 p.m. Bretton West to Hudd. As on weekdays from 1.23 p.m.

Penistone Road Garage, Waterloo, Huddersfield.   By Order, H. BURGIN, Manager.

WILSON & SON, Printers, "Crown Press," Horbury.

needed for these skeleton services. It is interesting to compare the weekly numbers of journeys on each route in the immediate prewar period with that during the emergency. The approximate percentage cut in mileage for each route can then be calculated.

Route	Prewar journeys	11.12.39 journeys	% Cut
Wakefield (direct)	107	100	7
Wakefield via Emley (Sat)	4	0	100
Dewsbury	126	96	24
Wakefield via Kirkburton	113	16(W) 97(B/S)	31
Barnsley via Emley	108	33(B) 14(E)	66
Grange Moor Chapel (Sat)	12	10	17
Brighouse-Horbury	58	0	100
(B) to Barnsley; (B/S) to Bretton or Springwood; (E) to Emley; W (to Wakefield)			

Taking into account the various route lengths it is possible to deduce that about 40% of the prewar route mileage had been lost by 11 December 1939. This of course ignores works and colliery services which had to continue despite the fuel shortage.

With such a surplus of buses, it is hardly surprising that nine were requisitioned from September 1939 onwards by the War Department. These were the surviving petrol engined Leyland Lions (39-47), dating from 1931-4. Most of these buses had been taken out of service in September 1939 at the time of the first cutbacks and all had gone to the War Department by July 1940. County then relied entirely on their very modern fleet of diesel engined Leyland Tigers (48-63). Of the requisitioned buses, 42/3/5 were never recovered, 39-41 returned late in 1941 and 44/6/7 reappeared during 1943 and 1944. All had been withdrawn by the end of hostilities, seeing little or no use with County after their return, but two were loaned to West Riding for the second half of 1942.

Towards the end of January 1940 very heavy snowfalls and subsequent drifting on the more isolated parts of County's routes caused severe disruption and cancellation of services. One bus was stranded at Emley Moor for several days and three days after the first snow buses could reach no further than Lepton, Kirkburton and Kirkheaton. It took almost two weeks to clear the roads before normal services could be resumed.

Ernest Mellor started with County in May 1940 and was to remain with the company to the end. Originally a conductor, the only male conductor at that time, he had suffered a serious foot injury which prevented him from being called up for the forces. He later became a mechanic.

From about 27 July 1940 onwards buses were

repainted with dark blue or grey roofs (instead of ivory) as a form of camouflage. Some buses were repainted entirely in unrelieved grey.

From July 1941 employers had to provide their employees with certificates to allow them to purchase workmen's return tickets on Sundays. In January 1942 scholars tickets of County and Huddersfield JOC became interavailable between Huddersfield and Kirkheaton.

As the war situation deteriorated and fuel became even scarcer from 1 September 1941 further service reductions were made. On the Dewsbury and Wakefield direct routes the last through buses operated an hour earlier (7.40 and 8.00pm respectively). The Barnsley service also finished earlier but more buses served the full route. On the Wakefield via Kirkburton route the one remaining through journey on Sunday to Friday at 8.20pm was curtailed at Bretton West and on Saturdays the last two through journeys (7.20 and 8.20pm) were curtailed at Springwood Colliery and Bretton West.

At a later date after September 1941 but by October 1944 the Wakefield via Kirkburton route suffered further

cuts with the Sunday service reduced to run every two hours. Also the Sunday to Friday 9.20pm Lord Street to Springwood Colliery and return were restricted to workpeople and travel permit holders. This was the company's only journey to leave Huddersfield after 9.00pm except for trips to the depot.

Eric Green, who had joined County from a firm of chartered accountants in June 1935 as chief clerk, was promoted to manager on 1 April 1942 to replace Herbert Burgin. Unfortunately he received his call up papers to the armed forces immediately afterwards and served in the RASC. Demobilised in 1946, he returned to his managerial duties at Waterloo where he was still in charge after County had been absorbed into Yorkshire Traction.

In order to increase their capacity, Leyland Tigers 54-9 were converted to perimeter seating at some stage during the war years. The number of standees carried was greatly increased and no doubt the discomfort suffered by the passengers was preferable to waiting an hour or more for the next bus, which might have been full. The conversions were carried out at the Wakefield depot of parent company West Riding.

In the latter part of 1943 Tigers 60-3 were temporarily withdrawn from service to have their bodies reconditioned by parent Yorkshire Woollen in Dewsbury. To replace them, Yorkshire Woollen 206/7 (HD 4617/8), a pair of lowbridge Leyland Titan TD2s with Leyland L27/24R bodywork came to Waterloo on loan on 1 November, the first double deckers operated by County. It is interesting to note that Huddersfield JOC had

The first double deckers to run for County, apart from the hired Yorkshire Woollen Leylands, were a pair of highbridge Guy Arab IIs with Park Royal utility bodies new in May 1944. 66 (CCX 702) is parked in Lord Street on the Wakefield via Flockton route, painted in the mainly dark blue livery derived from the prewar single deck colour scheme. [S.T. Harling collection]

Another County wartime utility Guy Arab in the mainly dark blue livery, this time with a Roe lowbridge body, is 69 (CCX 797) new in 1945. It is standing near a Yorkshire Traction Guy Arab utility and a Traction postwar single decker on the rough ground at the "bottom end of Town" to the east of Northgate (now Southgate). [S.T. Harling collection] The Publisher had some reservations about including this poor quality picture, but was convinced by the Authors that it was of signifcant importance to be included.

placed one lowbridge double decker in service on their otherwise single deck Kirkheaton route in the previous month. County may have been concerned about losing their share of the market in that area. The Titans were quickly returned to their owner at the end of February 1944 but they were a pointer to future fleet renewal policy.

Towards the end of the war many bus operators who had hitherto relied entirely on single deck buses obtained new utility double deckers in order to cope more effectively with increased loadings. As early as 14 April 1943 the company secretary had been instructed to apply for permission to obtain three double deckers but an offer of AEC engined Daimler CWA6 buses in September 1943 had been turned down. Parent companies West Riding, Yorkshire Traction and Yorkshire Woollen also rejected offers of AEC engined Daimler utilities, preferring to wait until they could obtain Gardner engined double deckers. On 16 December 1943 County again applied for three double deckers and this time they were satisfied with the outcome. In May 1944 Gardner engined utility Guy Arab II double deckers 65/6 with Park Royal highbridge bodies entered service, followed in July by 64 (actually received by the end of March) which had Roe lowbridge bodywork, all equipped with spartan wooden seats.

Yorkshire Woollen's timetable books included all the County timetables from the October 1944 issue onwards. These could be bought in Huddersfield at YWD agents such as the Palace Sweet Shop in Kirkgate or later Palace Motors in Venn Street.

A further batch of Guy Arabs, 67-70, also fitted with Roe lowbridge bodies, followed during 1945. At least two of the utilities were soon fitted with more comfortable seats from a withdrawn County Leyland Lion or from old West Riding buses. All the utilities (64-70) were originally painted mainly dark blue, with ivory bands.

4.4: COUNTY'S POSTWAR RECOVERY

After the war normal service was gradually resumed with earlier and later journeys added although as mentioned in the last chapter the Wakefield via Emley and Brighouse-Horbury routes were not reinstated. Over the years there were to be very few significant changes to the rest of the network. By October 1945 all journeys on the Wakefield via Kirkburton route had been re-extended beyond Bretton West to Wakefield on a daily basis; an hourly frequency was also offered daily.

Around 2 June 1946 a bright new "reversed" livery of mainly off white with mid blue bands (brighter than the dark blue previously used) was first seen – applied to single decker Leyland Tiger 62.

With high postwar ridership there were times when more double deckers would have provided much needed extra capacity. At Whitsuntide in May 1946 one passenger complained that on bank holidays double deckers seemed to be available whereas at other times miners were left behind by single deckers filled to capacity. He said that the 12.25pm Barnsley bus on Whitsuntide Tuesday was a double decker carrying only

twenty or so passengers, followed by a West Riding double decker on the Wakefield service five minutes later carrying even fewer passengers. On normal working days the County Barnsley bus was only a single decker with an inadequate capacity. The manager in reply pointed out that on normal working days some of the double deckers were off the road for servicing, which did not happen on bank holidays.

The problem was to some extent addressed in December 1946 when a further pair of Guy Arab IIs with Roe lowbridge bodies (71/2) entered service, increasing the double deck fleet to nine. These buses were painted in a double deck version of the new livery: mainly off white with three mid-blue bands, one band below the upper deck windows and the others above and below the lower deck windows. Roofs and mudguards were also painted mid-blue. These double deckers had a single line aperture blind over the rear platform entrance which soon fell into disuse, being permanently set to blank or Huddersfield. It is curious that future open platform rear entrance double deckers, plus the utilities after rebodying, continued to be delivered so equipped and ran their entire lives without the side blinds ever being used. Meanwhile the utility Guy double deckers were gradually repainted into the bright new livery and the single deck version of the scheme continued to appear on the prewar Leyland Tigers.

Significant timetable improvements were introduced in January 1947. The Dewsbury route was increased to half-hourly during the Monday to Friday evening peak and in Saturday shopping hours and there were extra shorts at the Huddersfield end in the morning peak. There were also extra Monday to Saturday peak hour shorts as far as Grange Moor or Flockton on the Wakefield direct timetable. The prewar Barnsley via Grange Moor, Flockton and Emley route was finally reintroduced (three return journeys) and Barnsley via Emley, Flockton and Midgley was improved to give a combined hourly frequency to Barnsley. Earlier Sunday journeys were added to all routes.

Buses arriving in Dewsbury had a 19 minute layover which, owing to rather cramped conditions in the bus station, was usually spent in the section of Long Causeway south of Vicarage Road. The January 1947 timetable, however, included an earlier departure from Huddersfield which arrived in Dewsbury at 7.06am and appeared to have an even longer 24 minute layover. In fact the bus immediately doubled back empty as far as North Road (Ravensthorpe) and returned to Dewsbury picking up local passengers on behalf of parent company Yorkshire Woollen. Only then did it form the 7.30am departure for Huddersfield. Similarly the bus timed to arrive in Dewsbury at 8.26am would then run empty to the Pildacre Mills housing estate at Earlsheaton and leave there at 8.35am, picking up en route to Dewsbury, before forming the 8.45am back to Huddersfield. During the evening rush hour the bus arriving in Dewsbury at 5.26pm would pull straight onto the Ossett stand where the YWD inspector would load it for Bywell Road via Earlsheaton. After running back empty, the bus formed the 5.45pm to Huddersfield. When working these trips the destination blinds were left unturned on arrival at Dewsbury.

Faretables for these workings were shown at the back of the County Motors Fares and Stages booklet under the heading "YWD fares to be charged only when working for YWD Transport Company Ltd". The method of accounting for the revenue collected when running for Yorkshire Woollen was as follows. On arriving in Dewsbury from Huddersfield the conductor would write 'YWD' across the ticket showing in the window of the Bellgraphic ticket machine and then eject it (the carbon copy remained inside the machine). The Yorkshire Woollen passengers would then receive a County ticket in exchange for their fares. On returning to the bus station and before resuming work on the County route the conductor would write 'CML' across the face of the ticket showing in the window of the machine and similarly eject it. Thus the value of the tickets between where the conductor had written YWD and CML would be apportioned (less costs) to Yorkshire Woollen when the duplicate tickets in the machine were processed in the office.

Despite the joint ownership, the County company was allowed a surprising amount of autonomy in day to day running. For example, for many years uniforms were supplied by James Beevers of Brook Street, Huddersfield and conductors' cash bags were the products of a local leather goods maker, Walker and Aldridge of Cloth Hall Street. The cash bags were identical to those supplied to Huddersfield Corporation and were of a distinctive design, closing at the top with a brass fastener featuring an inbuilt lock.

The winter of early 1947 was remarkable for its severity and, like most other operators, County experienced great difficulty in maintaining services. The blizzard of Sunday 2 February caused severe drifting with many roads blocked. Emley was completely cut

After heavy snowfalls the first bus to reach Emley for five days did so on 6 February 1947. 1937 County Leyland Tiger TS7/Roe 55 (VH 9930), still in the mainly blue livery, was driven by Inspector Bill Pickering, in uniform on the left. [Kirklees Image Archive K000442]

off on the Sunday, Hopton was also inaccessible and the last direct bus back from Wakefield was marooned in drifts between Middlestown and Flockton on the Monday night and had to be dug out later. Even by Wednesday 5 February Dewsbury buses could not run beyond Kirkheaton, the indirect Wakefield service was still terminating at Kirkburton and the Barnsley services were rerouted to omit Emley; only the direct Wakefield bus was running normally. On the Thursday a single deck bus, Tiger 55 driven by Inspector Bill Pickering, attempted to reach Emley. The bus charged one hill three times before it got through, thanks to a double track of scattered cinders. It was over a week before the service was resumed; meanwhile milk and papers were delivered to the village by sledge.

Even a month later buses were still running late because of snow on all routes except Wakefield direct. After fresh snowfalls there were always three major

problem areas. The section of route across Emley Moor was usually the first to be blocked by drifts, causing all Barnsley buses to run via Grange Moor. Often only one half of Jack Hill, on the stretch of road which approaches Emley Moor Cross Roads from Lepton Edge, was ploughed as Denby Dale council were responsible for the road surface on the Emley Moor side whereas Kirkburton UDC were in charge on the Flockton side. Vehicles stuck on Red Hill (part of Shelley Lane, between Kirkburton and Shelley) caused delays on the Wakefield via Kirkburton route and the exposed moorland roads near Hopton caused disruption on the Dewsbury route.

Adverse weather conditions could not be blamed for an accident which occurred near the Stag Inn on Wakefield Road at about 6.00pm on 7 July 1947. Dennis Roberts was at the wheel of a single deck workmen's special returning to Town from Kirkheaton which got out of

County's first lowbridge Guy Arab utility, 64 (CCX 696) new in 1944 with Roe bodywork, is seen after repainting in the brighter livery first seen in June 1946. After working into Huddersfield on the indirect route from Wakefield via Scissett, it is standing on the "bottom end of Town" parking ground next to a prewar Yorkshire Traction Leyland Tiger used on the 15 to Barnsley. [S.T. Harling collection]

control and collided with a trolleybus standard, causing considerable damage. The injured passengers, including the conductress, had to leave by the rear emergency door; the road was blocked and at one time over a hundred vehicles including a dozen or more trolleybuses were held up. It was three hours before the bus, which ironically had undergone a routine inspection earlier in the day, was towed back to Waterloo with its badly damaged front end raised on a bogey.

Fog was also a serious problem. In November 1948 County did not withdraw their buses at all during one bad week as they found the fog cleared on the high ground around Lepton and Flockton and drivers were able to make up some of the lost time. Later, however, one bus was involved in a serious accident. On 30 November a Barnsley bound bus driven by R Renshaw of Moldgreen was in collision with a heavy coal lorry outside the Black Bull at Midgley. The cab of the bus was practically ripped out and the unfortunate driver had to receive hospital treatment at Wakefield.

Yorkshire Traction's unwillingness to consider County's interests has already been touched upon in the matter of their unsatisfactory Barnsley terminus before the opening of that company's bus station. It is not therefore surprising that it was only in May 1948 that full interavailability of return tickets with Yorkshire Traction was introduced on common sections of route.

The bodywork of the utility Guy Arab double deckers had been built at a time when many inferior materials such as unseasoned timber had to be used in their

construction and signs of deterioration soon appeared. Guy 64 was withdrawn as early as 1949 and scrapped three years later. 65/6 were rebuilt by East Lancs and Park Royal respectively in late 1948 and fitted with new Roe highbridge bodies in October 1950; in this form they survived until 1961/2. The later batch of utility Guys (67-70) suffered similar problems. 67 was transferred to Yorkshire Woollen in 1949, who had it rebodied as

their 516. 68 was rebuilt by County in November 1947 and again in January 1949 (eventually 68-70 were rebodied in 1953 with new Roe lowbridge bodies, which prolonged their stay at Waterloo until 1966-8).

The bodywork of many of the prewar single deckers had also deteriorated because of neglect during the war, although the chassis often still had a future. In March 1948 County transferred two Leyland Tiger TS7s (50/3) dating from 1935/6 to West Riding. There they became 678/9 and, sporting new Roe bodies and reregistered BHL 879/80, lasted until 1961.

The resulting vehicle shortage was alleviated by the loan from Yorkshire Woollen of seven Roe bodied Leyland Tiger TS7 single deckers of 1937 vintage. From 389/90/6/7/9-401 (HD 6305/6/12/3/5-7) an average of six vehicles were on loan at any time between March 1948 and January 1949. More permanent relief was soon to hand and between December 1948 and December 1949 no less than fourteen new buses were placed in service. The first postwar single deckers were Leyland Tiger PS1s with Roe bodies (73-8), followed by PS2/Roe 83-6, while further Roe lowbridge bodied Guy Arabs were Mark IIIs 79-82. The post war single deckers did not feature side blinds. Generally speaking after the war County's single deck buying policy followed Yorkshire Traction's whereas double deck selection was in line with West Riding's choice until the mid 1960s. The

County Leyland Tiger TS8/Roe 63 (BVH 144), before the war their highest numbered bus but here repainted into postwar livery, is on the parking ground east of Northgate (now Southgate) and south of what was the eastern part of Northumberland Street. County 63 served from 1939 to 1950. [P. Watson]

Leylands were part of an order for 14 chassis "reserved" for County "postwar" as long ago as February 1941. After the new deliveries, only six of the prewar buses (Tigers 58-63) survived and they would all be withdrawn in 1950.

After permission had been granted by the traffic commissioners on 24 March 1950, the Dewsbury service was strengthened by the provision of hourly short workings, using one bus, between Dewsbury and the Working Men's Club at Hopton on Monday to Friday evenings. On Wednesdays, for the benefit of shoppers going to Dewsbury market, the extra bus operated also during the afternoon. On Saturdays the service over the full route was now half-hourly almost all day. A further improvement on "Summer Sundays" from Easter Sunday to the last Sunday in October was the provision of a half-hourly frequency. These seasonal enhancements lasted from Easter Sunday 1950 until the end of the 1959 season.

The very low bridge in Station Road, Mirfield was the scene of an accident in April 1951. A double decker was being driven back from the Yorkshire Woollen garage at Savile Town, Dewsbury where it had just been repaired. Intending to return via Hopton and forgetting he was driving a double decker, the mechanic, Harry Asquith, drove the 13' 4" lowbridge bus under the 10' 6" bridge. The roof was completely sheared off and the driver was subsequently fined £3 at Dewsbury (West Riding) court.

By September 1951 the annual mileage was around 900,000 with about 4 million passengers being carried. The bus service to Grange Moor Chapel still ran only on Saturdays; a petition for a daily service signed by 170 residents had been supported by Kirkburton UDC in August 1950 and forwarded to the County manager. Eventually he applied to the traffic commissioners in October 1951 to divert the daily Barnsley via Grange Moor, Flockton and Emley service (three return journeys) to double run from Grange Moor Cross Roads to Grange Moor Chapel. On the Wakefield direct route, similar diversions were to apply on a few journeys, some in the evenings and mainly Sunday to Friday. These amendments were granted by the commissioners on 16 November 1951 and probably came into effect later in the month. [As long ago as 1932 Huddersfield JOC had tried to sell their scarcely profitable Lepton route to County but the asking price was too high. Had that deal gone through, Grange Moor Chapel would probably have had daily buses many years earlier.]

By August 1952 County was running four highbridge

Leyland Titan double deckers, Leyland bodied PD2/3s 87-88 which had entered service in 1950 and two new Roe bodied PD2/12s, 89-90. The fleet now consisted of 25 buses: 10 Leyland Tiger single deckers and 15 double deckers, 9 lowbridge Guy Arabs, 2 highbridge Guy Arabs and the 4 highbridge Leylands. In Wakefield, the Westgate terminus was forsaken with passengers benefitting from an extension into West Riding's bus station which opened on 1 October 1952.

Above- The first (numerically) postwar single decker for County was 1948 Leyland Tiger PS1/Roe 73 (DVH 752). In this view 73 is on layover in Dewsbury between operating Hopton shortworkings. [P. Watson]

Below- Two of the Guy Arab utilities with Roe lowbridge bodies were withdrawn in 1949 after a very short life with County, owing to use of substandard material in their bodywork, and they are seen here together in Waterloo depot: 67 (CCX 715) of 1945 and 64 (CCX 696) of 1944. 67 was sold to Yorkshire Woollen and fitted with a new highbridge Roe body but 64 was scrapped. [A.B. Cross]

4.5: FIFTIES OVERVIEW OF COUNTY OPERATIONS

In a typical hour during the 1950s departures from Lord Street, Huddersfield were as follows:

Monday to Friday

9.00am	Wakefield direct
9.20	Kirkburton, Scissett and Wakefield
9.25	Emley, Flockton and Barnsley
9.30	Wakefield [West Riding - odd hours only]
9.45	Dewsbury

Saturday

1.05pm	Wakefield direct
1.15	Dewsbury
1.15	Emley
1.20	Kirkburton, Scissett and Wakefield
1.25	Grange Moor Chapel, Flockton, Emley and Barnsley
1.25	Grange Moor Chapel
1.35	Wakefield [West Riding]
1.45	Dewsbury

During the 1950s, on reporting to the depot, conductors would draw a metal ticket box appropriate to the duty they were to work which contained a ticket machine, waybill, a book of emergency tickets (for use if the machine developed a fault) and, according to route or duty, a supply of twelve journey tickets. Also in the box would be a canvas bag in which, at the end of the duty, the conductor would place his or her takings along with the waybill; the bag would be closed with a draw string and dropped into the night safe inside the garage. On starting his duty, the conductor would sign on his ticket machine by writing his name, date and duty number across the face of the ticket showing in the Bellgraphic machine. This ticket would then be ejected from the machine. For writing on the tickets the conductor had to use a special purple leaded pencil known by the brand name of 'Mephisto' Copying 73V which was purchased from the company's stores at his own expense.

For administrative purposes only the routes had been numbered as follows before the war:

1 Huddersfield-Wakefield direct (known as 'Straight Wakefield')
2 Huddersfield-Wakefield via Emley
3 Huddersfield-Dewsbury
4 Brighouse-Dewsbury (later Brighouse-Horbury)
5 Huddersfield-Barnsley via Grange Moor, Flockton and Emley (also Springwood Colliery)
6 Huddersfield-Barnsley via Emley and Flockton
7 Huddersfield-Wakefield via Kirkburton and Scissett (referred to as 'KB')

Numbers 2 and 4 had fallen out of use with the withdrawal of those services at the outbreak of war but by the 1950s "route 4" was being used for the Saturday only Grange Moor Chapel duty.

These route numbers were never shown in public timetables or faretables or on the vehicles themselves and bore no relation to the licence numbers used by the traffic commissioners (BC 51/8 etc.). They were, however, used in duty numbers; letters for early turn duties (denoted by a single letter) and late turn duties (double letter) were all prefixed by the route number of the appropriate service. For instance, "Straight Wakefield" required two buses and the two early turn duties were 1A and 1B whereas the late turns were 1AA and 1BB. Barnsley and 'KB' each required three buses so the Barnsley duties were 6A, 6B, 6C (early turns) and 6AA, 6BB and 6CC (late turns); the 'KB' duties were similar but prefixed 7. Verbally the late turns were always referred to as "1 Double A" etc. rather than 1AA. This was a simple but effective system whereby one could tell at once what route the duty number applied to and whether it was an early or late turn.

A County driver had to be quite dexterous. Even as late as 1955 the company still had no buses fitted with trafficators, all signals having to be made by hand. Most of the drivers also had to cope with the eccentricities of a crash gear box (in 1955 there were only four buses

County Leyland Tiger TS8/Roe 62 (BVH 143), new in 1939 but resplendent in postwar livery on 12 September 1950, is taking most of its lengthy layover in Dewsbury in cobbled Long Causeway before returning to the congested bus station. 62 was withdrawn later in the year along with the rest of the surviving prewar buses. [R. Marshall collection]

Before the opening of the original Wakefield bus station in 1952, buses loading in the county town of the West Riding for Huddersfield and Holmfirth did so in Westgate. In 1950 County 1949 lowbridge Guy Arab III/Roe 82 (ECX 608) on the Huddersfield via Flockton service is parked in front of older West Riding utility Guy Arab II 588 (AHL 45) – also a Roe lowbridge – en route from Pontefract to Holmfirth. The older West Riding utility outlived the County Guy by a year, not being retired until 1965. [A.B. Cross]

without crash boxes); the Leyland crash gear boxes were more temperamental than the Guy ones.

During the mid 1950s vehicle allocation to routes followed a certain pattern. The two newest highbridge double deckers, Leyland Titans 89/90, were used on the Wakefield direct service; their all day Saturday and Sunday evening duplicates were usually single deckers. The slightly older highbridge Titans (87/8), together with highbridge Guy Arabs 65 or 66 were allocated to the Barnsley service. On "Wakefield KB" any three lowbridge Guy Arab double deckers were used; the low railway bridge in Denby Dale Road, Thornes on the outskirts of Wakefield prevented the use of highbridge buses on this route. On Dewsbury up to four buses were required and these would be either lowbridge Guy Arabs or (sometimes) single deckers; low railway bridges in School Lane, Kirkheaton and Newgate, Mirfield prohibited the use of highbridge buses. The Saturday Grange Moor Chapel service was usually worked by a lowbridge Guy Arab.

Of course maintenance and breakdowns meant that this pattern would vary at times. When heavy snowfalls made the Emley section of the Barnsley route impassable all buses would travel via Grange Moor and on such occasions single deckers were sometimes used. The 6.00am Huddersfield to Wakefield direct was always a lowbridge bus. This was necessary because, on reaching Wakefield after a fast run taking only 48 instead of the usual 55 minutes, it formed the 6.50am ex Wakefield on the "KB" route back to Huddersfield, on which it worked for the rest of the day. The first County bus from Wakefield to Huddersfield on the direct route did not leave until 8.00am (7.00am from Huddersfield). West Riding, however, ran journeys to Grange Moor at 6.00am and through to Huddersfield at 6.30 and 7.30am.

Public timetables rarely give the complete picture. The first bus of the day on the Wakefield "KB" route was shown as a short working to Springwood Colliery (between Clayton West and Bretton) but it actually reversed at the bottom of Bentley Springs. No mention at all was made that at shift times buses would divert from the normal route at Bretton Bar and perform a 'double run' to Bullcliffe Colliery.

On the Dewsbury route the bus running empty from Waterloo to the Bridge Hotel at Lower Hopton, where it formed the 6.45am to Huddersfield, actually took a short cut on its outward journey. Between the Blacksmith's Arms at Kirkheaton Moor Top and the bottom of Jackroyd Lane at Hopton it ran via Hollin Hall Lane

Above- County Guy Arab II 66 (CCX 702) received this new Roe highbridge body in 1950 and lasted until 1961. 66 is on the Barnsley stand in Lord Street, Huddersfield. [P.J. Cardno collection]

Below- While many people will remember County Leyland Tiger 86 (EVH 214) as rebodied with a Windover coach body, this is what 86 looked like between 1949 and 1954. With a Roe bus body, it is parked out of service on the east side of Lord Street, Huddersfield. [R. Marshall collection]

on the blinds and could be seen until September 1959 when, following reorganisation of secondary education, the specials were no longer required.

At Waterloo depot buses were refuelled as they entered the garage from service, the last bus usually arriving at 11.15pm. There was a night staff who washed, cleaned and maintained the vehicles. Minor repairs and routine maintenance were carried out but for major repairs, overhauls and repainting buses were driven in alternate years to either Savile Town, Dewsbury (Yorkshire Woollen) or Belle Isle, Wakefield (West Riding). Yorkshire Traction were not normally involved in this work.

A van, known as a 'paddy bus', was kept at Waterloo to ferry in those employees on the early shift who lived to the east or south-east of Waterloo; similarly after the late shift it would take them home. Employees living on the Huddersfield side of Waterloo did not need such a facility. The trolleybus service from Town to Waterloo started at 5.15am and at night the last Yorkshire Traction bus returning from Sheffield passed the Waterloo depot at 11.25pm. There was also a trolleybus at 11.40pm which for many years connected in Town with a final

Awaiting departure for its home town at one end of the central platform of Yorkshire Traction's Barnsley Bus Station is County 65 (CCX 701). A Guy Arab II, 65 had been rebodied with this new Roe highbridge body in 1950. [P.J. Cardno collection]

instead of the normal route. For the return journey the blind would be set for John Taylor's Mill, situated at the junction of Firth Street and Queen Street South in Huddersfield. After depositing the mill workers, the bus ran via Queen Street South, Ramsden Street, Zetland Street and Venn Street to Lord Street where it formed the 7.20am departure on the Wakefield "KB" route. The evening return journey to Kirkheaton departed from the mill at 5.00pm. Other short workings on this route to Kirkheaton were for workers at the Broadhead and Graves mill, two stops before the Kirkheaton terminus at Moorbottom. Two specials were also provided from Waterloo for pupils who lived outside Huddersfield borough and attended Mirfield Grammar School. One followed the normal route as far as Ing Grove Park, Mirfield whereas the other was routed via Kirkburton (Turnshaws), Grange Moor, Liley Lane and Freemason's Arms where it regained the normal route; beyond Mirfield to the school buses ran via Doctor Lane. The destination Mirfield Grammar School actually appeared

Fitted with this new Roe lowbridge body in 1953, County Guy Arab II 69 (CCX 797) leaves Dewsbury for Huddersfield via Mirfield, Hopton and Kirkheaton. [R.F. Mack]

After the transfer to Yorkshire Traction of the two County Leyland Tigers rebodied as double deckers, two Traction Guy Arab IIs with Roe utility lowbridge bodies came to County in August 1956 as temporary replacements and lasted until 1958. They took the numbers of the Tigers so Traction 721 became County 78 (HE 9918). Here it is seen on the setting down platform at Wakefield Bus Station with destination blind already reset for the return to Huddersfield. [P. Watson]

One of County's two 1946 Guy Arab II/Roe lowbridge buses, 71 (CCX 931), is in Wakefield Bus Station as the duplicate on the "direct" service to Huddersfield. The service bus, highbridge Leyland Titan 89, can just be seen on the left. [P.J. Cardno collection]

County 70 (CCX 801), a Guy Arab II fitted with a new Roe lowbridge body in 1953 and not withdrawn until 1968, waits in Lord Street, Huddersfield on the Dewsbury via Kirkheaton route, which negotiated two low railway bridges. The Wakefield via Flockton routes of County and West Riding did not require lowbridge buses but most of West Riding's green fleet were of that layout. Sometimes, however, one of West Riding's small number of highbridge Leyland Titans would appear in Huddersfield, such as 684 (CHL 155), a 1949 Leyland bodied PD2/1 seen here on route 87. [P.J. Relf]

departure to most termini.

The company had many long serving employees, indicative of the good relations between management and staff. Arthur Heywood, who started as a conductor at the age of 16 in 1926, was exempted from military service in WW2 on the grounds that he was required to teach new drivers who replaced men who had been called up. Promoted first to inspector and then to chief inspector, he continued working for Yorkshire Traction after the takeover and when he retired in 1975 his career had spanned 49 years of unbroken service. After the war his fellow inspectors were Bill Pickering and Arthur Walker. Mr AE Scholes joined County as an apprentice mechanic in 1929; he became foreman engineer in 1946 and kept the position until the end. Miss Edith Brooke became a conductress in September 1930, a job she was to perform for 28 years before she moved into the garage as stores manager. Another lady with a long career with County was Mrs EM Denton who started conducting in August 1940; two years later she changed to fuel pump assistant and by 1945 had become stores clerk. Further promotion followed in 1957 when she became senior clerk.

4.6: COUNTY: INTO THE FINAL DECADE

Apart from in their earliest years, County did not operate excursions but they did cater for private hire. Two of the 1939 delivery of Leyland TS8s had been fitted with semi-coach bodies to meet this demand but they had received ordinary bus seating (32 seats) in November 1943. Eventually two of the 1949 Leyland PS2s (85/6) were rebodied in 1954 with full fronted Windover coach bodies (Ernest Mellor was one of two mechanics who drove them down to London to be fitted with their new bodies). They were used on private hires as well as on some service work until 1967. Fitted with sunshine roofs and heaters, these vehicles ensured comfortable travel irrespective of the weather. Reduced hire charges applied on weekdays, when a coach could be hired for day trips to Blackpool and Scarborough for £15 and £20 respectively in the mid 1950s. But even the full fronts of their new bodywork did not disguise their age effectively in a period when underfloor engined coaches had rendered their predecessors obsolete and they appeared to see relatively little use. During the period when the Monday to Friday morning peak turnout required 23 out of the fleet of 25 buses, it was usually the two Tiger/Windovers that were parked up at the depot as spares.

In the mid 1950s, in common with many operators County had too many low capacity single deckers in stock. Two of the 1948 Tigers (75/8) were prematurely withdrawn in 1955 and given new Roe double deck

In 1958 County's final delivery of both Guy Arabs and lowbridge buses took to the roads: four Roe bodied Guy Arab IVs. 91 to 94 had a decidedly traditional appearance – one concession to modernity was the fitting of platform doors. 94 (NCX 179) heads a line of vehicles in Lord Street, about to depart on a peak hour short working of the Dewsbury route as far as Kirkheaton. [P.J. Cardno collection]

lowbridge (L27/28R) bodies. They were duly painted by Roe in County livery with new fleet numbers 91/2. Unfortunately a change of policy resulted in them being repainted red and cream before leaving Roe's factory. The Huddersfield motor taxation office refused to permit them to have new registration numbers because they retained their original chassis numbers. The Barnsley

Until 1959 schoolday County bus routes ran from Waterloo to Mirfield Grammar School via Kirkheaton and via Kirkburton and Grange Moor. Seen outside the depot is 82 (ECX 608), a 1949 Guy Arab III/Roe lowbridge. [P.J. Cardno collection]

office, however, would allow this to be done so they entered service there with Yorkshire Traction reregistered KHE 649/50, running until 1965. As a temporary measure two elderly utility Guy Arabs (HE 9917/8) with Roe lowbridge bodies were transferred from Yorkshire Traction to County. Taking the numbers of the withdrawn Tigers (75/8), they remained at Waterloo until the delivery of new buses in 1958.

A dispute over a wage claim by the 76 drivers, conductors and fitters employed by County resulted in strike action being taken during the last week of July 1957. The strike also involved the crews of other company buses which operated into Huddersfield (Hebble, Yorkshire Traction and Yorkshire Woollen) and as a result Huddersfield railway station was so busy that trainspotters were banned for the duration of the strike! A promise of a pay increase of 11/- per week for the platform staff was sufficient to allow a resumption of normal working.

January and February 1958 saw the appearance of 91-4, the last lowbridge buses and Guy Arabs to enter the fleet. These were Mark IV Arabs and their Roe bodywork featured platform doors but exposed radiators were still favoured, contrasting with the large numbers of more modern looking concealed radiator Roe bodied Arabs recently placed in service by West Riding.

From 1959 onwards, however, County started to buy more modern looking buses which made the Arab IVs look even older. The first underfloor engined single deckers at Waterloo entered service in March 1959, Willowbrook bodied Leyland Tiger Cubs 95/6. These vehicles were also surprising on two counts. They were painted in a reversed livery, predominantly blue and were equipped with route number boxes. In view of the livery and destination equipment specifications, it has been suggested that they were part of an order originally intended for the small BET group Stratford Blue bus company and diverted to County at the last minute. As

request alighting stop with passengers being allowed to ride to the Lord Street stand.

A further pair of Leyland Tiger Cubs entered service in September 1960. Metro-Cammell Weymann bodied 97/8 were painted in standard livery and lacked route number boxes. Single deck stock had plummeted to a low of only six vehicles in the previous year and by now the front engined Leyland Tigers, with the exception of rebodied coaches 85/6, had all been withdrawn. 83/4 were transferred to Yorkshire Traction, where they subsequently appeared rebodied and reregistered as double deckers.

In this period the company was still following West Riding in placing new double deck orders so it is not surprising that they welcomed a Guy Wulfrunian demonstrator on loan. This revolutionary bus, which featured advanced suspension and managed to combine a front engine with an entrance right at the front of the bus, was developed for West Riding.

County placed two Guy Wulfrunians with high capacity (75 seat) front entrance Roe bodies (99/100) in service in July and September 1961 respectively. They were used alongside West Riding Wulfrunians on the direct service to Wakefield, where the extra seats were appreciated even if the lowheight design (without sunken gangway) was not necessary. Certainly very advanced in appearance, they gave the impression of being at the forefront of modern vehicle engineering and design. Wulfrunian 100 had a buzzer in the upper saloon and a bell in the lower saloon, to indicate the whereabouts of the conductor to the driver (in such a large vehicle, the management perhaps thought that the conductor might get lost!).

Underused Leyland Tiger coaches 85/6 did undertake more regular duties in 1962 as the whole fleet was gradually sent away for painting into a new colour scheme, which featured a greater area of cream and also a richer, more attractive shade of blue. The double deck livery was simplified to feature only one broad blue band above the lower deck windows. Single deckers sported just one blue band, below the saloon windows.

Heavy ridership on the direct Wakefield route still required the duplication of most departures on Saturdays

County Leyland Titan PD2/12 90 (FVH 166), new in 1952 with classic Roe highbridge body, leaves Lord Street on the "direct" Wakefield route while the conductor of a 1958 lowbridge Guy Arab IV/Roe resets its destination blind. The Yorkshire Traction booking office on the left features an impressive board listing the places which could be reached by express coach from Huddersfield. [P.J. Cardno collection]

we have seen, it was never felt necessary to number the County routes therefore the route number boxes were used to display a monogrammed "CM" with the M superimposed over the C. The vehicles were later repainted in standard livery.

Some frequency reductions on the Dewsbury route were granted by the traffic commissioners on 22 August 1959. The enhanced Summer Sundays timetable was to be abandoned; the basic hourly frequency would apply in future. Also the Monday to Friday evening Hopton-Dewsbury shorts were withdrawn. With changing social habits and increased car ownership these were no longer found to be necessary and again buses ran hourly over the whole route. Up to this point passengers had alighted from all inbound buses from the Waterloo direction at the bottom of Kirkgate with the buses then running empty to their stands in Lord Street. Kirkgate now became just a

County Willowbrook bodied Leyland Tiger Cub 95 (OVH 606) is standing at Grassington on a private hire. 95 still wears the reversed (mainly blue) livery in which 95 and 96, County's first underfloor engined single deckers, were delivered in 1959. [P. Watson]

The two Roe bodied Guy Wulfrunians entered service in summer 1961 and were used on the Wakefield via Flockton ("Direct") route. 100 (UCX 276) leaves Wakefield Bus Station in October 1961.
[C.W. Routh]

comprehensive "via" blinds, which emphasised their contemporary lines.

On the double deck front, however, all was not well. It soon became obvious that the day to day maintenance problems posed by the complexity of the Wulfrunians were beyond the resources of a small company. The disc brake pads had very short lives. The buses' advanced suspension also induced travel sickness in passengers and staff and on 28 April 1963 they completed their last journeys for County and were transferred to West Riding. [Their substantial fleet of Guy Wulfrunians later caused financial problems for West Riding which would result indirectly in the demise of County Motors.]

At first, two Yorkshire Traction Leyland Titan PD2s appeared on loan as replacements but these operated on the Barnsley routes rather than Wakefield direct. They were returned to Yorkshire Traction after the delivery in September 1963 of the second pair of Leyland Leopards (103/4). County's own Leyland PD2 double deckers 87/8, which the Leopards should have replaced, were retained until the actual replacements for the Wulfrunians arrived.

The final pair of double deckers to appear in the County fleet entered service in February 1964. These were more conventional machines in the form of Leyland Titan PD3As with Roe highbridge (H42/31F) bodies numbered 105/6. They were of course normally to be found working on the Wakefield direct service;

in the early 1960s but the last duplicate, 10.00pm from Wakefield, ran only as far as Waterloo depot. Any through passengers on board the duplicate were meant to be transferred to the service bus at Waterloo. On one occasion some passengers apparently unaware of this were turned off the duplicate at the depot without being transferred to the service bus and a letter of complaint followed. In his reply, manager Eric Green claimed that the passengers should have easily been able to distinguish between the service bus and the duplicate as the service bus was one of the new front entrance type with fluorescent saloon lighting whereas the duplicate was an older rear entrance bus! For even longer, right up to the end of operation Saturday duplication was provided on the Wakefield via Kirkburton route between Bretton and Wakefield. One single decker was able to cover all the journeys.

The company was quick to introduce a pair of the recently legalised 36 feet long single deckers in September 1962. 101/2 were the first Leyland Leopards at Waterloo and had 54 seater Willowbrook bodies. Their high seating capacity, equivalent to that of a lowbridge bus, plus of course much greater (unofficial) space for standees, boded ill for the future of the double decker in the County fleet. Single deckers from 101 onwards all featured the route number box, albeit glazed over and showing the fleetname. Eventually, under Yorkshire Traction ownership, the boxes would be used to display route numbers. 101/2 were of a rather

angular appearance but nine similar Leopards which entered service between 1963 and 1967 (103-4/7-12/4) featured Willowbrook, Marshall or Weymann bodywork of a more rounded and elegant appearance. These 53 seaters bore the classic BET style curved windscreen, which seemed ideally suited to the attractive livery; they were the most modern looking buses in Huddersfield. Later batches introduced lower case lettering on their

County's Guy Wulfrunian/Roe 99 (UCX 275) is seen at Shorehead, leaving the edge of Huddersfield town centre for Wakefield via Flockton.
[R. Marshall collection]

Guy Motors Wulfrunian demonstrator 8072 DA was often used by County in the early 1960s, not so much to demonstrate its excellent qualities as to deputise for an indisposed 99 or 100. 8072 DA leaves Wakefield Bus Station for Huddersfield via Flockton. It was later acquired by West Riding and dismantled for spares. [P. Watson]

In Lord Street on the Wakefield via Flockton stand, County Guy Wulfrunian 100 (UCX 276) is advertising Yorkshire Traction's coastal express coach services from Huddersfield and elsewhere. 99 and 100 were transferred to West Riding in April 1963. [R. Marshall collection]

the other routes could be served adequately by either single deckers or the lower capacity double deckers. This allowed PD2s 87/8 to be belatedly withdrawn but even then they were still to be seen in Huddersfield. They went straight on loan to Yorkshire Woollen, covering for a vehicle shortage until new Albion Lowlanders were delivered and were regularly used on Yorkshire Woollen's Dewsbury routes into Huddersfield.

Councils regularly came in for criticism even when they had done nothing wrong, as was the case with the new bus shelter constructed in Wakefield Road, Lepton in May 1964. Attractively faced in tough cedar wood and commanding panoramic views of Almondbury and Castle Hill and surrounding woodlands, the shelter was criticised for being much too good, even though it had cost £200 less than a conventional shelter.

In 1966, after receiving permission from the traffic commissioners on 21 January, County withdrew the evening service on the Saturday only Grange Moor Chapel route, diverting further occasional journeys on the Huddersfield-Wakefield direct route to double run from Grange Moor Cross Roads to Chapel as a replacement. The Saturday evening frequency on the Dewsbury route was also halved to hourly.

Five inspectors and drivers were presented with gifts to commemorate 40 or more years service with the company at a supper at the Friendly and Trades Club in Northumberland Street in December 1966. These were Harold Booth, Arthur Heywood, William (Bill) Pickering, Norman Fisher and Arthur Walker. Over the years these stalwarts had seen many changes and dealt

with many awkward situations but they had never had the experience of cleaner Ted Gerndt. While sweeping out the saloon of a bus, he was used to the usual rubbish of cigarette ends, newspapers, food wrappers and used tickets. He was, however, rather shocked on one occasion to be confronted with an 18 inches long snake lurking under the back seat! It was left to the police to remove the reptile, which was later identified by staff at Ravensknowle Museum as a harmless grass snake.

In January 1967 a shorter single decker was placed in service in the shape of 113, a Leyland Tiger Cub with 45 seater body by Marshalls of Cambridge, who built the bodywork on all the new buses from 1966 onwards. This vehicle had high backed "dual purpose" seating and soon afterwards 85/6, the elderly Tiger/Windover rebodied coaches, were withdrawn. By now County were subcontracting most private hire to West Riding. The last 53 seater Leopard to enter service (114) did so in July, whilst the very last new bus was another short single decker, Tiger Cub 45 seater 115, this time with standard seating, which appeared in April 1968.

The final utility was taken out of service in 1968 and it is interesting to chart the rise and fall of the double deckers. In 1961 the fleet had contained a maximum of 18 out of a total of 24 buses. The last lowbridge examples with offside sunken gangway were purchased in 1958. From 1962 with the introduction of the 36 feet long Leopards with a seating capacity comparable to that of a lowbridge bus, the number of double deckers began to dwindle.

Year	Bought	Nos	Disposals	Nos.	Total in stock
1944	3	64-6			3
1945	4	67-70			7
1946	2	71/2			9
1949	4	79-82	2	64/7	11
1950	2	87/8			13
1952	2	89/90			15
1956	2	75/8*			17
1958	4	91-4	4	71/2;75/8*	17
1961	2	99/100	1	66	18
1962			3	65,79/80	15
1963			2	99/100	13
1964	2	105/6	4	81/2/7/8	11
1965			2	89/90	9
1966			2	68/9	7
1968			1	70	6

* Obtained secondhand from Yorkshire Traction

During the last years of County's existence falling passenger numbers and increasing costs resulted in a search for economies, one of which was one man operation. All the single deckers were suitable for pay as you enter working and by March 1968 had been fitted with hinged plastic boards below the windscreens which could be displayed to advertise that the bus was one man operated. After initial resistance from the union, one man operation started with about four volunteer drivers paid "time and a quarter", working especially some duties on the Dewsbury route with its long layovers and the Wakefield via Kirkburton route which was not tightly

County highbridge Leyland Titan 87 (FCX 331), repainted in the simplified livery and returning from Barnsley, is waiting at the timing point in Flockton before turning off for Emley. Withdrawn soon afterwards, 87 (and 88) went on hire to Yorkshire Woollen early in 1964 when deliveries of Albion Lowlanders were delayed and appeared on the YWD workings between Huddersfield and Dewsbury. [A.J. Douglas]

timed and had quiet sections. Latterly drivers were expected to undertake one man duties and lightly loaded journeys on Sundays on most of the routes were being worked in this way. There were no timetable changes. One man operation was not tried on the busier direct Wakefield service - with its relatively short layovers it remained fully crew operated until the end.

Meanwhile the independent West Riding company had been experiencing serious financial problems, partly as a result of increasing difficulties with their large fleet of Guy Wulfrunians. In a climate of uncertainty engendered by proposals for passenger transport authorities and talk of nationalisation, West Riding had sold out voluntarily to the state owned Transport Holding Company on 30 October 1967. When in March 1968 the BET group holdings in Yorkshire Traction and Yorkshire Woollen followed suit to bring all three parent companies into common ownership there was no longer any justification for County to exist as a separate entity.

On 1 October 1968 Yorkshire Traction took over the management of County and by the end of December a third of the fleet had been repainted in Yorkshire Traction's red and cream livery but with County fleetname transfers on removable stick-on panels. Also the vehicles were renumbered into Yorkshire Traction sequences from 1 October onwards (see 4.8 for details) and this process was completed during November.

On 16 December 1968 the final route alteration was made to a County service. The Huddersfield-Wakefield via Kirkburton route was diverted between Bretton West and Calder Grove via Great Cliff (now serving Cliff

A second pair of Leyland Leopards was delivered to County in 1963 and these featured the B.E.T. style wrap-round windscreen, which was to appear on all subsequent single deckers. [B.E.T. owned Yorkshire Traction and Yorkshire Woollen.] Willowbrook bodied 104 (YCX 539) is in Lord Street awaiting departure for Dewsbury via Kirkheaton. The bus on the far right is a Sheffield J.O.C. Burlingham bodied Leyland Leopard. [P.J. Cardno collection]

Roe bodied Leyland Titan PD3A/1 105 (AVH 635B), one of the final pair of double deckers bought by County, enters a cobbled Lord Street from Kirkgate to complete the journey from Wakefield. [P. Watson

Soon after entering service in 1964, County Roe bodied Leyland Titan PD3A/1 105 (AVH 635B) is parked on Stand D in a still cobbled Lord Street on the Wakefield via Flockton route. Two Yorkshire Traction buses are on the Barnsley stand (B). The Leyland Tiger Cub is on single deck routes 33/33A via Penistone. The Leyland Titan in front would be on route 15 via Clayton West and Darton (route 235 from 1975 – until abandoned by Stagecoach in 2007). [Photobus]

Road and Blacker Lane, instead of Branch Road) to replace part of West Riding service 77 (Wakefield-Great Cliff). Although this County route was already largely if not entirely single decked, the rerouting prohibited the use of double decks altogether owing to a very low bridge near the bottom of Blacker Lane. West Riding 84 (Holmfirth-Wakefield) was diverted via Bretton West and Great Cliff at the same time.

With the formation of the National Bus Company on 1 January 1969 ownership of County and the 23 vehicles passed to Yorkshire Traction alone and the smaller undertaking was absorbed into the larger company with immediate effect. Yorkshire Traction obtained short term licences for the routes and route numbers appeared for the first time from 12 April 1969:

31 Barnsley via Emley, Flockton and Midgley
32 Barnsley via Grange Moor, Flockton and Emley
48 Grange Moor Chapel
61 Wakefield via Kirkburton and Scissett
62 Dewsbury
63 Wakefield direct

County manager Eric Green became area superintendent (Huddersfield) for Yorkshire Traction, also taking responsibility for the existing Traction depot in St Andrew's Road. County Motors (Lepton) Ltd. was a dormant company after 1968 until it was wound up in 1978. Brinton Farrar, one of the founders of the County Bus Service, died on 6 May 1971 at his home in Town End, Lepton.

By the later 1960s most County buses seen in Huddersfield's Lord Street were Leyland Leopards or Tiger Cubs. Leopard/Weymann 109 (FCX 287C), new in 1965, displays its very detailed "via" blind incorporating modern looking lower case lettering as it prepares to work the 2.25 departure for Barnsley via Emley and Flockton. In the background is the 2.20 bus for Wakefield via Kirkburton and Scissett. [P.J. Cardno collection]

4.7: COUNTY TICKETING

In the early days punch tickets were printed by Harland of Hull for the "County Bus Service". Their dimensions were 2.5 inches by 1.25 inches and they were printed with stages 1 to 24. All displayed the fare value in the form of a large red overprint whilst some had the fare printed in the usual way as well as the overprint. Single tickets from 1d to 1/6d probably existed but few have survived. Known values and colours were: 1d white; 2d green; 3d orange; 4d cerise; 6d grey; 9d lilac; 10d brown and 1/6d white. There was also a white exchange ticket.

From 1928, the company used composite punch tickets very much in the style of those used by co-owner Yorkshire Woollen (and later by Huddersfield JOC). These measured 3.5 inches by 1.25 inches and had a perforated lower tab. Punching at the top signified a return for adult, child or workman whereas punching at the bottom signified an adult or child single. The title printed in the central panel was County Motors (Lepton) Ltd and all tickets were overprinted CML in large red letters. Stage numbers 1 to 20 sufficed at first but stages 1 to 28 were printed on later issues; as a result the length of the ticket had to be slightly increased to 3.875 inches. Unlike the tickets of all the recognised ticket printers, many County punch tickets did not bear the name of the printer and it is possible that they were printed locally; others were printed by Williamsons of Ashton. Prewar tickets were supplied in packs of 50 but as a wartime economy measure much thinner paper was used, allowing the tickets to be supplied in stapled packs of 100. At the same period the fare appeared additionally as a large red overprint, possibly to help conductresses in the blackout. The reverse of the tickets was often blank as advertisements seem to have been only occasionally carried, contrary to the practice of many other operators.

Before 1952 maximum fares were as shown:

Stages	Route	Single	Ord. Ret.	Wrk. Ret.
1-15	Dewsbury	9d	1/3d	1/1d
1-22	Wakefield direct	1/5d	2/3d	1/10d
1-28	Wakefield via Kirkburton	1/6d	2/3d	2/-
1-25	Barnsley	1/6d	2/3d	2/-

Thus a range of tickets from 1d to 2/3d was required. Values and colours of surviving tickets are: 1d red (also white; also green); 1½d dark blue; 2d green; 2½d salmon; 3d cream; 3½d lilac; 4d pink; 4½d white; 5d sage; 6d buff; 9d pink; 1/1d magenta; 1/2d grey; 1/3d pink; 2/3d light blue. As the minimum fare for a child was 1d there was no ½ d ticket.

Exchange tickets had the fares printed down each side and were overprinted with a large red cross. A pink ticket with values from 1d to 1/3d was probably used only on the Dewsbury route. An apple green ticket had fares from 1½d to 2/3d and was intended for the longer routes. As all the routes were quite lengthy conducting staff had to update their waybills at intermediate points as well as at the termini; these booking up points were indicated by a cross in the fare tables and were as follows:

Dewsbury route: Kirkheaton, Hopton Fold, Mirfield Black Bull
Wakefield direct: Lepton Red Lion Garage, Angel Inn Flockton, White Swan Middlestown, Barclay's Bank Horbury
Wakefield via Kirkburton: Fenay Bridge, George Hotel Kirkburton, Scissett Church, Bretton Bar House, Calder Grove PO
Barnsley route: Lepton Red Lion Garage, Angel Inn Flockton, Emley Cross, Bretton War Memorial, Darton Pit Gate.

As fares started to rise, in keeping with the parent companies it became desirable for County to introduce mechanised ticket issuing. The Bellgraphic system had been tried first towards the end of the war and was used for a number of years but was replaced around 1959 by TIM machines, which lasted until the takeover.

4.8: COUNTY FLEET LIST

NO.	REG NO.	CHASSIS	BODY	NEW	OUT	NOTES
1	CX3248	AEC YB	Charabanc	1921	1925	*1
2	CX3439	AEC YB	Lorry with seats	1921	1925	*1
3	CX3376	AEC YB	Lorry with seats	1921	?	*1
4	CX3645	Karrier WDS	Charabanc	1921	1925	*1
5	CX5596	GMC K16	? B20F	1923	1924	
6	CX5863	AEC	? B30-	1923	1925	
7	used for 5 above (rebuilt as a goods vehicle)					
8	see 3 above, renumbered					
9	WU257	Reo Pullman	Taylor B20F	1925	1929	
10	WU557	Reo Pullman	Taylor B20F	1925	1929	
11	WU2464	Reo Pullman	Taylor B20F	1925	1929	
12	WU2713	Reo Pullman	Taylor B20F	1925	1929	
13	WU3149	Reo Pullman	Taylor B20F	1925	1930	*2
14	WU3335	Reo Pullman	Taylor B20F	1925	1929	
15/7	WU3612/3	AEC 411	Taylor B26-	1925	1931	
16	WU3671	Reo Pullman	Taylor B20F	1925	1929	
18	WU3672	Reo Pullman	Taylor B20F	1926	1930	
19	WU6538	AEC 411	Taylor B26-	1926	1931	
20	WU5929	AEC 411	Taylor B26-	1926	1934	*3
21	WU5928	Reo Pullman	Taylor B20F	1926	1930	
22	WU7677	AEC 414	Taylor B25-	1926	1933	
23	WU8029	AEC 414	Taylor B25-	1926	1932	
24	see 13 above (renumbered in 1926)					
25	WU7678	AEC 414	Taylor B25-	1926	1933	
26	WU8427	AEC 413	Taylor B26-	1926	1932	
27	WU8736	AEC 414	Taylor B25-	1926	1933	
28/9	WW5222/3	Leyland PLSC3	Leyland B35F	1928	1935	
30-2	VH2322/5/6	Leyland LT1	Brush B--	1929	1936	
33-6	VH2318-21	Leyland LT1	Leyland B-F	1929	1937-8	
37	see 20 above (renumbered in 1930)					
38	WW2280	ADC 416	? B32-	1927	1934	*4
39/40	VH3683/4	Leyland LT2	Leyland B32F	1931	1943	*5
41/2	VH4000/1	Leyland LT5	Leyland B32F	1931	1939-42	*5
43-5	VH5052-4	Leyland LT5	Roe B32F	1933	1939-44	*5
46/7	VH6541/2	Leyland LT5A	Roe B32F	1934	1943-4	*5
48-50	VH7551-3	Leyland TS7	Roe B32F	1935	1948	
51-3	VH8800-2	Leyland TS7	Roe B32F	1936	1948-9	
54-7	VH9929-32	Leyland TS7	Roe B32F	1937	1947-9	
58/9	AVH570/1	Leyland TS8	Roe B32F	1938	1950	
60/1	BVH141/2	Leyland TS8	Roe B32F	1939	1950	

NO.	REG NO.	CHASSIS	BODY	NEW	OUT	NOTES
62/3	BVH143/4	Leyland TS8	Roe DP30F	1939	1950	
64	CCX696	Guy Arab II 6LW	Roe L27/28R	1944	1949	
65/6	CCX701/2	Guy Arab II 6LW	Park Royal H30/26R	1944	1961-2	*6
67/8	CCX715/6	Guy Arab II 6LW	Roe L27/28R	1945	1949/66	*7
69/70	CCX797/801	Guy Arab II 6LW	Roe L27/28R	1945	1966-8	*7
71/2	CCX931-2	Guy Arab II 6LW	Roe L27/28R	1946	1958	
73-8	DVH752-7	Leyland PS1	Roe B32F	1948	1955-9	
79-82	ECX605-8	Guy Arab III 6LW	Roe L27/26R	1949	1962-4	
83-6	ECX211-4	Leyland PS2/1	Roe B34F	1949	1960-7	*8
87/8	FCX331/2	Leyland PD2/3	Leyland H30/26R	1950	1964	
89/90	FVH165/6	Leyland PD2/12	Roe H31/25R	1952	1965	
75/8	HE9917/8	Guy Arab II 6LW	Roe L27/26R	1945	1958	*9
91-4	NCX176-9	Guy Arab IV 6LW	Roe L27/28RD	1958	1968	**(685-8)
95/6	OVH606/7	Leyland PSUC1/1	Willowbrook B43F	1959	1968	**(594/5)
97/8	SVH354/5	Leyland PSUC1/1	MCCW B45F	1960	1968	**(596/7)
99/100	UCX275/6	Guy Wulfrunian	Roe H43/32F	1961	1963	
101/2	WVH230/1	Leyland PSU3/3R	Willowbrook B54F	1962	1968	**(389/90)
103/4	YCX538/9	Leyland PSU3/1R	Willowbrook B53F	1963	1968	**(391/2)
105/6	AVH635/6B	Leyland PD3A/1	Roe H42/31F	1964	1968	**(745/6)
107/8	BCX214/3B	Leyland PSU3/1R	Marshall B53F	1964	1968	**(394/3)
109/10	FCX287/8C	Leyland PSU3/1R	Weymann B53F	1965	1968	**(395/6)
111/2	GVH213/4D	Leyland PSU3/1R	Marshall B53F	1966	1968	**(397/8)
113	KCX263E	Leyland PSUC1/12	Marshall DP45F	1967	1968	**(598)
114	KVH557E	Leyland PSU3/3R	Marshall B53F	1967	1968	**(399)
115	NCX268F	Leyland PSUC1/12	Marshall B45F	1968	1968	**(599)

Notes

*1   3 was later renumbered 8 and between 1922 and 1924 1-4 were given bus bodies

*2   13 was renumbered 24 in 1926

*3   20 was renumbered 37 in 1930

*4   38 was acquired from Yorkshire Traction in 1930

*5   39-47 were requisitioned by the Ministry of Transport in September 1939 for the War Department

*6   65/6 were rebodied with new Roe H31/25R bodies in 1950

*7   68-70 were rebodied with new Roe L27/26R bodies in 1953

*8   85/6 were fitted with new full fronted 8 feet wide bodies (Windover FC35F) in 1954

*9   75/8 were acquired from Yorkshire Traction in 1956

**   Transferred to Yorkshire Traction after 31.12.68 (YT fleet numbers allocated from 1.10.68 shown in brackets)

    For more detailed information about the vehicles, including chassis numbers, see PSV Circle Fleet history PB 21 (Yorkshire Traction, part 2)

In 1922 Wakefield based Yorkshire (West Riding) Electric Tramways began running motorbuses in districts not served by trams and in 1923 the West Riding Automobile Company Ltd was formed to take over the bus operations. A fleet of over 100 green liveried Bristol single deckers was quickly built up and both Huddersfield and Holmfirth were soon seen as attractive destinations.

In December 1922 Huddersfield Watch Committee turned down their request for a licence for an indirect Wakefield-Shelley-Huddersfield service on the dubious grounds that Shelley was already adequately served, presumably by Harburn. Soon afterwards West Riding were operating three daily journeys between Wakefield and Shelley via Bretton, Scissett and Skelmanthorpe with a single journey time of 67 minutes. On 28 April 1923 they extended this service to Waterloo, where they had been granted a stand in March, with a through fare of 1/5d and the following timetable.

West Riding 133 (HL 1517), a Bristol 4-ton new in 1923 with 31-seater bodywork by Strachan & Brown, waits at the Holmfirth terminus at the Victoria Square end of Towngate before returning to Wakefield. The inclusion of Barnsley on the route boards refers to connecting services of Barnsley & District Traction. [G. Lumb collection]

Wakefield dep.	8.45am		8.45pm
Skelmanthorpe arr.	9.40am		9.40pm
Shelley arr.	9.52am	and	9.52pm
Waterloo arr.	10.10am	every	10.10pm
Waterloo dep.	10.15am	4 hours	10.15pm
Shelley arr.	10.33am	until	10.33pm
Skelmanthorpe arr.	10.45am		10.45pm
Wakefield arr.	11.40am		11.40pm

On the same date a second service was introduced, also running every 4 hours, following the same route from Wakefield as far as Scissett then continuing to Holmfirth via Denby Dale, Sovereign, Shepley and New Mill.

From 7 May 1923 a stand was allocated in Huddersfield on the east side of Castlegate, at the Seed Hill end, and soon afterwards the Waterloo route was extended to the centre of Huddersfield via Wakefield Road.

From 1 January 1924, however, the West Riding Wakefield-Scissett-Huddersfield route was withdrawn as part of a territorial agreement with Barnsley & District Traction. At the same time the Wakefield-Scissett-Holmfirth service was doubled in frequency to run every 2 hours (with a single journey time of 1 hour 45 minutes) and this offered a connection at Scissett by Barnsley & District bus to Skelmanthorpe, Shelley and Huddersfield. At 26 October 1925 the buses licensed by Holmfirth

UDC for use between Wakefield and Holmfirth were 12 of the larger 32 seat 4-ton Bristols: 201-12 (HL 2657-68).

Also new in January 1924 was a feeder bus which ran from Horbury tram terminus to Flockton every two hours. Through tickets were issued for a combined tram and bus journey of 55 minutes, the first ticket being surrendered for an exchange ticket on the second

WAKEFIELD, DURKAR, BRETTON COMMON, CLAYTON WEST, SCISSETT, DENBY DALE, SHEPLEY, NEW MILL & HOLMFIRTH. (Motor Omnibuses).

	Weekdays.								Sundays				
	a.m.	a.m.	a.m.	p.m.	p.m.	p.m.	p.m.	p.m.	p.m.	p.m.	p.m.	p.m.	p.m.
Wakefield (Cross Square), dep.	7-35	9-35	11-35	1-35	3-35	5-35	7-35	9-35	1-35	3-35	5-35	7-35	9-35
Durkar	7-49	9-49	11-49	1-49	3-49	5-49	7-49	9-49	1-49	3-49	5-49	7-49	9-49
Calder Grove	7-52	9-52	11-52	1-52	3-52	5-52	7-52	9-52	1-52	3-52	5-52	7-52	9-52
Bretton Cross Roads	8- 2	10- 2	12- 2	2- 2	4- 2	6- 2	8- 2	10- 2	2- 2	4- 2	6- 2	8- 2	10- 2
Clayton West	8-15	10-16	12-15	2-15	4-15	6-15	8-15	10-15	2-15	4-15	6-15	8-15	10-15
Scissett *	8-20	10-20	12-20	2-20	4-20	6-20	8-20	10-20	2-20	4-20	6-20	8-20	10-20
Denby Dale	8-30	10-30	12-30	2-30	4-30	6-30	8-30	10-30	2-30	4-30	6-30	8-30	10-30
Upper Cumberworth	8-39	10-39	12-39	2-39	4-39	6-39	8-39	—	2-39	4-39	6-39	8-39	—
Sovereign Inn	8-45	10-45	12-45	2-45	4-45	6-45	8-45	—	2-45	4-45	6-45	8-45	—
Shepley (Black Bull Inn)	8-50	10-50	12-50	2-50	4-50	6-50	8-50	—	2-50	4-50	6-50	8-50	—
New Mill	9- 5	11- 5	1- 5	3- 5	5- 5	7- 5	9- 5	—	3- 5	5- 5	7- 5	9- 5	—
Holmfirth, arr.	9-20	11-20	1-20	3-20	5-20	7-20	9-20	—	3-20	5-20	7-20	9-20	—
Holmfirth, dep.	9-30	11-30	1-30	3-30	5-30	7-30	9-30	—	3-30	5-30	7-30	9-30	—
New Mill	9-42	11-42	1-42	3-42	5-42	7-42	9-42	—	3-42	5-42	7-42	9-42	—
Shepley (Black Bull Inn)	9-52	11-52	1-52	3-52	5-52	7-52	9-52	—	3-52	5-52	7-52	9-52	—
Sovereign Inn	9-58	11-58	1-58	3-58	5-58	7-58	9-58	—	3-58	5-58	7-58	9-58	—
Upper Cumberworth	10- 3	12- 3	2- 3	4- 3	6- 3	8- 3	10- 3	—	4- 3	6- 3	8- 3	10- 3	—
Denby Dale	10-11	12-11	2-11	4-11	6-11	8-11	10-11	10-33	4-11	6-11	8-11	10-11	10-33
Scissett	10-20	12-20	2-20	4-20	6-20	8-20	10-20	10-42	4-20	6-20	8-20	10-20	10-42
Clayton West	10-25	12-25	2-25	4-25	6-25	8-25	10-25	10-46	4-25	6-25	8-25	10-25	10-46
Bretton Cross Roads	10-38	12-38	2-38	4-38	6-38	8-38	10-38	10-58	4-38	6-38	8-38	10-38	10-58
Calder Grove	10-47	12-47	2-47	4-47	6-47	8-47	10-47	11- 6	4-47	6-47	8-47	10-47	11- 6
Durkar	10-50	12-50	2-50	4-50	6-50	8-50	10-50	11- 8	4-50	6-50	8-50	10-50	11- 8
Wakefield (Cross Square), arr.	11- 3	1- 3	3- 3	5- 3	7- 3	9- 3	11- 3	11-20	5- 3	7- 3	9- 3	11- 3	11-20

* Note.—At Scissett connections are made with the Barnsley and District Traction Company's Omnibuses for Skelmanthorpe, Shelley, Kirkburton, Huddersfield, Cawthorne, and Barnsley.

West Riding timetable dated

vehicle. From 28 July 1924 the bus route was extended at both ends to run from Garforth to Huddersfield via Swillington, Wakefield, Horbury, Flockton, Grange Moor Cross Roads and Lepton, terminating at the stand in Castlegate. Between Horbury Bridge and Flockton Green alternate journeys ran via Middlestown and Overton (and so identical to the route already operated by County between Wakefield and Huddersfield) and via Netherton and Midgley. The 2-ton 20 seater Bristols were to be seen initially on this route. West Riding had applied to Huddersfield Watch Committee for licences for no less than 38 buses which could then be operated on this route; as a result of this the committee "resolved that hackney plates of other areas be recognised". Departures from Huddersfield on the one hour 50 minutes single journey were at two hourly intervals from 8.45am to 10.45pm (penultimate and final journeys to Oulton and Wakefield respectively). In March 1926 Leeds Watch Committee refused permission to extend the route from Garforth to Leeds. Early in that year [certainly by April; Barnsley & District moved in February] the Huddersfield terminus was moved to Lord Street.

West Riding acquired Waterloo based County Bus Service on 17 August 1927 jointly with Barnsley & District Traction (later renamed Yorkshire Traction) and Yorkshire Woollen of Dewsbury. The County company was retained as a separate business because the routes bordered the networks of the three larger companies. All three were "area agreement companies" with defined operating territories but, whereas Yorkshire Traction and Yorkshire Woollen were subsidiaries of the large BET organisation, West Riding was an independent bus company (like Hansons or Baddeleys) until 1967, albeit a very big one; it became the largest independent bus company in Britain.

The Holmfirth-Wakefield route may have been interworked with West Riding's Wakefield-Ackworth-Pontefract-Willow Park service as early as January 1924, although no through times or fares were advertised. By February 1927 these buses ran beyond Pontefract to Carleton, Moor Lane (instead of Willow Park) and by September 1927 a through service between Holmfirth and Carleton was officially advertised, still every 2 hours.

On 28 November 1929 West Riding management announced that they were now in a position to use more modern buses (presumably Leyland Lions and Bristol B types) on the Holmfirth route, which would allow the running time to Wakefield to be reduced from 92 to 70 minutes. Certainly by September 1930, by curtailing Holmfirth-Carleton at Pontefract town centre, West Riding were able to maintain the 2-hourly frequency with two faster buses, which were allowed 4 hours for the round trip.

By 1929 the Huddersfield-Wakefield-Garforth routes were also slightly accelerated with the through journey cut to 1 hour 42 minutes. From April 1932 on Saturdays only the Huddersfield frequencies were doubled but an application was made to the traffic commissioners in June 1934 to split the routes at Wakefield. In their October 1934 timetable booklet West Riding's Huddersfield routes were for the first time shown as running only as far as Wakefield but it is understood that this change did not actually take place until November. The traffic commissioners had received objections to certain fares alterations which the company planned to introduce at the same time, with the result that the new licences were not granted until 9 November 1934. There was [and is] a very low railway bridge beyond

HUDDERSFIELD, FLOCKTON, NETHERTON, MIDDLESTOWN, WAKEFIELD, STANLEY, OULTON and GARFORTH.

Weekdays and Saturdays.

		a.m.	a.m.	a.m.	a.m.		p.m.	p.m.	p.m.
Huddersfield (Lord St.)	dep.	—	7 45	8 45	1045		6 45	8 45	1045
Waterloo		—	7 57	8 57	1057		6 57	8 57	1057
Lepton		—	8 7	9 7	11 7		7 7	9 7	11 7
Flockton (Angel Inn)		6 38	8 19	9 19	1119	And	7 19	9 19	1119
Midgley		—	—	—	1126	every	7 26	—	1126
Netherton		—	—	—	1130	Two	7 30	—	1130
Overton		6 46	8 27	9 27	—	Hours	—	9 27	—
Middlestown		6 49	8 31	9 31	—	running	—	9 31	—
Horbury Bridge		6 54	8 36	9 36	1136	alternately	7 36	9 36	1136
Horbury (Highfield Road)		6 58	8 41	9 41	1141	via	7 41	9 41	1141
Wakefield (Nat. Prov. Bank)	a.	7 10	8 53	9 53	1153	Netherton and	7 53	9 53	1153
Wakefield (Springs)	dep.	—	—	9 55	1155	Middlestown	7 55	—	9 55
Ferry Lane		—	—	10 3	12 3	until	8 3	—	10 3
Stanley Station		—	—	10 8	12 8		8 8	—	10 8
Calverley Road		—	—	1018	1218		8 18	—	1018
Swillington Church		—	—	1027	1227		8 27	—	1027
Garforth (Town End)	arr.	—	—	1041	1241		8 41	—	1041

(Right-hand p.m. column marked: Sats. and Suns. only.)

West Riding timetable dated November 1930

HUDDERSFIELD, FLOCKTON, NETHERTON, MIDDLESTOWN, WAKEFIELD, STANLEY, OULTON and GARFORTH (continued).

Weekdays and Saturdays.

										Sats. & Suns. only.
Garforth (Town End)	dep.	—	—	—	—	10 42	12 42		8 42	—	10 42
Swillington Church		—	—	—	—	10 56	12 56		8 56	—	10 56
Calverley Road		—	—	—	—	11 5	1. 5		9 5	—	11 5
Stanley Station		—	—	—	—	11 15	1 15		9 15	—	11 15
Ferry Lane		—	—	—	—	11 20	1 20		9 20	—	11 20
Wakefield (Springs)	arr.	—	—	—	—	11 28	1 28		9 28	—	11 28
		a.m.	a.m.	a.m.	a.m.						
Wakefield (Westgate)	dep.	6 0	6 30	7 30	9 30	11 30	1 30		9 30		—
Horbury (Highfield Road)		6 12	6 44	7 44	9 44	11 44	1 44		9 44		—
Horbury Bridge		6 16	6 49	7 49	9 49	11 49	1 49		9 49		—
Middlestown		6 22	6 55	—	9 55	—	1 55		9 55		—
Overton		6 27	7 0	—	10 0	—	2 0		10 0		—
Netherton		—	—	7 54	—	11 54	—		—		—
Midgley		—	—	7 59	—	11 59	—		—		—
Flockton (Angel Inn)		6 37	7 10	8 10	10 10	12 10	2 10		10 10		—
Lepton		—	7 20	8 20	10 20	12 20	2 20		10 20		—
Waterloo		—	7 30	8 30	10 30	12 30	2 30		10 30		—
Huddersfield (Lord St.)	arr.	—	7 40	8 40	10 40	12 40	2 40		10 40		—

(Centre column text: And every two hours running alternately via Netherton and Middlestown until)

Note.—Sunday Service commences 9-30 a.m., Wakefield to Huddersfield.
Sunday Service commences 9-55 a.m., Wakefield to Garforth, then as above.

West Riding Leyland Titan PD2/12 750 (FHL 116), new in 1953 with classic Leyland lowbridge bodywork, is seen on the Huddersfield stand in the company's Wakefield Bus Station. Note the ornate and barely legible fleet number below the registration plate.
[R. Marshall collection]

been operated as part of the Yorkshire-Blackpool pool of the major operators (see Yorkshire Traction section of this book). In summer passengers were picked up and set down at the Hansons Weatherhill stand on the west side of Byram Street, between its junctions with St Peter's Street and Northumberland Street. Nearby was the Stubbs shop (newsagents, sweets and tobacco), which was for many years the B & S and later West Riding booking agent in Huddersfield. In the early 1930s B & S had picked up in Westgate.

Until 1 October 1952 the Huddersfield and Holmfirth stands in Wakefield were both in Westgate but on that date West Riding opened their bus station and these and almost all other services running into or through the county town of the West Riding of Yorkshire started to use it.

From 20 November 1961 the 86/7 (Huddersfield-Wakefield) timetables were changed so that most buses

Woodlesford which prohibited double deckers on the Wakefield-Garforth section and this may have been one reason for splitting the through services. At any rate West Riding started to use double deckers on the Huddersfield routes soon afterwards, surprisingly early (it will be recalled that County ran no double deckers at all on their parallel service or any other until the latter part of the war). "Gearless" Leyland Titans (models TD3c, TD4c and TD5c) with Roe lowbridge bodies laboured long and hard up the hills to Lepton and Grange Moor.

On the outbreak of war in September 1939 the Holmfirth-Pontefract route was curtailed at both ends for the duration, initially running in two sections: Wakefield-Ackworth and Wakefield-Bretton Bar-Bretton Village. The extension from Bretton Bar to the village (West Bretton) was a wartime extension which seems to have compensated for County Motors cutbacks. The Bretton-Holmfirth section was still served by County (as far as Scissett) and Yorkshire Traction (Clayton West to Holmfirth). Towards the end of the war a through Ackworth-Bretton route was started but it was not until January 1947 that there was any West Riding service beyond Bretton, when the full Holmfirth-Pontefract service was reinstated, again no longer serving West Bretton. On the other hand, the West Riding Huddersfield routes were subjected to only minor reductions during the war.

West Riding were late in introducing route numbers. The following were not shown in the timetable until November 1948:

Just after West Riding had taken the two County Guy Wulfrunians, in June 1963 the company also acquired a 1961 East Lancs bodied example from West Wales Motors of Tycroes, Carmarthenshire. As West Riding 959 (XBX 350) it is leaving Wakefield Bus Station on route 86 for Huddersfield via Middlestown and Flockton.
[A.B. Cross]

85 Holmfirth-Wakefield-Pontefract
86 Huddersfield-Middlestown-Wakefield
87 Huddersfield-Netherton-Wakefield

By 1950 route 85 was also normally operated by lowbridge double deckers. Most of West Riding's double deckers were of lowbridge layout, apart from those used on former tram routes. Buses running to Holmfirth had to pass under the low railway bridge at Thornes also encountered by County Motors.

In September 1950 a long distance coach service from Wakefield to Blackpool via Batley and Huddersfield was taken over with the business of B & S (Bullocks of Featherstone). In winter since 1 November 1935 this had

ran as 87 via Netherton (increased to every 2 hours, daily). 86 via Overton was correspondingly reduced to run mainly in Monday to Friday peaks and every 2 hours on Saturday. Previously alternate buses had run daily as 87 via Netherton and 86 via Overton. As the 86 route was also served hourly by the identical County service, it made sense for West Riding to concentrate on their Netherton version.

The company for many years demonstrated independence from the main bus groups by an unusual vehicle policy. Guys had been favoured for some time when, in the late 1950s, Guy Motors and West Riding got together with the aim of producing a revolutionary

One of the final (1965) batch of Guy Wulfrunians, Roe bodied West Riding 1023 (BHL 374C), waits in Lord Street, Huddersfield soon after entering service. In the background is Yorkshire Traction 1247 (YHE 247), a Leyland Tiger rebuild with Northern Counties forward entrance double deck body, a familiar type on the Kirkburton (80) route in the mid sixties. [Omnibus Society/P. Yeomans]

new double deck chassis, the Guy Wulfrunian. It was suitable for a high capacity body of low height, as required by West Riding, but without the need for the sunken offside gangway. It was also supposed to combine a better ride quality with ease of maintenance. In outward appearance from the front the new vehicle resembled the recently introduced rear engined Leyland Atlantean except that the Wulfrunian's engine was at the front and because of this the driver had to be provided with a cab door. West Riding purchased 132 of the 137 Wulfrunians built, including a few secondhand specimens (the County Motors pair, for example) and they were soon a familiar sight on the Huddersfield and Holmfirth routes.

Unfortunately development work by Guy Motors had been insufficient and problems began to arise, particularly with overheating brakes and heavy steering. Drivers noticed that the small cab soon overheated and conductors and passengers complained of travel sickness induced by the soft suspension.

From the mid 1960s West Riding bought large numbers of 36 feet long single deckers as well as double deckers, the latter no longer Guy Wulfrunians but rear engined types, initially the popular Leyland Atlantean. Their choice of rear engined single deck models was less fortunate, as unreliable Daimler Roadliners and AEC Swifts were followed by scarcely more satisfactory Leyland Panthers. In July 1966 the new Daimler Roadliners appeared on route 85 (Holmfirth-Wakefield-Pontefract) and from 22 August those based at Belle Isle depot (131-5) were used to convert the 85 and certain other routes to one man operation.

Spare parts for the Wulfrunians had become expensive and difficult to obtain and the West Riding company was in severe financial difficulties. There were also proposals to establish a passenger transport authority in the Leeds area or in other parts of the industrial West Riding and it was thought that this would involve compulsory nationalisation of independent bus operators. As a result the company sold out voluntarily to the state owned Transport Holding Company on 30 October 1967, consequently becoming part of the National Bus Company at its formation on 1 January 1969.

From 16 December 1968 the 85 (Holmfirth-Wakefield-Pontefract) was split at Wakefield. The Holmfirth-Wakefield section was renumbered 84 and diverted away from its direct route between Bretton Bar and Calder Grove via Bretton West and Great Cliff to replace withdrawn West Riding 77 (Wakefield-Great Cliff).

[The County Huddersfield-Wakefield via Kirkburton & Scissett route was rerouted via Great Cliff at the same time.] In addition routes 86/7 (Huddersfield-Wakefield) were converted to single deck one man operation with slightly more running time allowed. This of course meant that the Guy Wulfrunians could no longer be seen surging and swaying along Wakefield Road; our latest memory is of one passing Huddersfield's last trolleybus procession near Ravensknowle Park in July 1968. The motley collection of rear engined single deckers mentioned earlier now appeared in Huddersfield as well as Holmfirth although eventually some Bristol REs, which were much more reliable, were used (one man double deckers, Daimler Fleetlines, also belatedly turned up on the Huddersfield routes).

Further economies were made from 8 March 1971 when 84 (Holmfirth-Wakefield) was withdrawn on Sundays while 86/7 (Huddersfield-Wakefield) were withdrawn on Sundays and also on Monday to Friday evenings. To replace the 87 via Netherton, a few Sunday and Monday to Friday evening journeys on Yorkshire Traction 63 (the former County direct route and identical to 86 via Overton) were temporarily rerouted via Netherton. From 4 September 1971, however, the 86/7 were completely withdrawn and West Riding buses were no longer seen in Huddersfield. New Yorkshire Traction 64 provided a Monday to Saturday only replacement via Netherton and their 63 continued to run via Overton.

From 21 October 1972 route 84 (Holmfirth-Wakefield) was linked operationally with recently introduced Yorkshire Traction 58 (Holmfirth-Cawthorne-Barnsley) and both became jointly operated, with 58 conveniently renumbered 83.

New Plaxton bodied Daimler Roadliners, including 134 (FHL 827D) pictured here on the setting down stand in Wakefield Bus Station, were used by West Riding to convert route 85 (Holmfirth-Wakefield-Pontefract) to one-man operation in 1966. 134's apparently defective destination display would have been the least of their worries arising from these unreliable vehicles. [S.T. Harling collection]

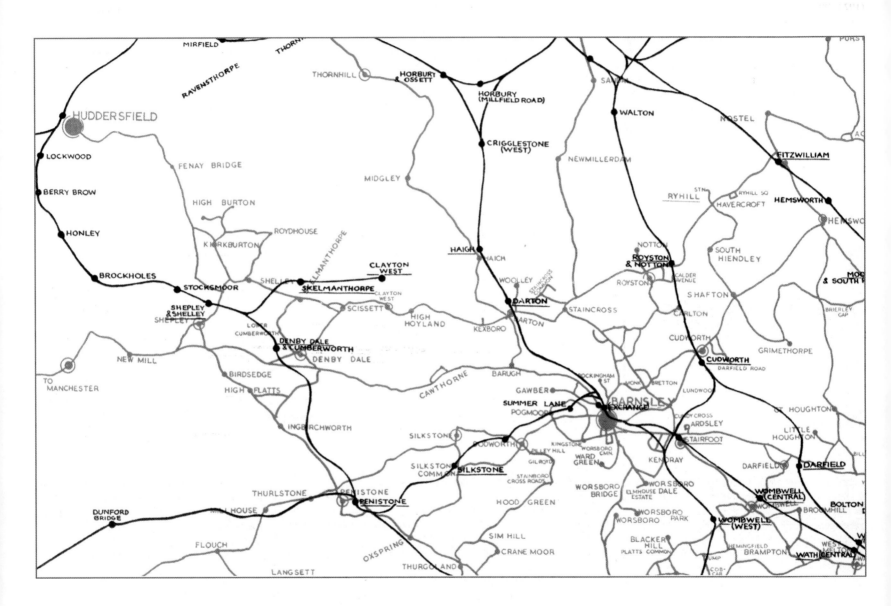

Section of a Yorkshire Traction 1961 map, showing the routes operated in grey and the railways in black.

6.1: BARNSLEY AND DISTRICT TRACTION (1923-28)

Tram operator Barnsley and District Electric Traction Company Ltd started motorbus operation on 3 May 1913 with a fleet of five Leyland S type single deckers with Brush bodies. By June 1914 the fleet size had increased to twenty and, among various route developments, a service from Barnsley to Barugh Green had been extended to Cawthorne. Later in the year the First World War caused a temporary halt to motorbus development from Barnsley and services were curtailed or discontinued owing to shortages of fuel, spares and staff.

During 1919 the growing importance of the motorbus operations led to a change of name to Barnsley and District Traction. In early May 1923 the Barnsley-Cawthorne route was extended via Denby Dale, Scissett, Skelmanthorpe, Kirkburton and Waterloo to reach Huddersfield (the service was running by 12 May). Frank Harburn (Blue & White) had pioneered the original Barnsley-Huddersfield route (via Penistone) in 1921. On 1 May 1923 Mitchell of Kirkburton had started running from Huddersfield to Barnsley via Denby Dale and Cawthorne while from the following day Harburn also introduced journeys via Cawthorne so Barnsley & District arrived in Huddersfield under very competitive circumstances.

Huddersfield Watch Committee in the usual parochial manner had at first refused Barnsley & District permission for a town centre stand for their proposed service as early as October 1922 but a change of mind allowed the use of a stand on the east side of Castlegate, just to the north of Seed Hill. Special conditions were imposed to the effect that a regular timetabled service had to be provided and no passengers could be both picked up and set down within the borough. Barnsley & District were soon in trouble with the chief constable for carrying more than the permitted five standing passengers and also for ignoring the restriction about local passengers. A through journey took 105 minutes. On Monday to Friday there were only four departures from Huddersfield; six trips were provided on Saturdays but only three on Sundays. Departures from Castlegate were at
9.30am (Not Sun), 1.30pm, 3.30pm (Sat), 5.30pm, 7.30pm (Sat) and 9.30pm.

As the table (right) shows, the number of journeys was progressively increased but travel was not encouraged on Thursdays (early closing day in Barnsley).

THE BARNSLEY & DISTRICT TRACTION CO. LTD.

Motor Coach Services.

BARNSLEY (Kendray Street) and HOLMFIRTH (Victoria Square)

Via Staincross,
Darton, Kexboro', High Hoyland, Clayton West,
Scissett, Denby Dale, Lane Head, Shelley,
New Mill,

Commencing January 1st, 1924.

Route No. 34 & 36	Not on Sundays		Every Day						Sats. only
	a.m.	a.m.	p.m.	p.m.	p.m.	p.m.	p.m.	p.m.	p.m.
BARNSLEY (Kendray Street) ...dep.	8 30	10 30	12 30	2 30	4 30	6 30	8 30		10 30
Staincross (Four Lane Ends) ... "	8 45	10 45	12 45	2 45	4 45	6 45	8 45		10 45
Darton (Rose and Crown) ... "	8 55	10 55	12 55	2 55	4 55	6 55	8 55		10 55
									arr.
Kexboro' (White Bear) ... "	9 0	11 0	1 0	3 0	5 0	7 0	9 0		11 0
High Hoyland (Globe Inn) ... "	9 10	11 10	1 10	3 10	5 10	7 10	9 10		
Clayton West (Guide Post) ... "	9 20	11 20	1 20	3 20	5 20	7 20	9 20		
Scissett Church ... "	9 25	11 25	1 25	3 25	5 25	7 25	9 25		
Denby Dale Schools ... "	9 35	11 35	1 35	3 35	5 35	7 35	9 35		
Sovereign Inn ... "	9 45	11 45	1 45	3 45	5 45	7 45	9 45		
Shepley (Black Bull) ... "	9 50	11 50	1 50	3 50	5 50	7 50	9 50		
New Mill (Duke of Leeds) ... "	10 5	12 5p	2 5	4 5	6 5	8 5	10 5		
HOLMFIRTH (Church) ...arr.	10 20	12 20	2 20	4 20	6 20	8 20	10 20		
HOLMFIRTH (Church) ...dep.	10 30	12 30	2 30	4 30	6 30	8 30	10 30		
New Mill (Duke of Leeds) ... "	10 45	12 45	2 45	4 45	6 45	8 45	10 55		
Shepley (Black Bull) ... "	10 55	12 55	2 55	4 55	6 55	8 55	10 55		
Sovereign Inn ... "	11 0	1 0	3 0	5 0	7 0	9 0	11 0		
Denby Dale (Prospect Inn) ... "	11 15	1 15	3 15	5 15	7 15	9 15	11 15		
Scissett Church ... "	11 25	1 25	3 25	5 25	7 25	9 25	11 25		
Clayton West (Guide Post) ... "	11 30	1 30	3 30	5 30	7 30	9 30	11 30		
High Hoyland (Globe Inn) ... "	11 40	1 40	3 40	5 40	7 40	9 40	11 40		
Kexboro' (White Bear) ... "	11 50	1 50	3 50	5 50	7 50	9 50	11 50	11 5
Darton (Rose and Crown) ... "	11 55	1 55	3 55	5 55	7 55	9 55	11 55	11 10
Staincross (Four Lane Ends) ... "	12 5	2 5	4 5	6 5	8 5	10 5	12 5	11 20
BARNSLEY (Kendray Street) ...arr.	12 25	2 25	4 25	6 25	8 25	10 25	12 25	11 40

The Company reserve the right to alter this Time Table without notice, but every endeavour will be made to adhere thereto.

TRAMWAY OFFICES,
SHEFFIELD ROAD,
BARNSLEY.
Tel. No. 159.
31/12/23

A PARCELS DELIVERY SERVICE ON ALL ROUTES.
Chief Parcel Office:
Eldon St., Barnsley. Tel. No. 86.

WALTER E. NICOLL,
General Manager.

E. Cheesman, Printer, Barnsley.

for the first time, with the original Huddersfield-Scissett-Cawthorne-Barnsley service initially route 31. On Saturday afternoons there were also now shortworkings between Huddersfield and Scissett (route 53) and a variant between Huddersfield and Clayton West branching off the existing route at Scissett (route 48); these were also advertised as running on Sunday afternoons by June. Four extra buses ran over from Barnsley (the Clayton West vehicles via Darton and High Hoyland) to provide a twenty minute frequency as far as Scissett, with departures from Castlegate at the following minutes past the hour:
xx10: 53 to Scissett;   xx30: 31 to Barnsley;   xx50: 48 to Clayton West.
On bank holidays during 1924 a twenty minute frequency was operated to Barnsley at the above times by extending the shortworkings.

A handbill announced the start of a new "motor coach" service on 1 January 1924 from Barnsley to Holmfirth (route 34). This ran every two hours via Staincross, Darton, Clayton West, Scissett, Denby Dale, Sovereign, Shepley and New Mill, with a journey time of 110 minutes and single fares from Holmfirth to Clayton West and Barnsley respectively of 1/- and 2/-. The parcel agent in Holmfirth was the hairdresser, Mr Kemp of 2 Victoria Square. This was Barnsley & District's 51st route, bringing the total route mileage up to 470, and over seven million passengers were being carried annually in a fleet of nearly 100 buses. Between Holmfirth and Scissett the Holmfirth to Barnsley timetable was coordinated with the West Riding company's Holmfirth-Wakefield bus route (introduced in 1923) to give a combined hourly

The increase in weekday journeys during 1924 possibly reflects a determination to overcome the competition in the form of Frank Harburn's business.

Meanwhile in January 1924 route numbers appeared

Number of journeys					
Day	May 1923	July 1923	Nov. 1923	June 1924	April 1925
Mon. to Wed.	4	4	6	12	13
Thursday	4	4	4	7	8
Friday	4	4	4	12	13
Saturday	6	6	10	13	14
Sunday	3	3	10	10	12

frequency. At the same time West Riding withdrew from the Scissett to Huddersfield corridor in favour of Barnsley & District.

Another "new motor coach service", in direct competition with Harburn, was started just before Whitsuntide 1924 from Barnsley to Huddersfield via Silkstone, Penistone, Ingbirchworth, Shepley and Kirkburton [Spring Grove] (route 33). This was actually an extension of a route already operating from Barnsley to Penistone and passed the new Barnsley Corporation reservoirs at Scout Dike. From Huddersfield (Castlegate) the service was every two hours from 10.00am to 10.00pm, with extra journeys between Penistone and Barnsley.

The first Huddersfield area premises were obtained in January 1925; a small garage in Dogley Lane (by the A629 between Fenay Bridge and Kirkburton) was rented for £50 per annum for a period of five years from Messrs Coals (Dogley) Ltd. The owner, JC Beaumont, had previously operated his charabancs ("The Mountaineers") from the premises; these were dual purpose vehicles, used also for carrying coal during the week. By the end of March 1925 at least three buses are likely to have been stabled at Dogley Lane overnight. The first bus from Barnsley arrived at 9.25am whereas the first departure for Barnsley left Castlegate at 7.30am. There was also a bus supplementing the main service as far as Denby Dale every two hours from 6.45am on Monday to Saturday. A third bus was required on Monday, Tuesday, Friday and Sunday for a recently introduced hourly service as far as Kirkburton. [On Saturdays from 12.45pm buses ran every 15 minutes between Scissett and Huddersfield but these entered service from Scissett and ran in from Barnsley depot.] The company had continued to standardise on Leyland single deckers; typical vehicles in this period were Leyland N and RAF types with forward entrance bodies by Brush.

From April 1925 a daily service running every 3 hours, route 57, linked Barnsley and Flockton via Barugh Green, Darton, Kexborough, Bretton and Midgley. With the possibility of connections at Flockton with the County and West Riding Wakefield-Huddersfield routes this shortlived Barnsley & District route was a forerunner of the County Motors Huddersfield-Barnsley route.

In a period of increasing competition it was no surprise that Harburn sold the bus side of his Blue and White business, including seven vehicles, to Barnsley &

THE BARNSLEY & DISTRICT TRACTION CO., LTD.
Motor Coach Services.

BARNSLEY & HUDDERSFIELD
VIA CAWTHORNE, DENBY DALE, SCISSETT, SKELMANTHORPE, SHELLEY AND KIRKBURTON.

Route Nos. 31, 35.					Every Day	Sats. only	Every Day	Not on Thurs.	Every Day	Not on Thurs	Every Day	Not on Thurs	Every Day	Not on Thurs	Every Day	Not on Thurs.	Every Day
			Not on Sundays														
	a.m.	a.m.	a.m.	a.m.	a.m.	a.m.	p.m.	p.m.	p.m.	p.m.	p.m.	p.m.	p.m.	p.m.	p.m.	p.m.	p.m.
Barnsley (Kendray St.) dep.	...	7 30	9 30	...	10 30	11 30	12 30	1 30	2 30	3 30	4 30	5 30	6 30	7 30	8 30	9 30	
Cawthorne (Church) ,,	...	7 50	9 50	...	10 50	11 50	12 50	1 50	2 50	3 50	4 50	5 50	6 50	7 50	8 50	9 50	
Denby Dale (Prospect Inn) ,,	...	8 15	10 15	...	11 15	12 15p	1 15	2 15	3 15	4 15	5 15	6 15	7 15	8 15	9 15	10 15	arr.
Scissett (Church) ,,	...	8 25	10 25	...	11 25	12 25	1 25	2 25	3 25	4 25	5 25	6 25	7 25	8 25	9 25	10 25	
Skelmanthorpe (Three Horse Shoes) ,,	...	8 35	10 35	...	11 35	12 35	1 35	2 35	3 35	4 35	5 35	6 35	7 35	8 35	9 35	10 35	
Shelley (Flockton Road) ,,	...	8 40	10 40	...	11 40	12 40	1 40	2 40	3 40	4 40	5 40	6 40	7 40	8 40	9 40	10 40	
Kirkburton (George Inn) ,,	...	8 50	10 50	...	11 50	12 50	1 50	2 50	3 50	4 50	5 50	6 50	7 50	8 50	9 50	10 50	
Huddersfield (Castlegate) { arr.	...	9 25	11 25	...	12 25p	1 25	2 25	3 25	4 25	5 25	6 25	7 25	8 25	9 25	10 25	11 25	
{ dep.	7 30	9 30	...	11 30	12 30	1 30	2 30	3 30	4 30	5 30	6 30	7 30	8 30	9 30	10 30	...	
Kirkburton (Post Office) ,,	7 55	9 55	...	11 55	12 55	1 55	2 55	3 55	4 55	5 55	6 55	7 55	8 55	9 55	10 55	...	
Shelley (Schools) ,,	8 5	10 5	...	12 5p	1 5	2 5	3 5	4 5	5 5	6 5	7 5	8 5	9 5	10 5	11 5	...	
Skelmanthorpe (Grove Shoes) ,,	8 15	10 15	...	12 15	1 15	2 15	3 15	4 15	5 15	6 15	7 15	8 15	9 15	10 15	11 15	...	
Scissett (Church) ,,	8 20	10 20	...	12 20	1 20	2 20	3 20	4 20	5 20	6 20	7 20	8 20	9 20	10 20	11 20	...	
Denby Dale (Schools) ,,	8 25	10 25	...	12 25	1 25	2 25	3 25	4 25	5 25	6 25	7 25	8 25	9 25	10 25	11 25	...	
Cawthorne (Church) ,,	8 45	10 45	...	12 45	1 45	2 45	3 45	4 45	5 45	6 45	7 45	8 45	9 45	10 45	11 45	...	
Barnsley (Kendray St.) arr.	9 15	11 15	...	1 15	2 15	3 15	4 15	5 15	6 15	7 15	8 15	9 15	10 15	11 15	12 15a	...	

On Saturdays the service between Scissett and Huddersfield is increased to a car every 15 minutes from 12-45 p.m., and to a car every 15 minutes from Huddersfield to Scissett from 1-30 p.m.

On Sundays, Mondays, Tuesdays, and Fridays, an extra car will be run between Huddersfield (Castlegate) and Kirkburton (George Inn), as follows:—

HUDDERSFIELD (Castlegate) depart 9-15 a.m. (Sundays excepted) 10-15 a.m. and every hour to 10-15 p.m.
KIRKBURTON (George Inn) depart 8-45 a.m. (Sundays excepted) 9-45 a.m. and every hour to 9-45 p.m.

Huddersfield and Denby Dale
Via Kirkburton, Shelley, Skelmanthorpe, Scissett.

	Not on Sundays.			EVERY DAY.					Saturdays only.
	a.m.	a.m.	a.m.	p.m.	p.m.	p.m.	p.m.	p.m.	p.m.
Huddersfield (Byram Street) ...dep.	6 45	8 45	10 45	12 45	2 45	4 45	6 45	8 45	10 45
Fenay Bridge (Star Inn) ... ,,	7 0	9 0	11 0	1 0	3 0	5 0	7 0	9 0	11 0
Kirkburton (Spring Grove) ,,	7 5	9 5	11 5	1 5	3 5	5 5	7 5	9 5	11 5
Kirkburton (Post Office).. ,,	7 10	9 10	11 10	1 10	3 10	5 10	7 10	9 10	11 10
Shelley (Commercial Inn) ,,	7 15	9 15	11 15	1 15	3 15	5 15	7 15	9 15	11 15
Skelmanthorpe (W.M. Club) ,,	7 25	9 25	11 25	1 25	3 25	5 25	7 25	9 25	11 25
Scissett Church ,,	7 30	9 30	11 30	1 30	3 30	5 30	7 30	9 30	11 30
Denby Dale (Prospect Hotel) ...arr.	7 35	9 35	11 35	1 35	3 35	5 35	7 35	9 35	11 35
" " ...dep.	7 45	9 45	11 45	1 45	3 45	5 45	7 45	9 45	11 45
Scissett Church ,,	7 50	9 50	11 50	1 50	3 50	5 50	7 50	9 50	11 50
Skelmanthorpe (W.M. Club) ,,	8 0	10 0	12 0	2 0	4 0	6 0	8 0	10 0	12 0
Shelley (Commercial Inn) ,,	8 5	10 5	12 5	2 5	4 5	6 5	8 5	10 5	12 5
Kirkburton (Post Office)... ,,	8 10	10 10	12 10	2 10	4 10	6 10	8 10	10 10	12 10
Kirkburton (Spring Grove) ,,	8 15	10 15	12 15	2 15	4 15	6 15	8 15	10 15	12 15
Fenay Bridge (Star Inn) ,,	8 20	10 20	12 20	2 20	4 20	6 20	8 20	10 20	12 20
Huddersfield (Byram St.) ...arr.	8 35	10 35	12 35	2 35	4 35	6 35	8 35	10 35	12 35

The Company reserve the right to alter this Time Table without notice, but every endeavour will be made to adhere thereto.

Tramway Offices,
Sheffield Road,
Barnsley.
Tel. No. 159.
8/4/25

A PARCELS DELIVERY SERVICE ON ALL ROUTES.
Chief Parcel Office:
Eldon Street, Barnsley. Tel. No. 86.

WALTER E. NICOLL,
General Manager.

E. CHEESMAN, PRINTER BARNSLEY

District in the first week of April 1925. Services taken over were Huddersfield-Penistone-Barnsley (Barnsley & District already ran alongside this) and Huddersfield-Shepley-Denby Dale. The last day of operation of the Blue and White timetable was 10 April. A special holiday timetable was in force for the Easter period (11-14 April) and a new one was introduced from 15 April. Over the Whitsuntide holiday a half hourly service operated for most of the day from the former Blue and White stand in Byram Street to Barnsley via Penistone. Another half hourly service operated from the Castlegate stand to Barnsley via Cawthorne and there were "frequent" buses to Kirkburton (advertised as convenient for visitors to Storthes Hall Hospital).

The August 1925 timetable showed the following routes in operation; use of the Byram Street terminal in Huddersfield had ceased.
33 Huddersfield-A629-Shepley-Penistone-Barnsley [increased frequency]
36 Huddersfield-Scissett-Denby Dale-Cawthorne-Barnsley [renumbered from 31]
38 Holmfirth-Scissett-Barnsley [renumbered from 34]
59 Huddersfield-A629-Shepley-Denby Dale [every 2 hours; ex Harburn]
66 Huddersfield-A629-Shepley-New Mill-Holmfirth [recently introduced]
Other numbers may have been used for shortworkings; numbering of "shorts" during this period was often inconsistent and changes were frequently made. The status of the Barnsley & District Kirkburton route at this stage is unclear.

On 1 December 1925, however, Tom Mitchell's "Red & White" Kirkburton Motor Services business was taken over. His Huddersfield-Kirkburton route, which also ran to Storthes Hall on Saturdays (a feature which Barnsley & District seem to have quickly abandoned), was numbered 80. The Mitchell vehicles were not operated but garage premises in Penistone Road, Waterloo were included in the deal. It is not clear whether this site was an operational depot for Barnsley & District in addition to being used as a store.

In February 1926 the Barnsley & District bus terminal stands in Huddersfield were moved from Castlegate to Lord Street, where they remained until 1975. Meanwhile the company had taken exception to another competitive operation, Richard Henderson's Huddersfield-Kirkburton service, and early in 1926 they started running a bus just in front of Henderson's to poach his passengers. Kirkburton UDC objected to this practice (on the

grounds that their bus was not running to a fixed timetable) but it obtained the desired result as Henderson seems to have abandoned the route by March, after being granted a licence for a Farnley Tyas via Almondbury route. An unexplained feature of the council's letter to Barnsley & District re Henderson was a curt reminder that they had not sought permission to run via Emley Moor.

By April 1926 route 66 (Huddersfield-Shepley-Holmfirth) was renumbered 86; 66 was to be reused in a new numbering scheme for buses between Barnsley and Sheffield. In July 1926 leasehold premises at Lincoln Street, off St Andrew's Road close to Huddersfield town centre, were bought from British Dyes for £3,500. This was used as a depot for up to 24 buses, replacing both the Waterloo and Dogley Lane sites. Along with Sheffield Corporation, application was first made for a licence for a service via Penistone to Sheffield in July 1926. This and several subsequent applications were rejected by Huddersfield Watch Committee.

An early example of an excursion operated by Barnsley & District from Huddersfield (Castlegate) was to York races on 24-26 August 1926. The pneumatic tyred new buses were advertised to depart at 10.00am each day, returning from York thirty minutes after the end of the final race. For those not particularly interested in the races, it was pointed out that this offered an excellent opportunity for visiting the historic city of York with its many attractions. At a return fare of 6/-, all seats were bookable in advance at Mr Lockwood's shop at 115 King Street. As more suitable vehicles entered the fleet in the later 1920s and the 1930s, the company expanded their excursion programmes from Huddersfield. From the late 1920s coastal expresses and regular long distance coach services were also developed; these are described in separate chapters.

As the route network developed, there were many changes in this early period to services and route numbers for the Huddersfield area. The following appeared in the February 1927 timetable:
31 Huddersfield-Penistone [every 2 hours; short working of 33]
33 Huddersfield-Penistone-Barnsley
36 Huddersfield-Scissett-Cawthorne-Barnsley
38 Holmfirth-Scissett-Barnsley
39 Huddersfield-Scissett [new number; shorts of 36]
55 Huddersfield-Shepley [new number; shorts of 31/3/86]
80 Huddersfield-Kirkburton

86 Huddersfield-Holmfirth
93 Huddersfield-Skelmanthorpe-Denby Dale [new number; shorts of 36]
There is no mention of Denby Dale via Shepley, which must have been withdrawn by then. Numbers for shortworkings (often untimetabled) were altered regularly but those for the main routes (33/6/8/80/6) lasted for a very long time.

Requests by Barnsley & District to run through buses from Huddersfield to Doncaster had also been rejected by Huddersfield Watch Committee but by June 1927 two cross-Barnsley extensions had been introduced. Every three hours a bus on route 36 via Cawthorne to Barnsley was extended to Doncaster via Marr and renumbered 14. Similarly every three hours a 36 journey was extended to Elsecar via Hoyland and renumbered 57. There was also a 36 terminating at Barnsley every three hours, giving a combined hourly frequency as far as there. The 57 was shortlived and by October 1927 had been replaced by new route 61 Huddersfield-Cawthorne-Barnsley-Sheffield, probably the unlicensed Sheffield route which incurred the wrath of the Huddersfield chief constable. More significantly in the long term, some of the journeys on 61 ran between Skelmanthorpe and Denby Dale via Lower Cumberworth (instead of Scissett). Also shown in the October 1927 timetable was 18 (Huddersfield-Scissett-Clayton West), a Saturday service similar to route 48 of 1924.

The company acquired County Motors jointly with West Riding and Yorkshire Woollen in August 1927 and County would be operated as a separate company for the next 41 years. From October the Waterloo premises acquired with the Mitchell business, latterly used for storage, were rented to County for £75 per annum.

In October 1927 Barnsley & District agreed to operate two routes in the Farnley Tyas area on a temporary basis on behalf of Huddersfield Corporation. This was to allow the municipal operator time to obtain consent from the Ministry of Transport to operate in this district, which was outside the borough boundary. The two small bus operators concerned, Richard Henderson, who had earlier competed on the Kirkburton route, and EH Sellers, were keen to sell; Henderson ran from Huddersfield to Thurstonland via Almondbury and Farnley Tyas while Sellers operated from Huddersfield to Farnley Tyas via Waterloo and Storthes Hall. The agreement ran from 18 October 1927 but the businesses and their routes, both numbered 77 by Barnsley & District, may not have been taken over until 6 February

1928 (Henderson) or 20 April 1928 (Sellers). In return the Corporation agreed to halve to hourly the frequency on their Huddersfield-Kirkburton route, which they had introduced in competition with Barnsley & District in March 1927. That there was a need for some détente on that corridor is shown by the incident described below. The Corporation also promised that Huddersfield Watch Committee would grant a licence to the company for the often requested through route to Sheffield via Penistone. 30 June 1928 was the last day of operation of Barnsley & District 77 after which the routes duly passed to Huddersfield Corporation.

Rivalry between drivers of different firms sometimes led to dangerous driving and speeding as they tried to reach a particular stop to pick up passengers before a competitor. A serious case involving Barnsley & District driver Thomas Dexter and Huddersfield Corporation driver Albert Smethurst was witnessed early in the morning on 23 April 1928 in Penistone Road when two intending passengers waiting at Rowley Bottom for a bus to Huddersfield had to jump over a wall to save their lives. As the company and Corporation buses passed Woodsome Road at speed they were abreast of each other; ten yards before Rowley Bottom the Barnsley & District driver cut in front of his rival in an endeavour to be first at the stop and caught one of the intending passengers on the shoulder as he tried to jump out of the path of the bus. The Corporation bus swerved out of control, striking road workers' equipment and tar barrels before hitting the wall on the other side of the road, and the driver fell out of his cab. In court the Barnsley & District driver was fined £2 while the Corporation driver, who claimed that his steering had failed after hitting the barrels, was found to be blameless.

The through service from Lord Street to Sheffield via Penistone, Wortley and Chapeltown (joint with Sheffield Corporation), every 2 hours Sunday to Friday but hourly on Saturdays, was due to start on 1 May 1928 but this was deferred until 14 May owing to a shortage of buses. The route number (68) was the one already used by Sheffield Corporation for their service between Sheffield and Penistone (from 4 May 1927).

It is likely that the projection of certain route 36 journeys beyond Barnsley to Sheffield as route 61 was abandoned at the same time or earlier. A few of these trips continued to run between Huddersfield and Barnsley via Lower Cumberworth instead of Scissett and by August 1928 were differentiated by use of new number 55; some were also extended beyond Barnsley to Doncaster via Marr like the 14. [Confusingly the Huddersfield-Shepley route, a shortworking of 31/3/68/86, continued to be listed in the timetable for several months also as route 55, although no timings were shown.] By August 1928 14/36/55 combined to offer an hourly service between Huddersfield and Barnsley; there were also hourly Saturday only Huddersfield-Shelley-Lower Cumberworth-Denby Dale shortworkings of 55 numbered 97. The 97 combined with two other hourly Saturday only routes, Huddersfield-Scissett-Clayton West (18) and Huddersfield-Scissett-Denby Dale (numbered 93 according to timetable index but shown as 39 in actual timetable; 39 was elsewhere described as Huddersfield-Scissett) to give three extra buses per hour on Saturdays between Huddersfield and Shelley. There were also positioning journeys to and from Barnsley as these extras were mostly worked by Barnsley depot.

Also by August 1928 alternate journeys on 33 (Barnsley via Penistone) had been diverted between High Flatts and Ingbirchworth via Denby Church (Upper Denby). Probably in August 1928 the 80 was extended in Kirkburton from the George Inn terminus to run via Turnshaw Road to the Junction Inn (Hallas Lane/ Paddock Lane). This is thought to have coincided with the similar extension of the Huddersfield Corporation Kirkburton route to Turnshaw in that month.

Various attempts were being made around this time to increase the company's presence in the Holmfirth area. In May 1927 they had been refused permission by Holmfirth UDC to extend the Barnsley-Holmfirth route to Holmbridge in direct competition with Huddersfield Corporation. In June 1928 they were similarly refused a licence application for a Holmfirth-Penistone route, which would have connected at Penistone with the new Huddersfield-Sheffield route. This request may have arisen in response to established operator Leonard Baddeley's recently started service between Penistone and Clayton West, which was in Barnsley & District territory. A month later a further application to extend the Barnsley-Holmfirth route, this time via Paris and Scholes to Jackson Bridge, was rejected. From 12 November 1928, however, a more significant presence was achieved by reorganising the Barnsley-Holmfirth (38) service, which ran every two hours. After each bus arrived in Holmfirth, before returning to Barnsley it now performed three short workings as far as New Mill (new service 48) to increase the frequency on that section to half hourly.

6.2: THE DEVELOPMENT OF YORKSHIRE TRACTION (1929-45)

In January 1929 the name of the company was changed from the rather parochial Barnsley & District Traction to Yorkshire Traction to reflect the widening scope of operations. The fleet had grown to about 145 single deck buses and centre entrance Leyland Lions purchased from 1926 onwards were particularly common.

By January 1929 the Saturday only Huddersfield-Scissett-Clayton West (18), which had featured positioning journeys from Barnsley via High Hoyland, was transformed into daily route 15 (every 2 hours) which continued beyond Clayton West to Barnsley via High Hoyland, Darton and Staincross. 14/36/55 (Barnsley via Cawthorne) were increased to run at a combined frequency of alternately every 30 or 60 minutes, still extending to Doncaster only every 3 hours (as 14 or 55). The new 15 filled the gap in the 14/36/55 timetable to produce a half-hourly service on 14/15/36/55 combined. Also the frequency of the 68 (Sheffield) route had been doubled on Sunday evenings (to hourly) and on Saturdays (to half-hourly), when 8 buses were required including Sheffield's contribution. The through Huddersfield-Barnsley-Doncaster facility (14/55) was improved to hourly by May 1929.

Two new limited stop services between Doncaster, Mexborough, Barnsley and Manchester, jointly operated with Stockport based bus company North Western Road Car, were introduced on 11 May 1929, each running every two hours; not all journeys served the Doncaster section. Between Barnsley and Manchester route 20 served Penistone, Flouch and Woodhead but the 19, routed via Sovereign, New Mill, Holmfirth and Greenfield, passed through the Holme Valley. The 19 also catered for local journeys to points beyond Parkhead on the Greenfield Road out of Holmfirth and was popular with walkers. The numbers 19 and 20 are those most closely associated with these services but up to 1939 the route numbering was inconsistent and confusing and we do not propose to list the frequent changes. Numbers 19 and 20 were originally used for journeys between Manchester and Barnsley, with 12 and 16 respectively denoting journeys via those routes running through to Doncaster. Six Leyland Tigers with Hall Lewis coach bodies were bought for these routes and the new coastal expresses. They were the first true coaches for Yorkshire Traction and also the very first in a long line of Tiger models for the company.

All journeys on 33 (Barnsley via Penistone) ran via Upper Denby by June 1929. The 33A variant of the latter, which diverted between Sovereign and Upper Denby via Denby Dale, had been introduced by November 1929; alternate journeys continued to serve the main road via High Flatts as 33. The separate route number 33A was not actually shown in the timetable until December 1929; this was one of Yorkshire Traction's first suffix lettered routes and the first of any bus operator in Huddersfield. Another enhancement advertised by November 1929 was the introduction of supplementary Saturday journeys on 36 (hourly, full route) and 55 (hourly, Huddersfield-Denby Dale only), replacing the Saturday only 39/93/97 routes which continued to be listed in the timetable books but without any timings.

The February 1930 timetable showed the following routes serving Huddersfield and Holmfirth. Only basic frequencies are given.

14 Huddersfield-Scissett-Cawthorne-Barnsley-Marr-Doncaster [hourly, incl. 55]

15 Huddersfield-Scissett-Clayton West-Staincross-Barnsley [every 2 hours]

19 etc. Doncaster-Barnsley-Holmfirth-Manchester [joint with North Western; every 2 hours]

31 Huddersfield-Penistone [infrequent; short of 33]

33 Huddersfield-Shepley-High Flatts-Penistone-Barnsley [every 2 hours]

33A Huddersfield-Shepley-Denby Dale-Penistone-Barnsley [every 2 hours]

36 Huddersfield-Scissett-Cawthorne-Barnsley [short of 14; every 2 hours]

38 Holmfirth-Scissett-Barnsley [every 2 hours]

39 Huddersfield-Scissett [short of 14/5/36]

48 Holmfirth-New Mill [short of 38/86; one or two buses per hour]

55 Huddersfield-Lower Cumberworth-Cawthorne-Barnsley-Marr-Doncaster [irregular]

68 Huddersfield-Penistone-Sheffield [joint with Sheffield; every 2 hours]

80 Huddersfield-Kirkburton [at least hourly]

86 Huddersfield-Shepley-Holmfirth [every 2 hours]

93 Huddersfield-Shelley-Scissett-Denby Dale [short of 14/36]

97 Huddersfield-Shelley-Cumberworth-Denby Dale [short of 55]

14/5/36/55 gave a combined 30 minute frequency to Barnsley and between Huddersfield and Skelmanthorpe; extra journeys on Saturdays increased this frequency,

This early 1930s Yorkshire Traction Leyland Lion bears a destination board for the Huddersfield-Penistone-Barnsley-Cudworth (33) route in this depot scene. [D. Dodd collection]

This Leyland bodied Leyland Lion LT2 was new to Yorkshire Traction in 1931 (348: HE 5232). Allocated to Huddersfield depot, it stands at the Exchange Street, Sheffield terminus of route 68 to Huddersfield, jointly operated with Sheffield JOC. [The Omnibus Society collection]

with 55 particularly enhanced. The Sheffield (68) service was also greatly enhanced at weekends.

In September 1930 the Barnsley via Penistone services (33/33A) were extended via Monk Bretton to Cudworth; the complete journey took almost two hours. The first double deckers appeared in the fleet in 1930, Leyland Titan TD1s with lowbridge bodies for tramway replacement routes. For some years, however, Yorkshire Traction's bus fleet would remain overwhelmingly single deck, partly because of a large number of very low bridges in the operating territory (for example, on the aforementioned 33/33A), with only single deckers allocated to Huddersfield depot. By May 1931 all the extra Saturday journeys on 36/55 ran through to Barnsley, providing a double (15 minute) frequency on that day (with route 15) between Huddersfield and Barnsley via Skelmanthorpe. The new licensing system

introduced as a result of the 1930 Road Traffic Act seems to have had little impact on Yorkshire Traction's Huddersfield area operations.

Crowther's tea rooms in Lord Street served as the first parcels agency in Huddersfield but by May 1931 a Yorkshire Traction sub-office had been established at 3 Lord Street. By August 1932 two rooms were leased from Fred Marshall and Co. Ltd at 7 Lord Street for use as a booking office at a rental of £50 per annum. This office across the road from the stands was to remain in use for over forty years until Yorkshire Traction buses and office moved into the new Huddersfield bus station in Upperhead Row in 1975.

At an unknown date between February and August 1932 most journeys (every 2 hours) on route 15 (Barnsley via Darton) were combined at Barnsley with alternate journeys on route 27 to Rotherham via Elsecar,

Wentworth and Greasbrough. The ride from Huddersfield to Rotherham took over two hours, there was a return fare of 4/9d and route numbers were changed at Barnsley. The other timings between Barnsley and Rotherham were operated by Rotherham Corporation, whose buses did not run through to Huddersfield.

From November or December 1932 two journeys on 80 (Kirkburton) were extended from Turnshaw to the village of Highburton, previously without buses (Huddersfield Joint Omnibus Committee extended a few of their Kirkburton journeys from 7 November 1932). Huddersfield JOC were strongly opposed to the use of return tickets, which were just as fervently supported by Yorkshire Traction. As the two operators could not therefore reach agreement on standardised fares which the traffic commissioners were trying to introduce under the new licensing system, Yorkshire Traction paid the JOC to withdraw their Kirkburton service and it ran for the last time on 1 April 1933. As a result the number of Yorkshire Traction buses running through to Highburton was increased to four; these journeys were eventually renumbered 80A.

Returning to Holmfirth, by August 1932 the Holmfirth-New Mill journeys (previously route 48) were shown as part of route 38 (Barnsley), off which they were of course worked. By November 1932 they were extended to Shepley every two hours throughout the day and once again renumbered 48. By November 1933 the 86 (Huddersfield-Shepley-Holmfirth), which had previously run direct between Spring Grove and Shelley Far Bank, was diverted via Kirkburton and Shelley villages and the Monday to Saturday afternoon frequency was doubled to hourly. As a result of the improvements on the 86, route 48 (Holmfirth-Shepley) was reduced to run only in the Monday to Saturday morning peak, when 86 did not operate. The 48 was another route which was regularly renumbered during the 1930s. By January 1934 it had become 48A but the "A" suffix had been dropped by 22 December 1938. By 27 May 1939, however, it had been renumbered 48B. These changes resulted from the reuse of 48 etc. for unrelated services to the east of Barnsley.

Also enhanced by November 1933 was 15 (Barnsley via Clayton West) which had been doubled to hourly. The extra journeys did not run through to Rotherham as 27.

In 1934 scheduled departures from Lord Street in a typical two hour period from Monday to Friday were as follows (by 1939 only minor changes had been made):

9.00am   33 High Flatts, Penistone, Barnsley, Cudworth

Traction's prewar single deck bus livery is shown on Eastern Coach Works bodied Leyland Tiger TS8 591 (HE 8244) of 1938, standing with a full load on the east side of Lord Street, Huddersfield. [J.F. Higham collection]

9.05am	80 Kirkburton
9.30am	14 Scissett, Denby Dale, Cawthorne, Barnsley, Doncaster
9.45am	68 High Flatts, Penistone, Sheffield
9.55am	15/27 Clayton West, Barnsley, Rotherham
10.00am	33A Denby Dale, Penistone, Barnsley, Cudworth
10.05am	80 Kirkburton
10.30am	14 Scissett, Denby Dale, Cawthorne, Barnsley, Doncaster
10.40am	86 Shelley, Shepley, Holmfirth
10.55am	15 Clayton West, Barnsley [change for Rotherham]

A two hour period after 11.00am on a Saturday would have produced twenty scheduled departures as well as duplicates and short workings:

11.00am	33 High Flatts, Penistone, Barnsley, Cudworth
11.05am	80 Kirkburton
11.15am	55 Cumberworth, Denby Dale, Cawthorne, Barnsley
11.15am	68 High Flatts, Penistone, Sheffield
11.15am	80 Kirkburton
11.30am	14 Scissett, Denby Dale, Cawthorne, Barnsley, Doncaster
11.45am	68 High Flatts, Penistone, Sheffield
11.45am	36 Scissett, Denby Dale, Cawthorne, Barnsley
11.55am	15/27 Clayton West, Barnsley, Rotherham

12.00noon	33A Denby Dale, Penistone, Barnsley, Cudworth
12.05pm	80 Kirkburton
12.15pm	55 Cumberworth, Denby Dale, Cawthorne, Barnsley
12.15pm	68 High Flatts, Penistone, Sheffield
12.15pm	80 Kirkburton
12.30pm	55 Cumberworth, Denby Dale, Cawthorne, Barnsley, Doncaster
12.40pm	86 Shelley, Shepley, Holmfirth
12.45pm	36 Scissett, Denby Dale, Cawthorne, Barnsley
12.45pm	68 High Flatts, Penistone, Sheffield
12.55pm	15 Clayton West, Barnsley [change for Rotherham]

By December 1934 the through journeys between Huddersfield and Rotherham on 15/27 had been discontinued. One long term disadvantage of through working would have been restriction to single deck operation on account of a very low bridge on the 27 route. It is not, however, thought that double deckers were introduced on the 15 as early as 1934.

Before the start of the 1935 summer season, the company obtained the express and excursion licences of the former Wilson Haigh business, which had been purchased by Huddersfield JOC the previous year. Regular cheap Sunday evening excursions of the "mystery" or "round the moors" type, picking up at Holmfirth, Honley, Meltham and Huddersfield were operated, together with a full programme of daily excursions during the local summer holiday weeks. September and October featured the inevitable trips to the illuminations at Blackpool and Morecambe.

From [probably] 3 October 1936 a faster variant of the 68 (Sheffield) route was introduced, a precursor of the X68 started in 1968. A few Tuesday and Saturday trips ran direct between Wortley and Sheffield via Grenoside as 68A, cutting ten minutes off the journey time. The company's bus station in Barnsley, which cost £40,000 to build, came into use in January 1939 and was used by all services running into the town. During the 1930s Yorkshire Traction had continued to standardise on Leyland buses, mostly forward entrance single deckers of both the Lion and Tiger ranges; there were also some Dennis Lancets. Relatively small quantities of Leyland Titan double deckers of both lowbridge and highbridge layouts also entered service and by the end of the decade these could be seen in Huddersfield.

On the outbreak of war drastic cuts had to be made to timetables in order to conserve fuel for the war effort. From 15 September 1939 the through services across Barnsley, 14 (Huddersfield-Cawthorne-Barnsley-Doncaster) and 33/33A (Huddersfield-Penistone-Barnsley-Cudworth), and the 68A variant on the Sheffield route were withdrawn and not reinstated after the war. The following services were temporarily withdrawn:

15 Huddersfield-Clayton West-Barnsley
19 Doncaster-Barnsley-Holmfirth-Manchester
33 Huddersfield-High Flatts-Penistone-Barnsley
48B Holmfirth-Shepley

55 Huddersfield-Cumberworth-Cawthorne-Barnsley
68 Huddersfield-Penistone-Sheffield
Reduced frequencies applied on other services. 36 (Huddersfield-Scissett-Cawthorne-Barnsley) ran every two hours. The 80 ran at 8.05am and 9.05am then hourly from 12.05pm to Kirkburton with no buses to Highburton. 86 (Huddersfield-Shepley-Holmfirth) was withdrawn between Shepley (Black Bull) and Holmfirth and ran every 2 hours. Works and schools services were continued but peak period duplicates could not be operated. The 33A still ran every 2 hours as far as Barnsley and 38 (Holmfirth-Barnsley) also retained its 2 hourly frequency.

These cuts proved to be too drastic and various amendments were soon made. The 68 (Sheffield) route was reinstated from 10 November 1939, running every two hours, followed from 17 November by 15 (Barnsley via Clayton West) likewise every two hours. Just two journeys (8.00am and 5.00pm) on 33 (Barnsley via High Flatts & Penistone) were reintroduced from April 1940.

While operating under blackout conditions it was imperative that the saloon lights should not be seen from outside the bus. On the evening of 9 December 1939 two policemen on duty in Lord Street found that one double decker at least was in breach of regulations as passengers in the bus were clearly visible from outside. Examining the lights, they found nine bulbs in the lower saloon and ten in the upper saloon, all of the 12 watt and 24 volt variety. Each bulb was surrounded by a black metal cylinder fitted with a frosted glass plate at the base. It transpired that twelve buses had been treated in this manner and that there had not been any other

complaints. The company had experimented with two other systems; on some buses cardboard containers had been fitted around each bulb but passengers had torn bits off to increase the illumination; on other buses the bulbs had been painted black so that only a pinpoint of light showed but passengers had scratched off some of the paint. At least the present system could not be tampered with but it was subsequently agreed to paint both the insides of the metal cylinders and the glass plates black. Also, to make them less visible from the air, the roofs of many buses were repainted red instead of the usual cream.

Surprisingly despite restrictions on the use of fuel several excursions were operated over Whitsuntide 1940 from Huddersfield:
Sunday to Tuesday (12-14 May): Blackpool dep. 8.00am (8/-), Scarborough dep. 7.00am (8/-) and Cleethorpes dep. 6.00am (9/-)
Sunday only: Circular Tour dep. 6.00pm (3/-) via Howbrook, Hoyland Common, Wentworth, Hemsworth and Nostell.
The company was also able to reintroduce the 19 (Barnsley-Holmfirth-Manchester) route but on a seasonal basis only. A limited timetable of three return journeys on Friday, Saturday and Sunday only (plus a similar service on the 20 via Penistone) was operated from 10 May to 7 September 1940 but thereafter these routes would seem to have remained suspended for the rest of the war.

For the company as a whole the mileage operated in 1940 was approximately 8 million, representing a decrease of 30% compared with 1938. The actual cuts in timetabled journeys from Huddersfield (excluding works services and duplicates) is as shown.

Total Number of Weekly Journeys

Route	Prewar	War time	%Cut
14/36/55	131	96	27
33/33A	120	69	43
15	97	48	51
68	76	48	37
80	147	88	40
86	83	47	43

Late in 1941 it proved possible to reinstate the withdrawn section of the 86 beyond Shepley to Holmfirth.

On Sunday 30 August 1942 an exhibition golf match was played at Woodsome Hall in aid of the National Air Raid Distress Fund. In anticipation of the numbers of spectators, permission was granted to duplicate the

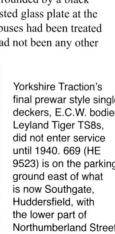

Yorkshire Traction's final prewar style single deckers, E.C.W. bodied Leyland Tiger TS8s, did not enter service until 1940. 669 (HE 9523) is on the parking ground east of what is now Southgate, Huddersfield, with the lower part of Northumberland Street in the background. [A. Douglas]

THE
YORKSHIRE TRACTION CO., Ltd.

CURTAILMENT
OF SERVICES

AT THE DIRECTION OF THE REGIONAL TRANSPORT COMMISSIONER, DRASTIC CURTAILMENT OF BUS SERVICES WILL COME INTO OPERATION COMMENCING SUNDAY, NOV. 1st, 1942. THE CHIEF EFFECTS WILL BE AS FOLLOWS:

WEEKDAYS: Last Buses from City or Town termini will not be later than 9 p.m. as shown on list below, except that later Buses will be operated on certain routes for the benefit of workpeople. Employers of labour will be given information in respect of the Special Buses upon application to this Company.

Route No.	FROM	Last Bus	FROM	Last Bus
15	HUDDERSFIELD	8-30	BARNSLEY ...	9- 0
33a	HUDDERSFIELD	9- 0	BARNSLEY ...	8-30
36	HUDDERSFIELD	7-30	BARNSLEY ...	8- 0
68	HUDDERSFIELD	7-45	SHEFFIELD ...	7-45
80	HUDDERSFIELD	9- 5	KIRKBURTON ...	9-30

SUNDAY SERVICES
ARE AS FOLLOWS:

HUDDERSFIELD—BARNSLEY (Via Cawthorne)—
1-30 p.m. and every two hours until 7-30 p.m.

HUDDERSFIELD—BARNSLEY (Via Staincross)—
2-30 p.m. and every two hours until 8-30 p.m.

HUDDERSFIELD—KIRKBURTON
1-0 p.m., 3-0 p.m., 7-0 p.m., 9-0 p.m.

HUDDERSFIELD—SHEPLEY
2-0 p.m. and every two hours until 8-0 p.m.

HUDDERSFIELD—SHEFFIELD
1-45 p.m. and every two hours until 7-45 p.m

HUDDERSFIELD—BARNSLEY (Via Penistone)—NO SERVICE

NO DUPLICATE CARS WILL BE RUN

five departures from Lord Street between 12.30pm and 2.05pm.

Sunday services were pruned further from 1 November 1942 with no buses at all to Barnsley via Penistone. From an unknown date between June 1942 and March 1943 a supplementary service started operating every two hours daily between Huddersfield and Shepley, direct via Penistone Road, similar to shortworkings on the 33A advertised in April 1940. This was presumably meant to compensate for reductions to the other services along this corridor and became route 74.

For Christmas 1942, in accordance with the Essential Work Order, the company paid the bus crews only a guaranteed 40 hour week instead of the customary 48 hours. As a result a strike started at Barnsley depot on the morning of 2 January 1943 and by midday the Huddersfield crews had also taken their buses off the road. Negotiations soon settled the problem for future holidays and the strike lasted for just two days. Military vehicles were used to transport essential war workers and collieries were given permission to use their own lorries to bring in the miners.

From March 1943 onwards 21 utility wooden seated Guy Arab double deckers, of both highbridge and lowbridge layouts, were placed in service. Leylands were of course unobtainable during this period but higher capacity double deckers of any breed were welcome in a fleet which had been heavily reliant on single deckers.

From 13 May 1943 platform staff again took strike

Parked on the waste ground east of today's Southgate was Traction 1944 Guy Arab II 710 (HE 9833) with Weymann utility highbridge bodywork. One of their prewar Leyland single deckers can also be seen.
[S.T. Harling collection]

action, this time in protest against the arbitration tribunal's rejection of their wage claim. In particular they wanted better rates of pay for split shifts, where they often received only nine hour's pay for duties spread over thirteen hours. Lasting for 22 days, this strike was very unpopular with women passengers whose servicemen husbands could not go on strike, irrespective of their conditions. Army lorries provided a well organised workers service in the Barnsley area and also between Kirkburton and Huddersfield. Nevertheless many would be passengers had to walk each day to Waterloo to catch a trolleybus into Town.

Workmen's special buses were known as "paddy buses" and at times of staff shortage during the war they had to be given priority even if this meant the cancellation of service buses. On at least one occasion even general manager Norman Dean drove a paddy bus. In 1938 paddy buses accounted for only 5% of the company's mileage but such was the contribution to the war effort that by 1945 this had increased to 18% (but the decrease in overall mileage would also to some extent have accounted for this increase). Annual mileage was over 1 million with over 6 million workers carried but revenue from the cheap workmen return fares was much less than operating costs; this was to be an ever increasing problem in later years. Producer gas units were used on some Barnsley local services but no vehicles based at St Andrew's Road were converted in this way.

6.3: POSTWAR PRIVATE ENTERPRISE (1945-68)

Shortlived route 74 (Shepley) was withdrawn by June 1945 and from 9 December 1945 the Saturday and Sunday frequency on 68 (Sheffield) was doubled to hourly. During 1946 services were restored almost to prewar frequencies; as mentioned earlier, through running beyond Barnsley was not resumed. By Easter the fuel situation was such that it was possible to offer a limited excursions programme and the extension of certain route 80 journeys beyond Turnshaw to Highburton was restored by August. Limited stop services 19/20 (Barnsley-Manchester via Holmfirth or Penistone) which had been entirely suspended for most of the war were finally reinstated on 19 August 1946. [Through running to Doncaster was not resumed until the late 1970s.] The Holmfirth-Shepley journeys worked by the 38 (Barnsley-Holmfirth) bus no longer had a separate number (latterly this had been 48B).

On 1 August 1948 Sheffield Joint Omnibus Committee's brand new Weymann rear entrance bodied AEC Regal I 146 (KWJ 146) was waiting at the Kirkgate end of Lord Street, Huddersfield on the joint (with Traction) service 68. The "C" under the fleet number indicates that the bus was part of the Sheffield C fleet, wholly owned by British Railways. [R. Marshall]

On 21 July 1949 an accident befell Traction's 1939 Leyland Tiger TS8/Roe 653 (HE 8943) in the section of Penistone Road where it passes near to Thunderbridge. The Huddersfield depot bus was travelling from Huddersfield to Barnsley via Penistone. To avoid tar spraying, the Tiger was being driven on the offside of the road when the causeway gave way. The bus has been secured to the steam roller on the right to prevent it from slipping down the bank. [Kirklees Image Archive ke01855]

After the austerity of wartime people were travelling for pleasure again. Maintenance difficulties and the shortage of spares during the war coupled with the heavy loads carried had taken their toll on the condition of the buses so fleet renewal was urgently required. Although there were some new Leyland Titan double deckers (PD1s and PD2s) the majority of the buses entering service in the late forties were Leyland Tiger single decks with 32 seat front entrance bodies. These front engined half cab saloons would soon become very unfashionable and their low capacity an embarrassment.

Thirty passengers had a narrow escape on 21 July 1949 when travelling on a Barnsley bound 33 or 33A on Penistone Road near Thunderbridge. 653 (HE 8943), a Leyland Tiger TS8 with Roe B32F body of 1939 vintage, was being driven by Stanley Haigh of Moldgreen and tar spraying between Kirkburton and Shelley meant that the bus had to use the offside of the road by Harley Bank

Wood. The causeway gave way and only the skill of the driver prevented the bus from toppling into the valley below; the passengers safely disembarked with the front end of the bus hanging precariously over the bank. After the incident the bus was secured to a steam roller to prevent it sliding further down the bank before arrival of the breakdown gang from Barnsley.

In July and August 1951 Yorkshire Traction excursions from Castlegate included trips to the Great Yorkshire Show, Castleton and Liverpool/Chester via the Mersey Tunnel as well as the usual seaside destinations. After three years of delays while the company and Kirkburton UDC negotiated about a turning point, three journeys on 80 (Kirkburton) were finally extended from Turnshaw to the tiny hamlet in Linfit Lane from 11 August 1951. Councillor Burt was the first passenger to make a round trip. Travelling on the first bus from Lord Street at 9.00am, he was met at the outer terminus by about a dozen people waiting in typically dreadful August rain to make the journey to Town. Kirkburton UDC had purchased land for the turning space at Lockwood Fold after Yorkshire Traction refused to apply to run up to Linfit Lane Top (where buses could have reversed at the Paul Lane junction) on the grounds that passengers might have been abstracted from County Motors.

By 1952, when the company's golden jubilee was celebrated, concern was being aired about the worsening problems associated with the operation of the many colliery specials. These buses often stood idle in pit yards for an hour or more and covered only 300 miles per week compared with the average of 800 miles. Operating losses on these services amounted to 3d a mile even though workmen's return tickets had been increased in price by 1d or 2d. The private hire side of the business was said to be doing very well particularly since underfloor engined higher capacity coaches were being taken into stock. From 1951 onwards new single deck service buses were also 30 feet long and underfloor engined with an entrance opposite the driver. Their increased seating capacity – up to 45 – was welcome on busy routes afflicted with very low bridges. The first of these were Leyland Royal Tigers but from 1954 lighter Tiger Cubs appeared. Although Huddersfield Joint Omnibus Committee used underfloor engined single deckers without conductors from January 1952, it would be over 14 years before Yorkshire Traction followed suit. On the double deck front, the classic Leyland Titan PD2s continued to be purchased until 1953.

After an application to the traffic commissioners

Traction 833 (BHE 763), a Roe bodied Leyland Titan PD2/1 new in 1949, rests on the Barnsley stand in Lord Street, Huddersfield. The "H" visible after the fleet number signifies "highbridge" – not Huddersfield depot! [P. J. Cardno collection]

had been granted in June 1952, some journeys on 86 (Huddersfield-Holmfirth via Shepley) were diverted between Kirkburton and Shelley to serve the tiny hamlet of Roydhouse, previously visited only by school buses, and renumbered 86A.

People living in Wakefield Road between Scissett and Clayton West had been complaining that all the bus operators (County, West Riding and Yorkshire Traction)

ran via Chapel Hill and Church Lane, missing their stretch of the main road. After much correspondence between Denby Dale UDC and Yorkshire Traction, the company finally agreed to divert the 15 (Huddersfield-Barnsley) via Wakefield Road and Scott Hill, at first as an 8 weeks trial from 5 September 1953. This longer routing was immediately made permanent. Certain journeys on 38 (Holmfirth-Barnsley) were diverted to

Traction's Leyland highbridge bodied Titan PD2 778 (BHE 139), new in 1948, waits in Lord Street on Stand B on 20 July 1952. The masked destination display presumably resulted from postwar shortages of materials. The bus could have been on any of the double deck routes to Barnsley (15, 36, 55) but in those days of stable and uncomplicated timetables most passengers would have known that, for example, the bus leaving at five past was always a 15. [R. Marshall]

Yorkshire Traction Leyland Tiger/Brush 32-seater 888 (CHE 722), new in 1950, stands out of service on the "wrong" (east) side of Lord Street in front of the company's Huddersfield booking office on 20 July 1952. Note the advert for the timetable booklet, which cost 6d for almost all the bus's time with Traction. From 1962 888 ran as a works bus for contractor Sir Alfred McAlpine. [R. Marshall]

serve Lower Cumberworth between Upper Cumberworth and Denby Dale after permission had been received from the traffic commissioners in April 1954.

During 1953 the Huddersfield garage in Lincoln Street off St Andrew's Road was extensively reconstructed with a new roof and a large forecourt; at this period there was accommodation for 20 buses. Two workshop pits were built but the stalls provided for horses, dating from the days when the building was in use as a livery stable, were left intact.

In the early to mid 1950s service requirements were fairly constant and both highbridge double deck and single deck vehicles were allocated to Huddersfield depot. The hourly 15 to Barnsley via Clayton West required three highbridge double deckers, two provided by Barnsley depot and one by Huddersfield. Routes 33 and 33A to Barnsley via Penistone also needed three buses for their combined hourly frequency but these were single deckers because of the very low railway bridge at Oxspring; two worked from Huddersfield depot and one from Barnsley. On weekdays an extra peak hour working was also provided by Huddersfield depot. Routes 36/55 to Barnsley via Cawthorne were usually highbridge double deck (two from Huddersfield depot

and one from Barnsley). The extra Saturday journeys on the 55 via Cumberworth additionally required three vehicles, one supplied by Huddersfield depot. During the week the two hourly route 68 to Sheffield, which also had to negotiate the Oxspring railway bridge, needed just two single decks, one from Huddersfield depot and the other from Sheffield JOC. On Saturdays the half hourly frequency demanded eight buses of which Huddersfield depot provided four. Service 80 to Kirkburton was run with one Huddersfield highbridge double decker plus an extra bus in the peaks. The maximum requirement on 86 to Holmfirth was two single deckers. [Barnsley depot continued to operate Holmfirth area routes 19 and 38.]

During the Suez Crisis the company had to reduce total mileage by 5% and service cuts came into effect from Saturday 29 December 1956. In the Huddersfield area, Saturday journeys on 55 (Barnsley via Cumberworth) were cancelled after 5.00pm, the 68 (Sheffield) Saturday frequency was halved to hourly, four off peak daily return journeys on 80 (Kirkburton) were cancelled (10.00 and 11.00am, 7.00 and 8.00pm) and the Sunday service on 86 (Holmfirth via Shepley) was suspended. On 19/20 (Barnsley-Holmfirth or Penistone-Manchester) the Monday to Friday timetable was operated on Saturdays and on Mondays to Thursdays all journeys were suspended.

After the crisis was over the normal pattern of services resumed except that on route 68 the reduced frequency was made permanent. The cuts on the 80 had still not been restored at the end of 1957, even though a petition had been handed in to Kirkburton UDC.

From 1955 "new" double deckers were obtained by having the chassis of surplus early postwar Leyland Tiger single deckers rebodied as double deckers, increasing their seating capacities from 32 to at least 59. The Barnsley licensing authorities allowed the use of new registrations so, in the eyes of the travelling public, these were new buses. No brand new double deckers appeared after 1953 until 1959 when the company's first batch of the revolutionary rear engined Leyland Atlanteans was bought. As these were lowheight buses, they were used on routes from Barnsley which needed them; they were not employed in Huddersfield until much later.

A dispute over a wage claim culminated in all 70 employees at the St Andrew's Road depot coming out on strike on 22 July 1957. The strike lasted a week, with no Yorkshire Traction (or County Motors, Hebble or Yorkshire Woollen) buses operated, and passengers

Traction's Lincoln Street depot, off St. Andrew's Road, Huddersfield, was used from 1926 to 1971. 999 (EHE 946) was one of ten 1953 Leyland Royal Tigers with Willowbrook bus bodies. [R. Marshall]

Above-
Yorkshire Traction 1015 (GHE 15), a Saro bodied Leyland Tiger Cub new in 1954 and allocated to Huddersfield depot, crosses tram lines in central Sheffield, returning home with a good load. [W.A. Haynes]

Below-
From 1955 Traction had surplus early postwar Leyland Tiger single deckers rebuilt and rebodied as double deckers. The resulting Roe bodied 1042 (HHE 323) was one of the first and was working from Huddersfield depot when seen on the Kirkburton (80) stand towards the Kirkgate end of Lord Street. [R. Marshall]

who had booked excursions or period returns had their money refunded at the Lord Street offices. Services were resumed on 29 July after platform staff had accepted an 11/- per week wage increase.

In October 1961 there was a proposal to revive Huddersfield-Doncaster through services but this did not come to fruition. From June 1962 the Monday to Saturday morning Holmfirth-Shepley short workings were transferred from the 38 (Barnsley-Holmfirth) route to the 86 (Huddersfield-Holmfirth), which meant that they were worked by Huddersfield depot instead of Barnsley.

From 1960 onwards the company had arranged for rebuilt Leyland Tigers to be fitted with 63 seat front entrance double deck bodywork equipped with driver operated folding platform doors. The final batch of these, Northern Counties bodied 1240-8 (YHE 240-8), rebuilds of chassis purchased from Yorkshire Woollen, entered service from 1 February 1963 mainly on the Huddersfield to Barnsley double deck routes 15/36/55. These seem to have been the first front entrance double deckers used by Yorkshire Traction in Huddersfield. Within a few days of entering service one of these buses had fallen into a twelve feet trench in Southgate, where the inner ring road was under construction, and suffered severe damage. Soon afterwards Leyland Titan PD3A/1s became a common sight on those routes. These 73 seaters were purchased by Yorkshire Traction between 1961 and 1965 and most had distinctive Northern Counties front entrance bodies; their sliding doors were an unusual feature in the Huddersfield area. Front entrance Tiger rebuilds were later used particularly on the 80/80A (Kirkburton) route but could still be seen on Barnsley journeys.

While Yorkshire Traction were still placing rebuilt Leyland Tigers in service, a change in the law permitted the introduction of 36 feet long single deckers. The company would buy many Leyland Leopard buses seating 54 or 53 from 1962 onwards and there were also coaches and dual purpose vehicles, the latter fitted with coach type seats in a bus shell, and later some shorter Leopard service buses. While County Motors at Waterloo used these higher capacity single deckers to replace double deckers on most of their routes, Yorkshire Traction tended to put them on existing single deck services plagued with low bridges to provide more capacity.

During these years there was a general shortage of labour in the Huddersfield area but at the same time

spare female labour in the coalfields around Barnsley. Some employers, such as Brook Motors, ran their own buses to bring in workers. One of the licences obtained by Yorkshire Traction on 1 January 1964 at the takeover of the Pickerill of Low Valley business was an express licence for a "mill girls' service" between Wombwell and the Huddersfield area.

Following a long period during which the route network had been very stable, the second half of the 1960s saw several rounds of service alterations and, with a constant need to make economies, this process has continued ever since. At the end of March 1965 the company obtained permission from the traffic commissioners to make limited reductions in the Kirkburton area. Almost all Sunday journeys on 80/80A (Turnshaw or Highburton or Linfit Lane) were consequently withdrawn. At the same time, however, the whole of the Sunday service on 86/86A (Holmfirth via Shepley) was altered to run as 86A via Roydhouse, providing a replacement for Turnshaw residents.

On 25 June 1966 new Saturday only limited stop route 1 between Huddersfield and Barnsley via Shelley and Denby Dale was introduced, advertised as bringing Huddersfield 20 minutes nearer to Barnsley (compared with route 15). Five round trips were provided every two hours usually using one Barnsley depot single decker (double deckers could be used); running time was

55 minutes each way. The route was similar to the 55 (Barnsley via Cumberworth) but it bypassed Cawthorne and also ran direct between Shelley and Lower Cumberworth (avoiding Skelmanthorpe); as a result the extra Saturday journeys on 55 were withdrawn. The 15 route was speeded up from the same date and allowed 70 minutes for the journey to Barnsley instead of 75 minutes. The new limited stop route 1 was conductor operated like all other Yorkshire Traction bus routes at that time. This situation was, however, about to change as the company's first one man conversion took place in the following month.

Yorkshire Traction were relatively late in introducing pay as you enter buses. Penistone Rural District Council had actually suggested that such buses might at least prevent future fare increases. Although they had a large fleet of single deck service buses, most were required not on account of light passenger loadings but because of the proliferation of very low railway bridges in the Barnsley and Penistone areas, for example on Huddersfield routes 33/33A/68. The first one man conversion took place on 16 July 1966 when routes 19/20 (Barnsley-Manchester via Holmfirth or Penistone), operated jointly with North Western, lost their conductors. The vehicles used at first were Plaxton bodied Tiger Cub coaches and some Tiger Cubs with Alexander bus bodies, equipped with Almex ticket machines. It would be another year before the use of Almex machines spread to other routes. These routes passed through some very sparsely populated areas such as the Parkhead to Greenfield section and miles of open moorland had provided little to occupy the conductor's time.

More rear engined Leyland Atlantean double deckers were placed in service in 1966 and these started to run in Huddersfield on Barnsley routes 15/36/55. This batch of buses (1334-43; 618-27 in the lowheight sequence from the following year when the whole fleet was renumbered and a more contemporary style of fleetname introduced) had very modern looking Northern Counties bodies of two subtly different designs. Vehicles of the same chassis/body combination with yet another bodywork design were to enter service until 1969; there would also be some Daimler Fleetlines of similar external appearance.

From 12 November 1966, recently introduced Saturday limited stop 1 (Huddersfield-Barnsley) was diverted between Shelley and Lower Cumberworth via Skelmanthorpe and Ponker Lane (the 55 route). Presumably experience had shown that there was some

slack in the running time and also spare seats.

From the same date the existing 86 (Huddersfield-Holmfirth via Shelley) service was withdrawn and its journeys were transferred to sister route 86A via Roydhouse, which itself dropped the "A" suffix and became 86. This was at first sight a surprising development, given the very small number of houses served by most of this considerable increase in mileage, but two factors seem to have played a part. Firstly, if Yorkshire Traction were already planning to dispense with the 80/80A (Kirkburton) route, the new 86 provided an alternative regular hourly service for Turnshaw (just as most of the Sunday 80/80A had been replaced by 86A in the previous year). Secondly, the 86 was converted to one man operation soon afterwards. On the withdrawn version of the 86, it was impossible for buses travelling along the main road through Shelley from the Huddersfield direction to make the sharp turn into Far Bank Lane (or to carry out the manoeuvre in the opposite direction) so they had to continue along the main road and turn round by reversing into Flockton Road under the conductor's supervision before approaching the junction from the opposite direction. As buses serving Roydhouse approached Shelley via Flockton Road, there was no need for them to reverse. Longer buses appeared on the 86 in the shape of 53 seater Weymann bodied Leyland Leopards 1319/20 (FHE 319/320D), which were downseated to 45 seaters by the removal of front

seats to make them acceptable to the drivers for one man operation.

After experiments with one man buses by joint operator Sheffield JOC on 68 (Huddersfield-Sheffield) from Tuesday 7 March 1967 (a Sheffield Leyland Leopard working the 3.45pm Sheffield to Huddersfield and return was their first pay as you enter bus), this route too was officially converted to one man operation by the two operators from 2 July 1967. Both undertakings used Leopards; Setright Speed tickets were issued on Sheffield JOC 1015-8 while Yorkshire Traction favoured the Almex ticketing system. From 1 April 1968 the 68 service was extended on a limited stop basis from Huddersfield to Halifax via Elland ; a second route (X68), running limited stop throughout and more directly between Wortley and Sheffield, was introduced. Halifax JOC and Huddersfield JOC became additional joint operators because the extension to Halifax encroached on their territory. On Monday to Saturday the combined 68/X68 provided an hourly frequency between 7.45am and 5.45pm from Huddersfield, falling to two hourly in the evenings. Typically an X68 left Huddersfield at 45 minutes past the even hour and reached Sheffield in only 70 minutes, a valuable saving of 40 minutes in comparison with the 68. Stops were made only at Moldgreen, Waterloo, Spring Grove, Shelley Far Bank, Shepley (Black Bull), Birdsedge, Ingbirchworth, Penistone Church, Oxspring, Thurgoland, Wortley

Wakefield Road, Huddersfield between Green Cross and Aspley is the location of Traction 729 (3282 HE), a Northern Counties bodied Leyland Titan PD3A/1 new in 1964 as fleet no.1282. The photograph dates from the period between the adoption of a new fleet numbering scheme and style of fleet name in April 1967 and the removal of the trolleybus wiring in September 1968. Note the sliding door and the semi-permanent destination display, common on route 80 and others, which shows the two terminal points – the bus is travelling towards Huddersfield. [A.B. Cross]

and Sheffield. All journeys were limited stop between Halifax and Huddersfield. Yorkshire Traction would tend to use Leyland Leopards with Marshall or Alexander 49 seater dual purpose (semi-coach) bodywork on the lengthy 68/X68 although more mundane Leopard buses were regularly seen. Sheffield also continued to send Leopards but rear engined AEC Swifts were also used for a period.

Yorkshire Traction continued to offer excursions from the Huddersfield area (between April and October). For 1968 the Huddersfield pick up point was Pine Street, off Leeds Road and some excursions were also available from Clayton West, Scissett, Skelmanthorpe, Shelley, Kirkburton, Fenay Bridge and Waterloo. As well as the inevitable Blackpool, Blackpool Illuminations (day or half day) and Scarborough, destinations visited less frequently from Huddersfield were not particularly adventurous either, comprising Belle Vue, Bridlington, Castleton, Cleethorpes, Doncaster Races, the Great Yorkshire Show, Harrogate & Knaresborough, Morecambe, Southport, York Races and the Yorkshire Dales.

From 23 November 1968 a package of economy measures was implemented in the Huddersfield area. All journeys on 33/33A (Huddersfield-Penistone-Barnsley) were now one man operated (some journeys had been one man since 8 October 1967). The 33 was also rerouted to run direct between High Flatts and Ingbirchworth in order to save time, omitting Upper Denby, but there was an outcry, even though 33A still served Upper Denby, and from 9 December 1968 it reverted to serving Upper Denby [but soon afterwards, by April 1969, the 33 was permanently removed from Upper Denby!]. The major change, however, was the withdrawal of route 80 (Kirkburton). Linfit Lane was left without any buses but all journeys on 36/55 (Barnsley via Cawthorne) were either diverted to double run to Turnshaw Road from the centre of Kirkburton or rerouted between Dogley Bar and Kirkburton via Highburton and Turnshaw as a replacement. This latter route entailed for the first time the ascent by buses of the steep Far Dene, which seems to have been too much for some of them. The last official route 80 journey had been made by Leyland Atlantean 619 on the 10.35pm from Lord Street the previous day but it was not long before it was found necessary to run untimetabled extras between Lord Street and Kirkburton at busy periods.

6.4: PROUD TO BE PART OF THE NATIONAL BUS COMPANY (1969-74)

Yorkshire Traction had been 100% state owned since March 1968 with the sale of the BET group's UK bus and coach operations. As all the owners of County Motors were now under common ownership, it was decided that Waterloo based County would be absorbed by Yorkshire Traction. From 1 October 1968 Yorkshire Traction took over the management of County and began to repaint the buses in red and cream but with County fleetnames. The buses were also renumbered in the Yorkshire Traction sequences (see County section for details). Apart from four lowbridge Guy Arabs, the County fleet consisted of Leyland buses which fitted in well with Yorkshire Traction's existing stock: Leopards, Tiger Cubs and a pair of PD3A/1 Titans. From 1 January 1969 ownership of County Motors (Lepton) Ltd passed to Yorkshire Traction and the smaller company was immediately absorbed with the rest of the buses quickly repainted. Short term licences were obtained for all routes (see below for details) and Yorkshire Traction became part of the newly created National Bus Company.

Four months before this Norman Turner of Kirkheaton, the long serving Yorkshire Traction Huddersfield Area Superintendent, had retired. Turner had joined Barnsley & District as a driver in 1925 and was later promoted to inspector. During the war he moved to Doncaster but had returned to Huddersfield as Area Superintendent in 1947. Thus former County manager Eric Green became the company's new Huddersfield Area Superintendent,

responsible for operations from both St Andrew's Road and Waterloo (Penistone Road). Buses from the existing Yorkshire Traction fleet soon appeared at Waterloo, initially 54 seater Leopard/Willowbrook single deckers 302/6 of 1962 vintage deputising for former County stock sent away for repainting, while older Tiger Cubs and Guy Arabs moved away from Waterloo.

Extra journeys were run to Emley on Saturday 1 February 1969 on the occasion of an amateur cup tie between Emley football club and Barking. The special buses comprised single deckers Leopard 396 (ex-County) and Tiger Cub 506 and double deckers Guy Arabs 685/6 (ex-County) and Leyland Titan 724. Roads in the Emley area were blocked by snow from 13 March 1969 so that the ex-County Barnsley bus services had to be rerouted until the 18th and even then the roads were still treacherous. Worse was to follow on the following day when, owing to the weight of ice on its structure, the 1264 feet ITV mast at Emley Moor came crashing to the ground at 5.00pm.

From 12 April 1969 numbers were allocated to the former County routes as follows:

31 Barnsley via Highgate Lane, Emley, Flockton, Midgley and Haigh

32 Barnsley via Highgate Lane, Grange Moor Chapel, Flockton, Emley and Haigh

48 Grange Moor Chapel via Lepton (Saturday only)

61 Wakefield via Kirkburton, Scissett, West Bretton and Great Cliff

62 Dewsbury via Kirkheaton, Upper Hopton and Mirfield

63 Wakefield via Lepton, Flockton, Overton and

Traction 397 (GVH 213D) is a 1966 Marshall bodied Leyland Leopard recently transferred from County when photographed in Dewsbury Bus Station still on an ex-County route on 22 March 1969. The County Motors name has been removed from the aperture to the right of the destination blinds but the vehicle is not yet able to display route numbers, which were only introduced on the former County routes in April 1969. [R. Marshall]

Horbury

These routes were hourly (31/2 combined were hourly and 62 was half hourly at times) and ran all day daily (except for 48). The 63 was worked by the Leyland Titan PD3A/1s but all other duties could be covered by single deckers and some of these had latterly been one man operated off peak. Highbridge buses could not be used on the 62 because of a low bridge in Mirfield and double deckers were prohibited altogether on the 61 on account of an even lower bridge encountered between Great Cliff and Calder Grove on a new section of route introduced in the previous December.

From the same date 33A (Barnsley via Denby Dale and Penistone) was renumbered 34 and some of the journeys on 36 recently rerouted to double run in Kirkburton to Turnshaw ceased to do so as it had been realised that there were buses on 86 at similar times.

From 1 October 1969, as part of the deal which saw Huddersfield Corporation absorb the Joint Omnibus Committee by acquiring the National Bus Company's share, the JOC's share of the Huddersfield-Bradley-Dewsbury routes passed to local NBC company Yorkshire Traction. Thus the two NBC subsidiaries Yorkshire Traction and Yorkshire Woollen now shared the double deck operation of the 26 via Stocks Bank Road, Nab Lane and Savile Arms and 27 direct via the main road. The first Yorkshire Traction bus to run on these routes was Daimler Fleetline 643 and they were operated from the former County depot at Waterloo. In order to distinguish the 26/7 from existing Yorkshire Traction routes in the Barnsley area already using those numbers, the Huddersfield area services were shown as H26/7 in some publicity but the "H" prefix was never shown on buses. At the same time Yorkshire Traction also took over Huddersfield JOC's tiny share in 68/X68 (Halifax-Sheffield). Sheffield JOC also ceased to exist after 31 December 1969. From the next day Sheffield Transport Department followed Huddersfield's lead and absorbed the JOC "B" fleet plus part of the "C" fleet operations, including their share of the 68/X68 services.

On 8 August 1970 the company extended the use of one man operation considerably. One man single deckers were introduced on 1 (Barnsley, limited stop), 31/2 (Barnsley via Emley) and 48 (Grange Moor Chapel). Double deck routes 36/55 (Barnsley via Cawthorne) were also converted to one man, using a mixture of single and double deckers, the latter the first to be used in this way in Huddersfield by Yorkshire Traction. Former County routes 31/2 had already seen some one

Above- With Leyland Leopard/ Marshall dual-purpose saloons such as 216 (JHE 516E) new in 1967, Yorkshire Traction regularly offered passengers a luxurious ride to Sheffield. On the X68, limited stop throughout, the Lord Street to Sheffield section took a mere 65 minutes; the 68 was much slower at 106 minutes. 216 in Lord Street on 21 November 1969 wears the much missed predominantly cream semi-coach livery of the period. [H.J. Black]

Centre- Yorkshire Traction 746 (AVH 636B), one of the pair of ex-County Roe bodied Leyland Titans, picks up at the Amby Place timing point in Flockton on the Huddersfield-Wakefield route for which they were obtained. The destination display has not yet been modified to show a route number. [S.T. Harling collection]

Bottom-1962 Leyland Titan PD3A/ Northern Counties 717 (XHE 224), originally no. 1224, was typical of Traction buses used on the former Huddersfield J.O.C. share of the Huddersfield-Bradley-Dewsbury routes (26/7), joint with Yorkshire Woollen, from October 1969. Standing at the terminus in the original Dewsbury Bus Station, it exhorts passengers to go by coach to "lively London". [D.F. Parker]

man working at quiet times. The first one man bus used on each route is shown below (plus, in brackets, the last crew operated bus, where known)

Route 1: short Leopard 509 (Titan 743)
Route 31: Leopard 394 (Tiger Cub 595)
Route 36: Tiger Cub 507
Route 32: Leopard 325 (Tiger Cub 595)
Route 55: Atlantean 648 (Titan 724)
Route 48: Tiger Cub 594

From the same date the Sunday service on 33 (Barnsley via High Flatts and Penistone) was withdrawn.

On Friday 25 September 1970 industrial action was taken in support of a union pay claim for a minimum wage of £20 per week and no services at all were operated from the Huddersfield depots. It was reported that over 700 pupils were absent from Penistone Grammar School alone because of the strike while David Brown's at Penistone ran a shuttle service of their own lorries to bring in the workers. The one day strike was repeated the following Friday and a dozen pickets from St Andrew's Road depot made a vain attempt to prevent a Huddersfield Corporation bus from leaving Lord Street for Lepton. They were angry because Corporation buses were crossing what they claimed was the boundary at Waterloo into their territory and only after police intervention was the bus able to leave. A spokesman later accused the Corporation of "blacklegging" over parts of the Kirkheaton and Lepton routes.

West Riding withdrew Monday to Friday evening and Sunday services from their 86/7 (Huddersfield-Wakefield) routes from 8 March 1971 and, as a temporary measure pending widespread changes to the Yorkshire Traction route network, a few journeys on 63 (Wakefield via Overton) in those periods were diverted via Netherton instead of Overton to replace the 87 (West Riding 86 was identical to the standard version of the 63).

In April or May 1971 the St Andrew's Road depot was closed with all Huddersfield operations from now on based at Waterloo, where more use had to be made of outside parking in the depot yard.

NBC cousin Yorkshire Woollen made substantial changes to the whole of their route network from 14 August 1971 and alterations affecting Huddersfield are shown in detail in the Yorkshire Woollen section. To summarise, Yorkshire Traction acquired a greater presence on Leeds Road, becoming joint operators with Yorkshire Woollen on the following routes:

1 to 3 Huddersfield-Dewsbury-Leeds

Sheffield 51 (DWB 51H) was an AEC Swift/Park Royal ordered for Sheffield Joint Omnibus Committee but delivered to the Corporation in 1970 after the JOC's dissolution. 51 featured a 5-speed gearbox for motorway operation. Returning home on slower route 68, it displays its contemporary fleetname style in Lord Street on 16 September the same year. [H.J. Black]

21 Huddersfield-Mirfield-Heckmondwike-Batley-Birstall-Leeds
60 Huddersfield-Cleckheaton-Bradford

1-3 replaced the 26/7 (Huddersfield-Dewsbury) routes of which Yorkshire Traction had inherited Huddersfield Joint Omnibus Committee's share two years earlier. 1-3/21 were interworked using one man double deckers while one man single deckers appeared on the 60. As with the 26/7 before them, 1-3/21 were shown in publicity only with an "H" prefix as H1-3/21 to distinguish them from Mexborough or Barnsley area

routes with the same numbers. For subsequent changes on these routes, see under Yorkshire Woollen.

As if all this were not enough, increasing costs and falling passenger numbers resulted in a major reorganisation in the western part of Yorkshire Traction's own territory, implemented on 4 September 1971, also involving West Riding. Reduced frequencies were the order of the day but careful timetable adjustments together with some new routes ensured that most villages continued to be served at least once an hour. New facilities were provided for some villages by extra

New in 1963 as County 104 and taken over in 1969, Traction 392 (YCX 539), a Willowbrook bodied Leyland Leopard, is still running into Lord Street, Huddersfield but on an old established Traction route from Barnsley via Penistone. 392 can now display route numbers and has been fitted with a YTC style "pay as you enter" sign below the windscreen. [D.F. Parker]

connections and the use of through transfer tickets. Where through fares were available, passengers had to retain both their ticket and a yellow transfer slip to be collected by the driver of the second bus boarded. The remaining Huddersfield area conductor operated services were converted to one man operation from this date with the exception of 15 (Barnsley via Clayton West) and 63 (Wakefield via Flockton), on which traditional front engined Leyland Titan double deckers could still be seen.

Route 36 (Barnsley via Scissett and Cawthorne) was halved in frequency to run every two hours, with all journeys double running via Turnshaw but none via Highburton, which appears to have been left unserved for several months. Route 55, the infrequent variant of 36 (via Lower Cumberworth instead of Scissett) was withdrawn. Former County 61 (Wakefield via Kirkburton and Scissett), which was now one man operated, was also halved in frequency to every two hours. The 61 reverted to the pre-December 1968 County Motors route to run direct between West Bretton and Calder Grove, omitting Great Cliff and the very low bridge; this allowed double deckers to be used once again. Between Huddersfield and Scissett the timings of routes 15/36/61 were coordinated to give a roughly 30 minutes frequency and 36/61 became interworked, using double (and some single) deckers from Huddersfield (2 buses) and Barnsley (1 bus) depots.

The long established combined hourly service to Barnsley via Penistone on 33/4 was also halved to two hourly as the 33 was withdrawn between Huddersfield and Penistone. The 34 was diverted between Upper Cumberworth and Denby Dale via Lower Cumberworth (as a replacement for the 55), between Upper Denby and Ingbirchworth via Denby Lane (instead of Falledge Lane; to replace the 33) and on Sundays via Green Road in Penistone.

Former County route 32 (Barnsley via Grange Moor and Emley) was withdrawn while 31 (Barnsley via Emley and Midgley) was reduced to a two hourly frequency; at the same time West Riding 86/7 (Wakefield) were withdrawn. Out of the ashes came new Yorkshire Traction 64 running every two hours Monday to Saturday only between Huddersfield and Wakefield, which followed 31 as far as Flockton via Emley, then replacing the former West Riding 87 through Midgley, Netherton and Horbury. The introduction of the 64 also allowed the 63 (Wakefield via Flockton) evening and Sunday journeys temporarily diverted via Netherton to revert to the standard route through Overton, although

64 did not operate on Sundays. There was a combined hourly frequency on 31/64 to Flockton via Emley on Monday to Saturday.

Previously former County services 31/2 and 61 connected in both directions every hour at Bretton Cross Roads; 31 and 61 would now connect only every two hours. New connections were, however, also advertised at Midgley between 31, the new 64 and the 109 (Barnsley-Dewsbury) service; the 109 was also included in the much publicised Bretton connections.
Odd hour connections at Bretton:
31 from Huddersfield to Barnsley at 20 mins past
61 from Huddersfield to Wakefield at 20 mins past
109 from Barnsley to Dewsbury at 20 mins past
Odd hour connections at Midgley:
31 from Huddersfield to Barnsley at 18 mins past
64 from Wakefield to Huddersfield at 22 mins past
109 from Barnsley to Dewsbury at 22 mins past
Even hour connections at Bretton:
31 from Barnsley to Huddersfield at 20 mins past
61 from Wakefield to Huddersfield at 22 mins past
109 from Dewsbury to Barnsley at 22 mins past
Even hour connections at Midgley:
109 from Dewsbury to Barnsley at 18 mins past
31 from Barnsley to Huddersfield at 22 mins past
64 from Huddersfield to Wakefield at 22 mins past

Also withdrawn was service 38 (Holmfirth-Scissett-Clayton West-Barnsley). It was partly replaced by a new more direct one man single deck route 58 (Holmfirth-Denby Dale-Cawthorne-Barnsley), also running every two hours. The 58 followed the old 38 route as far as Denby Dale, after which buses ran via Miller Hill and the 36 route via Cawthorne into Barnsley, compensating for the reduced frequency on the 36.

The 62 (Huddersfield-Kirkheaton-Dewsbury) route, which was now one man operated, lost its Wednesday (market day) Hopton-Dewsbury shorts. A further change was the renumbering of Saturday only limited stop 1 (Huddersfield-Barnsley) which became 101 to avoid confusion with the recently introduced route 1 (Huddersfield-Dewsbury-Leeds).

From 27 September 1971 the existing Barnsley-Manchester routes, 19 via Holmfirth and 20 via Penistone, were withdrawn and replaced by new limited stop 19 (Barnsley-Penistone-Holmfirth-Manchester) branded as the Pennine Rose Express. Although this was still advertised as jointly operated with North Western, in practice all journeys were usually operated by Yorkshire Traction, using 49 seater dual purpose (semi-coach)

Leyland Leopards. From Barnsley the former 20 route was followed as far as Penistone, after which the service ran direct via Ingbirchworth to the Sovereign Cross Roads; beyond the Sovereign the old 19 route through Holmfirth to Manchester was used except for a diversion between Ashton-under-Lyne and Manchester via Denton and Hyde Road to serve the Belle Vue entertainment centre. For the first time special cheap day returns to Manchester (and Belle Vue) were available from Barnsley, Penistone and Holmfirth. There were just three return trips from Monday to Thursday but this was increased to four on Friday and Sunday and six on Saturdays. The route was later referred to as X19.

Services operating in the area from 27 September 1971 were as follows; Monday to Saturday daytime frequencies are shown:
1 to 3 Huddersfield-Dewsbury-Leeds [every 20 mins, combined]
15 Huddersfield-Scissett-Clayton West-Staincross-Barnsley [hourly]
19 Barnsley-Penistone-Holmfirth-Greenfield-Manchester, limited stop [infrequent]
21 Huddersfield-Heckmondwike-Batley-Leeds [hourly]
31 Huddersfield-Emley-Flockton-West Bretton-Barnsley [every 2 hours]
34 Huddersfield-Denby Dale-Penistone-Barnsley [every 2 hours]
36 Huddersfield-Turnshaw-Scissett-Cawthorne-Barnsley [every 2 hours]
48 Huddersfield-Grange Moor Chapel [Saturday only; hourly]
58 Holmfirth-Denby Dale-Cawthorne-Barnsley [every 2 hours]
60 Huddersfield-Cleckheaton-Bradford [hourly]
61 Huddersfield-Scissett-West Bretton-Wakefield [every 2 hours].
62 Huddersfield-Kirkheaton-Hopton-Mirfield-Dewsbury [hourly; every 30 mins Saturday]
63 Huddersfield-Flockton-Overton-Wakefield [hourly]
64 Huddersfield-Emley-Flockton-Midgley-Netherton-Wakefield [every 2 hours]
68/X68 Halifax-Huddersfield-High Flatts-Penistone-Sheffield [hourly, combined]
86 Huddersfield-Turnshaw-Roydhouse-Shelley-Shepley-Holmfirth [every 2 hours]
101 Huddersfield-Lower Cumberworth-Denby Dale-Barnsley, limited stop [Sat; every 2 hours]
Routes 1-3/21/60 were jointly operated with Yorkshire Woollen; route 19 was notionally joint with North

Western; 68/X68 were jointly operated with Sheffield Transport and Calderdale Joint Omnibus Committee, as Halifax JOC had been renamed. Barnsley depot ran services 19/58/101 while 15/34/6/61 were provided by both Barnsley and Huddersfield. All the other routes listed were run by Huddersfield depot including the 31. Another service operated from Waterloo since the Yorkshire Woollen changes of 14 August was one man single deck 59 (Dewsbury-Three Nuns-Brighouse-Elland-Rastrick), a new Yorkshire Traction route running in the Dewsbury company's territory which had replaced various Yorkshire Woollen services.

To restore a service to Highburton, further changes had to be made from 22 January 1972. Certain journeys (daily except Saturday) on 36 (Barnsley via Cawthorne) were once again diverted via Highburton instead of Spring Grove, as were a few trips on 61 (Wakefield via Scissett), and on Saturdays only new circular services were started. One extra one man single decker was used to operate an eight hour shift, running alternately on the new Kirkburton circulars 80 and 80A (each route every two hours):
80 Lord Street-Penistone Road-Dogley Bar-Spring Grove-Kirkburton-Turnshaw-Highburton-Far Dene-Dogley Bar-Penistone Road-Lord Street
80A as 80 but running in the opposite (clockwise) direction beyond Dogley Bar
The 61 was also once again diverted via Great Cliff but this time only on Sundays (when West Riding 84 did not operate); this meant that all journeys on 36/61 had to be single deck on Sundays.

From 21 October 1972 route 58 (Holmfirth-Cawthorne-Barnsley) was renumbered 83. On Monday to Saturday a double run from Denby Dale to Scissett, where buses turned in a loop via Highbridge Lane and Busker Lane, was introduced to offer a connection with 61 (Huddersfield-Scissett-Wakefield). As this considerably increased the running time, for operational reasons the route became interworked with the long established West Riding 84 (Holmfirth-Wakefield) service. Two West Riding buses from Wakefield and one Yorkshire Traction vehicle from Barnsley were needed for the jointly operated 83/4. The Sunday timetable and route of 83 was unchanged; 84 did not run on Sundays.

1972 was the last year in which Yorkshire Traction maintained what might be termed their traditional look. The vehicles allocated to Huddersfield depot on 15 July 1972 are listed in section 6.9 and were the usual Leylands, apart from a pair of Daimler Fleetlines with

When Traction 479 (SHE 151), a Metro-Cammell bodied Leyland Tiger Cub new in 1960 as no.1163 and withdrawn in 1972, was photographed near the Kirkgate end of Lord Street late in its career, the 33/4 (Huddersfield-Penistone-Barnsley) routes had been temporarily relocated to share the Holmfirth via Shepley (86) stand. [D.F. Parker]

Leaving Stand E in Lord Street, Huddersfield, 527 (WHE 527J), one of the shorter (45 seats) Leyland Leopard service buses with Willowbrook body bought by Traction in 1971, typifies the style of the company just before the drab and tasteless "image" of the National Bus Company was inflicted upon it late in 1972. The 86 route to Holmfirth was an extremely indirect hour's ride via Kirkburton, Roydhouse and Shepley. [A.J. Douglas]

Alexander dual doorway (front entrance, centre exit) single deck bodies designed to carry large numbers of standees. These were unsuitable for Huddersfield depot's routes and were more commonly found on urban and interurban routes around Barnsley and Rawmarsh. The short and long Marshall bodied Leyland Leopards which entered service in 1972 were the last in a long line of service buses from the Leyland "zoo", although Leopard coaches and dual purpose vehicles would continue to enter service. All these vehicles, however, would wear the new National Bus Company poppy red and white colours, introduced to the press on a Leopard bus in September 1972, which looked insipid alongside the traditional red and cream soon to be removed from the existing fleet. 1973 saw standard NBC buses delivered in the shape of Leyland National single deckers (soon in use on 83/4) and Bristol VRT double deckers. Three of the first batch of Bristol VRTs entered service at Waterloo early in the year.

From February 1974 Saturday only Kirkburton circulars 80/80A were upgraded to operate Monday to Saturday with early morning journeys. Two Monday to Friday variant routes which restored a bus service to Linfit Lane were added and this time the company had no qualms about running through to Linfit Lane Top and beyond:

80B Lord Street-Lepton-Paul Lane-Linfit Lane-Highburton-Far Dene-Dogley Bar-Penistone Road-Lord Street
80C as 80B but running in the opposite (anticlockwise) direction beyond Waterloo

The entirely limited stop X68 version of the Halifax-Huddersfield-Sheffield service was withdrawn on 3 March 1974 by joint operators Yorkshire Traction,

Sheffield and Calderdale JOC. The 68 version was increased in frequency to run every 90 minutes and diverted between Elland and Ainley Top via Blackley and between High Flatts and Ingbirchworth via Upper Denby.

With local government reorganisation in April 1974 all Yorkshire Traction's operations fell within new metropolitan counties with Passenger Transport Executives. As this change fundamentally affected the planning and operation of services in what had become West Yorkshire and South Yorkshire, it is an appropriate point at which to bring the story to a close.

6.5: TICKETING

Until 1929 Barnsley and District Traction used Bell Punch tickets; they measured 2.5 by 1.25 inches and had the value overprinted in large red figures. Initially they were printed only with stages 1 to 10. Values and colours known for single tickets include: 1½ d beige; 2d yellow; 3d grey; 4d pale yellow; 5d green; 6d light brown; 8d salmon; 9d mauve; 10d green and 2/7d cream.

From 1929 composite tickets measuring 3.5 by 1.25 inches with tear off perforated tabs came into use. They carried the new title "The Yorkshire Traction Co Ltd." in the central panel. Stages 1 to 20 were now used and values and colours known included: 1d blue; 1½ d stone; 2d yellow; 2½ d salmon; 3d pink; 4d pale green; 5d sage; 6d beige; 7d yellow; 8d orange; 9d buff; 10d grey (also plum); 1/- stone; 1/2d white; 1/3d grey; 1/3½ d (child) white (short length); 1/4d magenta; 1/6d white; 1/9d steel blue; 2/- mauve; 2/3d salmon; 2/7d beige; 2/10d orange; 3/6d dark fawn; 4/3d yellow and 5/6d sepia. Tickets in this series overprinted YTC in large

red letters are believed to have been for use by Sheffield JOC conductors on the joint routes from Sheffield to Huddersfield, Bradford and Leeds.

Until 1951 the following fares applied from Huddersfield. Very cheap workmen and special ordinary returns existed for certain journeys.

	Single	Workmen ret.	Special ret.
Kirkburton	5d	6d	8d
Skelmanthorpe	10d	10d	
Penistone	1/2d	1/6d	
Denby Dale	1/-	1/3d	1/6d.
Cawthorne	1/7d		
Barnsley	1/11d		2/6d
Sheffield	2/7d		4/4d
Cumberworth	11d		1/3d
Shepley	8d	9d	
Shelley	7d	8d	

When Bell Punch tickets fell from favour they were gradually replaced by the Willebrew system, with tickets printed by Williamson of Ashton under Lyne from October 1934. Single tickets were white with fares from ½ d to 9d on one side and from 10d to 2/- on the other side. This was adequate for all but the Sheffield route from Huddersfield. For use on longer routes another white ticket showed fares from ½ d to 1/1d on one side. The other side was printed in 1d increments from 1/2d to 2/- then in 3d increments to 3/9d. There were at least two colours for return tickets. A salmon ticket covered values up to 2/6d; values up to 5/- were printed on a mauve ticket. In turn the Willebrew system was replaced by TIM machines and later by Almex, particularly for one man operation.

6.6: PROGRESS MOTORS AND THE BLACKPOOL POOL SERVICES

William Armitage was born in Huddersfield but moved to Blackpool in 1913. He opened a garage in Dickson Road and started running a Commer charabanc named "The Progress". After the war the business expanded and, probably during 1924, the coaching operations were split off to be run by William's sons CB and J Armitage, using the fleet name "Progress Motors".

During the period 1924-32 some 21 coaches were purchased, including 14 Albions and 5 AEC Regals. It is thought that this was facilitated by a cash investment from Josiah Olivant Mann, a Bradford based road haulier who became an additional partner and general manager. Livery was dark blue with 'Progress' in gold script on the sides and route branding over the windows on a typical coach read "Blackpool-Huddersfield-Dewsbury-Bradford-Leeds". The Burlingham bodied AEC Regals of 1931 (FV 1685-8) carried the words "Yorkshire Express" and "Limited Stop" on their roof luggage pods.

On Saturday 1 November 1924 one of the first weekend excursions to "Yorkshire" left Blackpool at 9.15am. The route was via Burnley, Todmorden, Hebden Bridge, Halifax, Huddersfield and Bradford to Leeds, the return fare to Huddersfield was 9/- and the return journey was to be made on the Tuesday afternoon. One might wonder what became of the coach and driver while the passengers were enjoying their weekend break in Yorkshire. In fact the coach picked up a second party from the Leeds area and took them for a weekend in Blackpool, returning on the Tuesday morning. The advertising for the Yorkshire passengers may well have been handled by Wilks' Garage in Leeds. These weekend excursions proved popular as by Saturday 3 October 1925 an additional route was in operation via Bolton, Manchester, Oldham and Huddersfield but this had ceased by May 1926.

For the first week of July 1926 a daily service was operated to the Yorkshire towns, leaving Blackpool at 9.00am and returning in the afternoon. This, however, proved too ambitious and the service was reduced to operate on Monday, Wednesday, Friday and Saturday only for the rest of the summer season. Operation was then continued for the winter on Wednesday and Saturday only.

Summer service was improved for 1927 and from 12 June departures from Huddersfield were:
Monday, 8.00am & 4.00pm

FV 1687, one of four AEC Regal/Burlingham coaches new to Progress Motors (W. Armitage & Sons Ltd) in March 1931, has its indicator set to Huddersfield and is lettered "Blackpool Huddersfield Dewsbury Bradford & Leeds" and "Yorkshire Express". The vehicle is not, however, on a Blackpool to Huddersfield working. It is parked outside the 17th century Whoop Hall Inn, a mile or so south east of Kirkby Lonsdale on the A65, the road used by many operators' coaches between Huddersfield and the Lake District. The name Progress was derived from Blackpool's motto. [R. Marshall collection]

Wednesday and Friday, 4.00pm
Saturday, 8.00am, 3.00pm & 6.00pm
Sunday, 8.00am.
On Tuesdays and Thursdays a service was provided by the Blackpool firm of Walker Taylor and Sons, who traded as Pride of the Road, while on Saturdays both firms ran in competition. Tickets could be booked in advance from Longley's the confectioners at 27 John William Street, Huddersfield.

Progress excursions were operated daily at 1.30pm from Huddersfield to the illuminations during September and October. The fare of 7/- included a hot supper and a drive through the illuminations which were said to feature a quarter of a million coloured lights. Following a 10.00pm departure from Blackpool, passengers were dropped off as near to their homes as possible.

The "Progress Motor Station", situated on the west side of Venn Street, was opened on 19 May 1928. At least two coaches could now be stabled overnight in Huddersfield and these were used for day excursions to Windermere on Whit Sunday and Scarborough on Whit Monday. A daily Blackpool summer service started on 1

June; in October the daily 8.00am coach was extended to serve Cleveleys and Fleetwood. Further competition was provided from 24 September 1928 by a third Blackpool operator, Wood Bros. trading as John Bull.

The Huddersfield Watch Committee had refused to license the Progress Blackpool service in July 1928. Two years later a Ministry of Transport inquiry held in Leeds investigated the reasons for the continued refusal by both the Leeds and Huddersfield authorities to licence the services. The Huddersfield town clerk, Mr Procter, suggested that with a Road Traffic Bill before Parliament it was not an appropriate time to grant new licences.

Meanwhile Monday 29 July 1929 saw the start of a new daily service operated by Yorkshire Traction from Doncaster via Barnsley and Huddersfield to Blackpool. The departure time from Lord Street, Huddersfield was 10.00am with the Coliseum bus station reached at 1.30pm. The coach's return journey from Blackpool initially started at 4.00pm but was soon retimed to 3.30pm. Other competitors on the road to Blackpool were Hansons, whose full story will be told elsewhere, and Bullocks (B & S) of Featherstone. Their service from Wakefield and Ossett called in Huddersfield at

BOOKING OFFICES.

HEAD OFFICE: Walker Taylor & Sons, Clarence Garage, Albert Road, Blackpool. Tel. 1618.

JUBILEE GARAGE, Lytham Rd., B'pool. Tel. S.S. 41620.

NEWMAN'S, Eclipse Garage, Bloomfield Road, Blackpool. Tel. 1802.

KILBURN'S, Waterloo Road (opp. Waterloo Hotel). Tel. S.S. 41450.

DUNES HOTEL Petrol Station, Blackpool. Tel. S.S. 42382.

ST. ANNES: Moore's, St. Albans Road. Tel. 1013.

LYTHAM: Parkinson's, 44, Clifton Street. Tel. 113.

LEEDS: St. Ann's Service Depot, 14, St. Ann's Street (off Cookridge Street). Tel. 28746.

BRADFORD: Mortimer, 26, Brook Street, Bradford. Tel. 598. 221, High Street, Wibsey. Tel. 169 Low Moor.

BRIGHOUSE: Rider, 7, Houghton Street. Tel. 490.

HUDDERSFIELD: Lion Cafe (opp. St. Georges Square). Tel. 2127.

ELLAND: Mitchell, 54, Huddersfield Road. Tel. 487.

HALIFAX: Scott's Garage, Powell Street. Tel. 2169.

TODMORDEN: Marshall, 7, Halifax Road.

PRESTON: Sergeant's, 245, Fylde Road.

Fares and Times are subject to alteration. While everything possible will be done to adhere to these times, we do not hold ourselves responsible for delays, etc., and we reserve to ourselves the right to alter time of departure or cancel same.

If any person is not carried by any reason whatsoever no liability will be accepted by us or any of our Agents, beyond the fare returned. Should Passengers arrive late at the Starting Point, no liability whatever can be entertained.

Luggage will be taken free but the Proprietors do not accept any responsibility for loss or damage to same. All luggage to be labelled. Prams not allowed.

Any Passenger not giving the time and date for the return journey when they book, must give 24 hours' notice at the Head Office.

Passengers can only be picked up at our recognised starting places.

Children paying half-fare are not guaranteed a seat until all adults are seated.

Dogs will be charged for.

Pride of the Road
LUXURY COACHES
BLACKPOOL & YORKSHIRE.

TIME TABLE.   June 1st to September 30th, 1931

DIRECT SERVICE to Halifax, Bradford and Leeds.

DIRECT SERVICE to Halifax, Elland, Huddersfield and Brighouse.

Burnley, Todmorden, Hebden Bridge, Halifax, Elland, Huddersfield, Brighouse, Bradford and Leeds.

With connections to Harrogate, York, Darlington, Middlesbrough, Newcastle, Sheffield, Barnsley, Wakefield, Doncaster and other Yorkshire Towns.

TIME TABLE OVERLEAF.

Walker Taylor & Sons

Clarence Garage, Albert Road, B'pool. Tel. 1618.

BLACKPOOL TO YORKSHIRE.

With Connections to All Yorkshire Towns.

DAILY SERVICE.

	a.m.	p.m.	p.m.
BLACKPOOL Clarence Garage.	9-0	2-0	6-0
ST. ANNES Ashton Gardens.	9-10	2-10	6-10
LYTHAM Parkinson's, Clifton Street.	9-20	2-20	6-20
BURNLEY Mitre Hotel.	10-50	3-50	7-50
TODMORDEN Town Hall.	11-15	4-15	8-15
HEBDEN BRIDGE Tram Terminus.	11-30	4-30	8-30
HALIFAX Harrison Road.	11-45	4-45	8-45
ELLAND Town Hall.	12-0	5-0	9-0
HUDDERSFIED St. Georges Square.	12-15	5-15	9-15
BRIGHOUSE Royal Hotel.	12-30	5-30	9-30
BRADFORD Chester Street.	12-15	5-15	9-15
LEEDS 14, St. Ann's Street, off Cookridge Street.	12-45	5-45	9-45

FARES:

	Single	Ret.	Day Trip		Single	Ret.	Day Trip
Burnley	4/-	6/-	5/-	Elland	6/-	10/-	8/-
Todmorden	5/-	7/-	6/-	Huddersfield	6/-	11/-	8/-
Hebden B.	6/-	8/-	7/-	Brighouse	6/-	11/-	8/-
Halifax	6/-	10/-	8/-	Bradford	6/6	11/-	9/-
				Leeds	7/-	11/-	9/-

YORKSHIRE TO BLACKPOOL.

DAILY SERVICE.

DAILY Except Saturday.				Saturdays.		
	a.m.	p.m.	p.m.	a.m.	p.m.	p.m.
LEEDS 14, St. Ann's Street, off Cookridge Street.	8-0	1-15	6-0	7-0	1-45	6-0
BRADFORD Chester Street.	8-30	1-45	6-30	7-30	2-15	6-30
BRIGHOUSE Royal Hotel.	8-15	1-30	—	7-15	2-0	—
HUDD'FLD St. Georges Square.	8-30	1-45	—	7-30	2-15	—
ELLAND Town Hall.	8-45	2-0	—	7-45	2-30	—
HALIFAX Harrison Road.	9-0	2-15	7-0	8-0	2-45	7-0
HEBDEN BRIDGE Tram Terminus.	9-15	2-30	7-15	8-15	3-0	7-15
TODMORDEN Town Hall.	9-30	2-45	7-30	8-30	3-15	7-30
BURNLEY Mitre Hotel.	9-55	3-10	7-55	8-55	3-40	7-55
BLACKPOOL Clarence Garage.	11-45	5-0	9-45	10-45	5-30	9-45

HEAD OFFICE:

Walker Taylor & Sons

ALBERT ROAD, BLACKPOOL.   'PHONE 1618.

PRIDE OF THE ROAD COACHES.

9.30am.

The Progress bus which left Huddersfield at 4.00pm on 30 October 1930 with seventeen passengers and a conductor on board was involved in a serious accident. Approaching the Halfpenny Bridge over the River Ribble near Preston, the bus mounted the kerb and knocked down a telegraph pole before crashing head on into the stone parapet. It finally came to rest with a front wheel hanging over a 20 feet drop into the river below. Such was the force of the impact that the man sitting immediately behind the driver was killed and five other passengers were injured.

Under the new licensing system, early in 1931 the three Blackpool operators lodged an application to the North Western Area Traffic Commissioners to continue their Yorkshire express services as before and this was duly granted. Unfortunately the Yorkshire Area commissioners refused to give the required backing to the application. They were of the opinion that as most of the traffic originated in Yorkshire it should be carried by Yorkshire operators. Following an appeal to the Minister of Transport in September 1932, the decision of the Yorkshire commissioners was upheld. Meanwhile the Armitages sought new day excursion licences from Huddersfield in an attempt to recoup the anticipated loss of revenue from their Yorkshire express services but because of the number of objectors this application was withdrawn before the scheduled hearing.

In April 1933 the three Blackpool operators agreed to pool their services with a proposed saving of 30% in the annual mileage; receipts were to be shared on an agreed basis. The pool arrangement proved acceptable to the traffic commissioners in both areas but, almost before the ink was dry, Wood Bros. offered their business for sale - with the Ribble company being the likely purchaser. As a result of this the two remaining partners themselves entered into negotiations with Ribble, who already operated Yorkshire-Blackpool services jointly with West Yorkshire Road Car. Ribble, acting jointly for themselves, West Yorkshire, Yorkshire Woollen and Yorkshire Traction, agreed to a total price of £24,200 (the Armitage share being £10,700) for the purchase of the Armitage and Walker Taylor businesses, backdated to 15 April 1933.

During 1933-34 the two Blackpool firms operated as subsidiaries to the consortium of large company operators. As far as Huddersfield travellers were concerned, the 10.00am (8.00am ex Doncaster) departure continued to be operated by Yorkshire Traction together

Hebble 196 (PCP 804), an Alexander bodied AEC Reliance service bus new in 1962, is masquerading as an express coach while negotiating Shorehead roundabout, Huddersfield. It is en route from Barnsley to Blackpool on a Yorkshire-Blackpool pool working. [W.J. Haynes]

commissioners for both areas agreed to a reduced pool of joint operators for the Yorkshire-Blackpool services in the winter timetable of 1935. The two Blackpool firms, Progress (Armitages) and Pride of the Road (Walker Taylor), were excluded and their licences withdrawn; as a result they ceased trading. The percentage shareholdings of the pool members were Ribble 28%, Hebble 9%, West Yorkshire 28%, Yorkshire Traction 23% and Yorkshire Woollen 11%. The various routes into Yorkshire were given numbers in the sequence J1 to J14; originally Huddersfield was served by J2/5/7/11.

Following the outbreak of war in September 1939 services were at first drastically pruned and ran Friday to Monday only. They were suspended completely in 1941 and did not restart until Easter 1946 (two daily journeys from Huddersfield from 18 April). The former Progress Garage in Venn Street, Huddersfield was in use during the war as an emergency ambulance station by Civil Defence.

Gradually over the years the routes and numbers of the daily Blackpool services changed. By the 1950s the through services from Huddersfield were J7/12/14. The J14 ran via Brighouse and Elland in winter, when it was also jointly operated by Hansons and West Riding; that Wakefield based concern had inherited their share by taking over Bullocks (B & S) of Featherstone in 1950.

In certain periods express services picked up and set down in Lord Street, Huddersfield. Yorkshire Traction 110 (OHE 721), a 1959 Leyland Tiger Cub/Plaxton coach which had been numbered 1148 until 1967 and was in use until 1970, is on the Blackpool service in the late 1960s, followed by a Hebble AEC Reliance/ Alexander coach. [P.J. Cardno collection]

with the corresponding return at 3.30pm from Blackpool. All other timings between Huddersfield and Blackpool were operated by Progress or Pride of the Road with connecting services between Huddersfield and Doncaster provided by Yorkshire Traction. Passengers at Blackpool had to be aware that Yorkshire Traction buses used the Coliseum bus station whereas Progress and Pride of the Road used the Dickson Road garage. Refreshment stops were made at the Hare and Hounds Hotel at Todmorden.

Eventually after much further deliberation the traffic

South Yorkshire Motors of Pontefract started a coach service from Leeds to London via the Great North Road on 22 October 1926 in time for the opening of the International Motor Exhibition at Olympia. The Studebaker coach made outward journeys on Wednesdays and Saturdays with corresponding returns on Thursdays and Mondays. Allowing for a lunch stop at Stamford, the marathon journey lasted 8 hours. By May 1928 three weekly return journeys were made and the route was extended to serve Bradford.

From 24 June 1928 the first direct service from Huddersfield to London was provided by Wilks' Parlour Cars of Leeds who operated a small fleet of Gilford coaches. The daily coach actually started at Halifax, picking up in Elland before reaching Huddersfield. All seats had to be booked at least 24 hours in advance and Longley's the confectioners of John William Street were the local agents. Fares from Huddersfield to the Kings Cross terminus were 16/- single and 26/- return. The route lay via Brighouse, Dewsbury and Wakefield to Doncaster then via the Great North Road, with refreshment stops at the Picture House café, Grantham and at Suttle's cafe in Biggleswade for lunch.

A misleading newspaper advertisement stated that from 15 October 1928 the "express service" to London was to be taken over by Progress Coaches (William Armitage). Departure from Huddersfield was daily at 9.00am and the route was via the Midland cities of Nottingham and Leicester. Armitage did stable two buses in his Venn Street garage but it appears most likely that he merely provided a feeder service to either Leeds or Doncaster as and when required. Another possibility is that the feeder coach started from the Progress Garage but was not operated by Progress at all. By this time the Doncaster firm of Bentinck and Ensign Motor Services (B&E) were operating feeder services to and from Bradford and Leeds in conjunction with the London coaches of South Yorkshire Motors and Wilks' and it is possible that they also served Huddersfield.

A night service (operator unknown) commenced on 8 July 1929 from Bradford and Leeds, running every night via the Midland route to London. A feeder coach departed from Huddersfield at 11.30pm to connect with the main service at Doncaster.

From the end of September the services settled down to a regular pattern. The day services via the Midland

TRAVEL BY
WILKS' PARLOUR CAR SERVICE

HALIFAX, ELLAND, HUDDERSFIELD, BRIGHOUSE, DEWSBURY, WAKEFIELD
AND LONDON

DAILY SERVICE

Leaves Halifax			8-30 a.m.		Leaves London:	
,, Elland	...	...	8-40 ,,			
,, Huddersfield	...	...	9- 0 ,,		28, Caledonian Road,	
,, Brighouse	...	...	9-10 ,,			
,, Dewsbury	...	...	9-30 ,,		King's Cross	9-0 a.m.
,, Wakefield	...	...	9-50 ,,			

					'Phone :
Halifax	- - - - -	Scott's, Victoria Motor House, Powell Street.			2169
,,	- - - - -	Warburton's, 92a, King Cross Road.			—
Elland	- - -	Armitage, Tobacconist, South End.			—
Huddersfield	- - -	J. Longley, 27, John William Street.		,,	3079
Brighouse	- - - -	Wood, Herbalist, Bradford Road.		,,	429
Dewsbury	- - -	C. H. F. Hill, Market Place.		,,	754
Wakefield	- - -	Bon Bon, Kirkgate.		,,	2889
London	- - - - -	Keating's, 28, Caledonian Road, Kings Cross, N.1.		Tel. North	4348

FARES:

To				S.	R.	To				S.	R.
Grantham	...	...	...	6/6	11/-	Buckden	...	...	...	5/6	8/-
Stamford	...	...	...	9/-	14/-	Stilton	...	...	...	6/6	10/-
Stilton	...	...	...	9/6	16/-	Stamford	...	...	...	8/-	14/-
Buckden	...	...	...	10/6	18/-	Grantham	...	...	...	9/6	17/-
Biggleswade	...	...	...	12/-	21/-	Newark	...	...	...	10/6	18/6
Baldock	...	...	...	12/6	22/-	Retford	...	...	...	12/6	21/6
Stevenage	...	...	...	13/-	23/-	Doncaster	...	...	...	14/-	24/-
Welwyn	...	...	...	14/-	24/-	Halifax	...	...	...	16/-	26/-
Kings Cross	...	...	...	16/-	26/-	Huddersfield, etc....	...	...	...	16/-	26/-

CHILDREN UNDER 12 HALF FARE.

Luggage must be labelled and is carried Free at Owner's Risk. All Seats must be booked 24 hours in advance.

The Proprietor will make every effort to maintain the services shown in this Time Table, but reserves the right to alter, to suspend, or withdraw any service or any vehicle without notice. He will not be liable for any loss, damage, injury or inconvenience that any passenger may sustain through the withdrawal of any service, for failure of any car to perform its service, for want of punctuality, delay or detention. The acceptance by passengers of Tickets issued by the Proprietor or his Agents shall be held to constitute a contract between the proprietor and the passenger, subject to the foregoing conditions.

Proprietor: E. WILKS, Central Bus Garage, Templar Street, Vicar Lane, Leeds.

route from Leeds/Bradford and Halifax/Huddersfield connected at Doncaster and operated every day of the year. The night service, also via the Midland route, ran from Easter to the end of September and also over the Christmas period. The day service via the Great North Road (Wilks') operated throughout the summer period but not over Christmas or during winter, possibly as a result of competition provided by West Yorkshire Road Car who in July 1929 started a Harrogate-Leeds-London service running daily via the Great North Road.

Three major Yorkshire bus companies, West Yorkshire, Yorkshire Woollen and Yorkshire Traction, started their own joint "Yorkshire Services" to Birmingham and London in July 1930. There were five routes as follows, with many connecting facilities:

Bradford-Barnsley-Sheffield-Chesterfield-Derby-Birmingham

Harrogate-Leeds-Doncaster-Nottingham-Tamworth-Birmingham

Scarborough-York-Leeds-Barnsley-Sheffield-Chesterfield-Derby-Birmingham

Harrogate-Leeds-Doncaster-Newark-Grantham-Biggleswade-Barnet-London

Keighley-Bradford-Wakefield-Barnsley-Sheffield-Chesterfield-Nottingham-Leicester-Luton-London

Huddersfield passengers were catered for by a feeder service which left Kirkgate at 10.15am to connect with the through coaches at Barnsley. Arrival times at Birmingham and London by the first and last routes above were 4.15pm and 8.00pm respectively.

Such was the competition that early in 1933 B&E Motor Services absorbed the operations of Wilks' Parlour Coaches and by May there was a change of name to London, Midland and Yorkshire Services Limited (LMYS). Joint operation of the London services with South Yorkshire Motors continued as before.

A media correspondent of the time had very happy memories of travelling with B&E and was pleased to see that the two winged blue crest of the old firm was retained on four new cream Leyland Tigers with Beadle coach bodies purchased in 1932. Travelling from London on the day service and returning via the night service, he found the coaches luxuriously appointed and with sufficient leg room to ensure a comfortable journey. He judged the scenery of the Midland route via Northampton infinitely superior to that along the Great North Road and the halts well chosen; there were vivid memories of the dim hazy birth of a spring dawn in the vast openness of the Dukeries. The writer felt

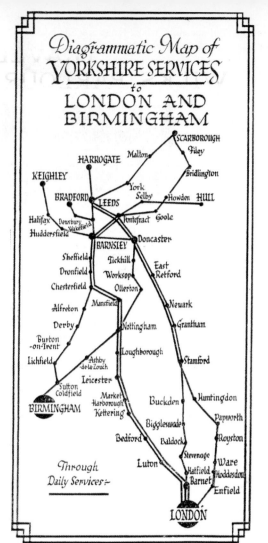

Diagrammatic Map of YORKSHIRE SERVICES to LONDON AND BIRMINGHAM

Through Daily Services:-

Interior View of Luxury Coach

operated by

YORKSHIRE SERVICES

The WEST YORKSHIRE Road Car Co. Ltd.
The YORKSHIRE (W.D.) Electric Tramways Ltd.
The YORKSHIRE TRACTION Co. Ltd.
The EAST YORKSHIRE Motor Services Ltd.

Return Tickets are available on either Company's Bus.

AGENT.

D. 35m 5/33.

that the advantages of coach travel over the railways were considerable and he appreciated the beauty of the quaint unspoilt villages through which the coaches passed as well as the bustling market squares of Market Harborough and Pontefract.

As a regular traveller he personally knew the former B & E proprietors, Mr and Mrs Heath, who were now directors of LMYS. From Mr Heath he had heard that "Philco" radio sets were to be fitted in the new coaches. The garage and head office remained at Bentinck Street but a new booking office in the established blue and cream colours had been opened in Watergate in the centre of Doncaster. The Heaths at this time were concerned at the loss of passengers on the night services, caused by a reduction in railway fares.

Unfortunately competition from the pool of major bus companies began to affect the profitability of the LMYS and South Yorkshire joint services and as a result in November 1934 both operators sold their London services to the Yorkshire Pool companies. The Yorkshire Pool operators, whose ranks now included East Midland and East Yorkshire, issued a revised 1935 summer timetable which featured the services previously operated by the LMYS.

Additional services were added to the timetables which were arranged so that Birmingham and London routes converged at Barnsley, Doncaster or Nottingham to provide extra connectional facilities. There were many feeders and soon route numbers YS1 to 12 were in use. As far as Huddersfield passengers were concerned, there were two direct services. The YS9 departed at 8.20am via the Midland route (Sheffield, Derby, Leicester, Kettering and St Albans), arriving in London at 5.55pm. The YS4 departed at 10.10am via Chesterfield and Derby for Birmingham, with a connection at Barnsley for London via Nottingham on the YS2. Apart from suspension during and immediately after the war these services continued to be operated by the pool until they became the responsibility of National Travel in 1974.

Yorkshire Traction 1939 Leyland Tiger TS8/Burlingham coach 629 (HE 8919) picks up for London on 6 August 1948. This stand is on the east side of Venn Street, Huddersfield, which was a southerly extension of Lord Street; note the position of the Parish Church clock in the background
[Kirklees Image Archive Ke00268]

OHE 720 was Yorkshire Traction 1147, a 1959 Leyland Tiger Cub/Plaxton coach. In this 1962 scene it is picking up for London on the east side of Venn Street. The "Midland route" to London via Sheffield, Nottingham, Leicester, Northampton and Luton took nearly nine hours. The former Progress garage and (in the distance) the Parish Church are on the left. [Kirklees Image Archive Ke16988]

Parked at Victoria Coach Station, London is the coach for Halifax via Huddersfield. Yorkshire Traction 1962 Leyland Leopard semi-coach 1232 (XHE 232) had rather angular bodywork by Willowbrook. Some of these vehicles were later used by Huddersfield depot as one-man buses on the Sheffield route. [R. Marshall collection]

6.8: OTHER YORKSHIRE TRACTION COASTAL EXPRESSES (HUDDERSFIELD AREA)

Barnsley & District had run seasonal coastal expresses since 1927. A daily service for the 1929 season from Huddersfield to Scarborough via Penistone and Barnsley commenced on 29 July. The journey time to Scarborough was over 5 hours, allowing for a refreshment stop at the Fox and Hounds Hotel at Copmanthorpe near York. For the Summer of 1930 the Scarborough express was reintroduced (7/- single or 11/- period return) and a daily coastal express service was started to Cleethorpes via Barnsley, Doncaster and Scunthorpe with a journey time from Huddersfield of nearly 5 hours. Fares to Cleethorpes were 7/6d single and 11/- period return.

In time for the summer 1935 season, Yorkshire Traction obtained the express and excursion licences of the Holmfirth based Wilson Haigh business, which had been purchased by Huddersfield JOC the previous year. Saturday express services were operated to Blackpool, Morecambe, Bridlington and Scarborough with picking up points at Holmfirth, New Mill, Honley and Meltham. The Morecambe and Bridlington coaches were also licensed to pick up in Huddersfield A new summer Saturday and Sunday express service from Huddersfield to Skegness was also introduced.

With the wartime "emergency" in September 1939 coastal services were generally suspended for the duration of the war, although it proved possible to run to Scarborough, Skegness and Cleethorpes, as well as Blackpool, between May and September 1940. It was not until Easter 1946 that the fuel situation had improved sufficiently to allow their limited resumption. Passengers were told to book in advance and day trippers were advised to take their own supplies of food to avoid the inevitable long queues in cafes at the resorts.

A daily Scarborough service resumed from 7 July 1946 but was operated only until 8 September; on Saturday and Sunday through bookings were allowed to Bridlington and Filey but passengers from Huddersfield had to change at Barnsley. The Cleethorpes service restarted on 7 June, operating mainly on Saturdays and Sundays but daily in August. The Skegness service resumed on 8 June and also ran mainly Saturday and Sunday until 21 September.

Later summer Saturday coastal expresses from Doncaster via Barnsley and Huddersfield were started to Morecambe (from 1950) and Southport (from 23 June 1951). Two more new summer Saturday coastal express services began in July 1956. One ran from Huddersfield to Hornsea and Withernsea while the second, originating from Barnsley, served North Wales from Holmfirth. A Huddersfield to Whitby "non-stop" express running on Saturdays in July and August was new from 2 July 1960.

Left- In 1952 Yorkshire Traction placed three "new" coaches in service, Leyland-Beadle chassis (incorporating units from withdrawn prewar Leyland Tigers) with Beadle bodywork. 972 (EHE 382) lasted until 1962 and is seen here before returning to Huddersfield on an express service. [R.F. Mack]

Right- Traction 974 (EHE 921), a Windover bodied Leyland Royal Tiger new in 1953, is parked in Scarborough before returning to Huddersfield on a coastal express service. As the entrance was towards the rear, passengers in the nearside front seats enjoyed a truly panoramic view. [R. Marshall collection]

6.9: YORKSHIRE TRACTION WATERLOO DEPOT ALLOCATION, 15 JULY 1972

coaches
6 (CHE305C) Leopard/ Plaxton		1965

dual purpose
224 (NHE24F) Leopard/ Alexander		1968

long single decks
338/9 (FHE320/1D) Leopard/ Weymann		1966
356 (WHE356J) Leopard/ Willowbrook		1970
362/3 (WHE362/3J) Fleetline/ Alexander		1970
381 (CHE381K) Leopard/ Marshall		1972
391/2 (YCX538/9) Leopard/ Willowbrook *		1963
393/4 (BCX213/4B) Leopard/ Marshall *		1964
395/6 (FCX287/8C) Leopard/ Weymann *		1965
397/8 (GVH213/4D) Leopard/ Marshall *		1966
399 (KVH557E) Leopard/ Marshall *		1967

short single decks
527 (WHE527J) Leopard/ Willowbrook		1970
529/36/7 (CHE529/36/7K) Leopard/ Marshall		1972
599 (NCX268F) Tiger Cub/ Marshall *		1968

double decks (lowheight, one man)
611 (RHE812) Atlantean/ Weymann		1959
637/8 (JHE637/8E) Atlantean/ NCME		1967
647-50 (NHE47-50F) Atlantean/ NCME		1968

double decks (highbridge, conductor)
724 (3277HE) Titan PD3A/1/ NCME		1964
745/6 (AVH635/6B) Titan PD3A/1/ Roe *		1964

total: 32
* ex-County. NCME- Northern Counties

All were Leylands except for the two Daimler Fleetlines. Former County Leopards 389/90 and Tiger Cub 598 had been transferred to Barnsley depot and their earlier Tiger Cubs and the Guy Arabs had already been withdrawn, in some cases after transfer to another depot.

Above-
But for the simplified livery, this 13 September 1968 image of the 1958 batch of lowbridge Guy Arab IV/Roe 91-4 (NCX 176-9) could pass for a typical fifties County depot scene. The Guys and County's more typical modern Leylands were soon to be transferred to Yorkshire Traction along with the Penistone Road premises. Much later Waterloo depot passed to Stagecoach but was soon sold off to Centrebus Holdings.
[H. J. Black]

Top right-
County 89 (FVH 165) a Leyland Titan PD2/12 with well proportioned Roe highbridge body new in 1952, is on the Huddersfield stand in the Wakefield Bus Station of West Riding, one of whose red Guy Wulfrunians (for ex-tram routes) is seen in the background. 89 and 90 were regular performers on the "Wakefield Direct" route for most of the 1950s and beyond – until the arrival of the County Wulfrunians. [Photobus]

Above- In its last four years County Motors bought only single deckers, all Leylands with attractive B.E.T. style bodywork. 113 (KCX 263E) was new in January 1967, a 45-seater Marshall bodied Tiger Cub. In this view in Lord Street, it is about to depart on the indirect route to Wakefield via Kirkburton and Scissett as a one man bus. [Photobus]

Left- One of the pair of Leyland Tiger PS2/1 County had rebodied by Windover in 1954, 85 (EVH 213) is leaving Dewsbury Bus Station on one of the hourly shortworkings to Hopton. These journeys ran mainly on Wednesdays, a Dewsbury market day. [Photobus]

All photographs taken by H. J. Black

Left-
Yorkshire Woollen Leyland Tiger PS2/3 51 (HD 8554) has left the Brook Street terminus on 28 May 1969 and is turning from Lord Street into Northumberland Street en route for Leeds via Norristhorpe (18A). Originally single decker 700, 51 had been rebuilt and rebodied by Roe as a double decker in 1963. Its appearance has been improved by the addition of a cream band.

Right-
Dispersal of theNational Bus Company owned Sheffield JOC "C" fleet in 1970 brought Roe bodied Leyland PD2/30 3157 WE to Yorkshire Woollen. 136 is waiting to depart from Lord Street on 5 May 1970 on main road route 27 to Dewsbury – note the terminus stop sign of Huddersfield JOC, former joint operator. Passengers would have appreciated the very comfortable seating, provided for riders on long routes such as Sheffield to Leeds or Bradford.

Left-
Not a common sight in Huddersfield, a Yorkshire Woollen AEC Regent V/ Metro-Cammell new in 1958, 56 (CHD 605), displays the traditional fleetname on the Dewsbury stand in Lord Street on 17 September 1970. Withdrawn in the following year, it later worked in Hong Kong.

Below left-
In Byram Street stands Yorkshire Woollen Leyland Titan PD2/20 143 (YWB 153) on 25 August 1971. Bound for Leeds on route 18, this secondhand bus unusually bears Eastern Coach Works bodywork, supplied to original operator Sheffield JOC by virtue of British Railways ownership in 1957 during the period when ECW built bodies only for state owned firms. On the right you can see standard YWD street furniture: a red timetable case and stop signs listing the many places served.

Below-
After Yorkshire Woollen's route network was totally recast in August 1971, the 18 and 19 to Leeds via Heckmondwike were their only conductor operated routes in Huddersfield. Albion Lowlander/Weymann 526 (KHD 409) new in 1964 carries the livery and plainer fleetname used just before the adoption of standard National Bus Company colours. The once fashionable illuminated advertising panel is disused in this 14 August 1972 Byram Street view.

Right-
YWD 1964 Leyland Leopard/Weymann 176 (AHD 118B) had lost its sixties mainly cream livery when photographed in Byram Street on route 18 to Leeds on 10 August 1973. This mainly red version for single deckers with modernised fleetname was used until NBC poppy red was applied.

Below-
On 13 August 1973 YWD Fleetline/Alexander 593 (BHD 214C) leaves the original Dewsbury Bus Station for Huddersfield on route 1 from Leeds. 593 carries the styles of fleetname and fleet number used just before NBC corporate identity was applied.

Below right-
In 1972 Yorkshire Woollen placed in service a batch of Fleetlines with Eastern Coach Works bodywork which appeared regularly on routes 1 to 3 (Leeds via Dewsbury). 703 (LHD 313K), proud to be part of the National Bus Company, leaves Dewsbury Bus Station for Huddersfield via Nettleton Road on 13 August 1973.

Left-
YWD's final batch of Alexander bodied Fleetlines entered service in 1971 and could be distinguished by their Scottish Bus Group/Ribble style destination and route number display. 684 (JHD 325J), which had originally been ordered for the Hebble company, is in Byram Street on route 18 to Leeds on 16 August 1973.

Below left-
Yorkshire Woollen 700 (LHD 310K), a 1972 ECW bodied Fleetline, stands in Byram Street on route 1 (Leeds via Dewsbury) on 10 May 1974. The (single) fare to Leeds had risen to 22p and 700 would soon become just another NBC double decker wearing NBC corporate identity.

Below-
24 July 1974 saw an unusual YWD vehicle in Byram Street on route 3 to Leeds via Dewsbury. 275 (KCP 808G) was a Marshall bodied AEC Reliance new to Hebble in 1969 which passed to YWD in 1971 and to independent South Yorkshire of Pontefract in 1975. The NBC dual purpose (semi-coach) livery of poppy red with an almost equivalent area of white was more tasteful than the bus version of red relieved by a single white band or not at all on some single deckers.

YORKSHIRE TRACTION

All photographs taken by H. J. Black

Upper-
Yorkshire Traction Leyland Atlantean/ Northern Counties 649 (NHE 49F) is in Lord Street on 29 October 1969 operating the main road route 27 to Dewsbury. Huddersfield JOC's share of routes 26 and 27 had been acquired at the beginning of the month. This simplified style of fleetname and destination display was introduced in 1967 when the bus fleet was renumbered.

Centre-
Yorkshire Traction Leyland Tiger Cub/Willowbrook 594 (OVH 606) had been new as County 95 in 1959. On 26 August 1970 it was leaving Dewsbury Bus Station for Hopton on a short working of ex-County route 62; no route number is yet being displayed.

Lower right-
In 1968 the long established Huddersfield to Sheffield route was much altered and extended on a limited stop basis to Halifax. Yorkshire Traction 341 (FHE 323D), a Leyland Leopard/Weymann bus new in 1966, is waiting in that town's Crossfield Bus Station on 30 August 1970 before departing on slower service 68 which observed all stops between Huddersfield and Sheffield via Penistone and Chapeltown.

Lower left-
After Traction's 1959 Leyland Atlanteans, it was 1966 before further rear-engined buses were obtained, Atlanteans with more rounded Northern Counties bodies. 618 (FHE 334D) waits in Lord Street on 17 September 1970 on route 27 to Dewsbury. There would be no intermediate destination on the blinds appropriate to the 27 (or 26) taken over from Huddersfield JOC less than a year earlier.

Upper-
As well as Atlanteans Traction bought Northern Counties bodied Daimler Fleetlines. New in 1969, 663 (RHE 663G) with panoramic windows is on the Dewsbury stand in Lord Street on 3 May 1971. Previous operator Huddersfield JOC's stop sign is still in use but with what looks like a Yorkshire Woollen timetable case.

Centre-
Yorkshire Traction's final choice of front engined double deck chassis was the Leyland Titan PD3A/1, mostly with Northern Counties bodywork. 724 (3277 HE), new in 1964, leaves Dewsbury Bus Station for Huddersfield on route 27 on 14 May 1971. The "destination" display shows both origin and destination.

Lower left-
Also leaving Dewsbury Bus Station for Huddersfield on 14 May 1971 was another 1964 Traction Leyland PD3A/1, ex-County Roe bodied 745 (AVH 635B). 745's destination display has been modified to show also route numbers. Routes 26 and 27 would be replaced by new one-man operated services 1 to 3 in August after which conductor operated Titans would no longer ply between Huddersfield and Dewsbury.

Lower right-
An ex-County bus on a former County route, Yorkshire Traction 393 (BCX 213B) was a Marshall bodied Leyland Leopard new in 1964 as County 108. On 12 July 1972 it was leaving Dewsbury Bus Station for Huddersfield via Hopton and Kirkheaton on route 62 – the present 262. The destination display is not as helpful as that of County.

Upper left- Although still based at Waterloo depot, Traction ex-County 1966 Leyland Leopard/Marshall 398 (GVH 214D) is venturing outside County and indeed outside traditional Traction territory on route 60 to Bradford via Cleckheaton. The YWD Albion Lowlander in the background allows us to compare the two companies' liveries in this 14 August 1972 Byram Street scene just before the National Bus Company's corporate liveries were unveiled.

Upper right- Yorkshire Traction Leyland Atlantean/Weymann 611 (RHE 812) has arrived in Byram Street on route 1 from Leeds via Dewsbury on 14 August 1972. New in 1959 with box-like bodywork typical of early rear-engined double deckers, this was a lowheight bus with lowbridge type seats at the rear of the upper saloon. Early Atlanteans were not often seen in the Huddersfield area until late in their careers and 611 was the only one allocated to Waterloo at this date.

Lower left- Advertising products lethal to the bus industry seems to have been more important to Yorkshire Traction than displaying a complete fleetname in this 27 July 1973 Byram Street view of 1970 Leyland Leopard/Willowbrook 349 (WHE 349J). For a car showroom on the edge of Barnsley, the advert was perhaps particularly inappropriate on a Huddersfield depot working to Bradford via Cleckheaton.

Lower right- Yorkshire Traction 1965 Plaxton bodied Leyland Leopard coach 6 (CHE 305C) was allocated to Waterloo depot for some time. Standing in front of an ex-Huddersfield Corporation Seddon RU of the newly formed West Yorkshire PTE in St George's Square on 16 April 1974, it still wears full pre-NBC coach livery. In spite of the destination display and the National Travel route number shown in the windscreen, the location outside Huddersfield Station suggests railway replacement work.